M. ANNAEI LVCANI
DE BELLO CIVILI
LIBER I

T0382020

M. ANNAEI LVCANI
DE BELLO CIVILI
LIBER I

Edited by

R. J. GETTY, M.A.

Formerly Fellow and Classical Lecturer of
St John's College, Cambridge
Professor and Head of the Department of Classics
University College, Toronto

CAMBRIDGE
AT THE UNIVERSITY PRESS

1955

CAMBRIDGE UNIVERSITY PRESS

Cambridge, New York, Melbourne, Madrid, Cape Town,
Singapore, São Paulo, Delhi, Mexico City

Cambridge University Press
The Edinburgh Building, Cambridge CB2 8RU, UK

Published in the United States of America by Cambridge University Press, New York

www.cambridge.org
Information on this title: www.cambridge.org/9781107632738

First edition 1940
Reprinted with corrections 1955
First published 1955
First paperback edition 2013

A catalogue record for this publication is available from the British Library

ISBN 978-1-107-63273-8 Paperback

ROBERTO MITCHELL HENRY

LATINITATIS

DOCTISSIMO ANTISTITI PRAECEPTORIQVE HVMANISSIMO

HAS PRIMITIAS GRATO ANIMO

DISCIPVLVS

PREFACE

For sixty-four years the defects as well as the merits of the
predecessor of this edition have been obvious to all students
of Lucan. Based upon the already antiquated text of Weise,
the slender volume of W. E. Heitland and C. E. Haskins did
little for the continuous interpretation of the First Book of
the *De Bello Ciuili*, though here and there sane and helpful
remarks are to be found. The same blemishes may be seen in
the larger edition by Haskins of the whole poem which
appeared in 1887; but this substantial volume had the good
fortune to be prefaced by Heitland with a learned and stimu-
lating *Introduction*, which will be commended repeatedly to
the reader of the present edition. Haskins, however, had the
misfortune to undertake his task at the end of a long period of
stagnation in the study of Lucan, and, with progressive contributions to knowledge from other scholars at home and
abroad, such value as it had in 1875 has been continuously
diminished.

The merits and demerits of the three Teubner editions of
C. Hosius (1892, 1905, 1913), of Heitland's recension in
Postgate's *Corpus Poetarum Latinorum* (1905), of C. M.
Francken's text and commentary (1896–7), and of Haskins's
own contribution have been nakedly but not unjustly set
forth by A. E. Housman on pp. xxxiii–xxxv of his edition;
but there is one work embodying considerable merit of which
Housman does not make overt mention, because it is concerned with Book I alone. This is the text, critical apparatus,
commentary, and scholarly introduction which appeared at
Paris in 1894 under the skilful direction of P. Lejay. The
editor sometimes fails to explain or even to see certain difficulties which confront him, but in the main he stocks his
commentary with much useful learning and displays little of

the haste for which he excuses himself. His great service to the critical study of the poet was the collation of a number of MSS of dates ranging from the ninth to the eleventh century in the Bibliothèque Nationale, and his reminder that the same library with its thirty-nine complete or fragmentary MSS is ready to furnish the future editor of Lucan with a not inconsiderable body of evidence.

In 1896 the first edition by J. P. Postgate of the Seventh Book appeared in the Pitt Press Series, where it was followed by a second edition in 1913 and by an even fuller treatment of the Eighth Book in 1917. The care, learning, and penetration revealed in these volumes suggest that Postgate was fitted as no other scholar before him to edit Lucan, and in them is afforded the best possible model for any subsequent edition of an individual Book, should it be of similar scope.

The first volume of the edition designed for the series of the *Association Guillaume Budé* was completed in 1926 by Monsieur A. Bourgery, but its text does not repose on the sure foundation of a wider knowledge of the MSS such as might have been expected from a fellow-countryman and follower of Lejay. It contains a rendering in prose which is sometimes misleading. Recent translations into the verse of modern languages include those by V. Ussani (1899–1912) into Italian, Demogeot (1866) and Gallot (1894) into French, and Sir E. Ridley (1896, 1905, and 1919) into English; but these do little for the interpretation of the poem. Ridley's third edition is, however, often right where Haskins is wrong. The most useful version in his own language for the English-speaking student is that of Mr J. D. Duff (1928), whose work is based on that of Housman. At the same time, thanks to his grasp of some at least of the conventions of ancient rhetoric and his realization of the absurdity of repeating them in a modern language, his is one of the few readable versions of a Latin poet in modern English prose.

Not since the days of Oudendorp, Cortius, and Burman has a weightier and more commanding contribution been made to the study of Lucan than the well-known volume produced by Housman in 1926 *editorum in usum*, and the editor who is the first to make use of even a part of this work may be permitted to assess its value for him. On its appearance it was greeted with a masterly review in *Gnomon*, ii, 1926, pp. 497–532 by Professor Eduard Fraenkel, who rightly disagrees with Housman's view that 'the manuscripts collated by Mr Hosius for his second and third editions are amply sufficient', and that Lucan 'does not profit by the discovery of new material'. Mr Fraenkel's justification for this opinion proceeds from an examination of selected passages in several MSS now in the Biblioteca Laurenziana at Florence, and particularly from a complete collation of Laur. 35, 10 (*saec.* xii). Of the 250 or 300 MSS of Lucan in existence no library contains a higher percentage than the Bibliothèque Nationale, and to its officials I am indebted for permission not merely to re-examine the codices which Lejay employed, but also to inspect the many so-called *deteriores* of dates ranging from the twelfth to the fifteenth century. I am grateful also to Professor A. Souter for kindly examining two British Museum MSS, namely Royal 15 A xxiii (*saec.* xii) and Add. 14799 (*saec.* xiv–xv), both of which supply the good reading *obstrinxit* in 5. 197 (see *C.R.* xliv, 1930, p. 174). It seems to me that Par. Lat. 8265 and 10315 merit further study, and for this reason their readings are mentioned occasionally in the Critical Apparatus. Their scholia may also deserve attention. The former is a Colbert MS of doubtful provenance, and it was written probably in the second half of the tenth century—not in the thirteenth as is stated in the catalogue. I am glad to have this opinion confirmed by Dr R. W. Hunt of the University of Liverpool, who has been kind enough to consult both MSS. He has secured the valuable opinion of Dr B. Bischoff, to whom also my best thanks are due, to the effect that Par. Lat. 10315, like its neighbour 10314 (*Z*), is certainly from Echternach (see the catalogue of H. Degering in *Aufsätze Fritz Milkau gewidmet*, Leipzig, 1921, pp. 98sqq.), and that it was at some time or another in the possession of Ludolf of Encheringen. It is the only MS I know which furnishes irreproachable evidence for *lingonas* in 1. 398.

Now *deteriores* are not always to be despised, as indeed may be seen from Housman's own preference for their readings in 1. 491, 507 (*conciperet* for -*erent*), and 569 (*tum* for *tunc*); and their accumulated evidence may lead sometimes to a considerable modification of views preconceived and suggested by his Ω. In 1. 18 *Scythicum glaciali* is vouched for not merely by *V*, but by at least twenty-six other MSS which I have seen, some of them of respectable date; and a similar story could be told about 54. Nor does it happen rarely that through fuller knowledge a different emphasis may be placed upon the rival merits of two readings, as in 304, where *transcenderet* is attested by twenty-eight of the Paris MSS, including *ENPQRST*. As Professor G. Pasquali well observes (*Storia della Tradizione e Critica del Testo*, Florence, 1934, p. 432 n.), such labour on the *De Bello Ciuili* as Mr Ulrich Knoche has bestowed already on Juvenal is urgently needed.

To those who are not satisfied with a text based upon the six MSS (*ZMPGUV*) only out of a number considerably greater which are prior in date to the twelfth century, Housman's discussion of their merits will seem excellent in itself, but an inadequate part of the whole story. His observation that *UV* 'agree together almost as much as any two manuscripts' is interesting in view of some places in this Book where they seem to me to supply the right reading, namely in 54, 89, 101, and possibly 681. To his citation of the one place in Book 1 where *V* alone of these six is right, namely 423 *Suessones*, there should be added 538 *ore* and 631 *monetis*; and the unique testimony of U in 368 is yet another place where that MS alone is probably correct.

Housman's text has been justly praised for a punctuation which is superior to that of any of its predecessors, but there are passages where there is still room for improvement, notably 140, 478–80, and 569. It is in the choice between two or more variants, however, that the future editor of Lucan will find no inconsiderable portion of his task. In many cases Housman's selection will afford him little help, for it is made frequently without due consideration of all the evidence which lies to hand. The same story may be told of many of his emendations, and a more profound scrutiny of many of them must endorse the conservative attitude which Heitland so cogently expresses in $C.R.$ xi, 1897, p. 42, although his Paulinism is now discredited. The amelioration of the text of such a poet as Lucan does not always mean attainment to what he wrote. For example, the interchange of 9 and 12 would produce a more natural sequence, but I have not ventured on so tempting an improvement because of 47–50 (see 12 n.). Only in 623–4, 641, 681, and possibly 446 do I regard as obvious some necessity for improvement other than that suggested by the tradition. Housman's edition, indeed, is characterized by brilliant and penetrating observations (which, however, not infrequently convey but half of the truth) on many passages, and complete silence on many more which, as one may be permitted to think, could have been illuminated from his great familiarity with Latin poetry.

If a reading is to be defended, recourse must be had (in the following order of merit) to the practice of (a) Lucan himself elsewhere, (b) his predecessors, notably Vergil and Ovid, and finally (c) his successors. It is dangerous to fall into the habit of despising unduly the evidence (for what it is worth) of a poet's successors who imitate him at every turn, and to make such contemptuous remarks as 'to say "8 et 9 recte disiungi probat Drac. $Rom.$ 5. 1" would be equally false but less absurd' (Housman in *C.R.* xli, 1927, p. 191).

The text of this edition of the First Book has been reconstituted entirely without more dependence on Housman than on any of his predecessors, and each reading of importance is discussed on its merits in the Critical Apparatus, where all the reasons which occur to the editor for acceptance or rejection are set forth. Here every question upon which it is possible to make some new observation is discussed as fully as possible, and I have omitted discussion only of places where the preference of Housman as the latest editor is obviously sound (*e.g.* 646 *an tollet* against *attollet*). The emendations of older scholars and editors, of whom Cortius is easily the most useful, are generally rejected or accepted within the Critical Apparatus, though here and there such comment is included in the Explanatory Notes when it can be separated only with difficulty from the main exposition.

The relationship of Lucan to his predecessors in the field of Roman poetry has still to receive the full treatment which this question deserves. In this respect Vergil has been dealt with substantially by Heitland on pp. cviii–cxxi of his *Introduction*, Manilius by F. S. Schwemmler (*De Lucano Manilii Imitatore*, Giessen, 1916), and Seneca not only by H. Diels (*Abh. d. k. Acad. d. Wissensch.* Berlin, 1885) but also by Hosius (*Neue Jahrb.* Leipzig, 1892, pp. 337–56), who later surveys the whole matter in his *De Imitatione Scriptorum Romanorum imprimis Lucani* (Greifswald, 1907). To no earlier poet, however, is Lucan more akin than to Ovid, but his debt to him, though very great, has never been discussed adequately. In the commentary every effort has been made to indicate such indebtedness as there appears to be to Vergil, Ovid, and other poets; and it will be found that Ovid's influence is so great that no criticism of the *De Bello Ciuili* is possible without painstaking attention to him. Nor is the *tour de force* of Petronius in chapters 119 sqq. of the *Satyricon* to be overlooked, for it vouches not only for the title of Lucan's poem, but also for such readings as *Enyo* (Petron. 62, Luc. 1. 687).

For the *Realien* of the scenes where Roman religion and divination are described, my debt has been great to such accessible and informative works as Sir J. G. Frazer's *The Fasti of Ovid* and Professor A. S. Pease's edition of Cicero's *De Diuinatione* (*Univ. of Illinois Studies in Language and Literature*, 1920 and 1923), and the reader is constantly referred to them.

In the text the orthography is usually in conformity with Housman's practice. However, for the sake of clarity the accusative plural of the third declension in -*es* has been adopted everywhere, and in this respect I follow the habit of G. W. Mooney in his invaluable *Index to the Pharsalia of Lucan* (Dublin, 1927). The Introduction is mainly concerned with material not to be found in other editions or essays on Lucan, and one section deals with an aspect of his rhetoric which Postgate alone among his editors did not neglect to the peril of satisfactory interpretation. It has seemed to me, however, unnecessary to discuss the construction on rhetorical principles of such speeches as that of Caesar in this Book on account of the careful treatment by R. Faust in his dissertation *De Lucani Orationibus* (Königsberg, 1908).

In passing it may be observed that students of Lucan should not continue to neglect what is probably the oldest translation of the *De Bello Ciuili* made in these islands. I refer to a medieval adaptation in Irish, which has been edited and translated by Whitley Stokes in E. Windisch's *Irische Texte* (4te Serie, 2. Heft, Leipzig, 1909), and is entitled *In Cath Catharda* or *The Civil War of the Romans*. Some of its renderings are worthy of a more sophisticated age, *e.g.*:

1. 15 (p. 23) 'from the point near which the sun rises to the place at which he sets'.

1. 218 *tertia...pluuialis Cynthia* (p. 35) 'it was the third (night) as regards the moon's age, when abundant moisture is usual'.

1. 397 (p. 55) 'Came there to the battle the dwellers of the land about the *river* Vogesus,...'.

1. 479–80 (p. 61) 'far greater and more soldierly...is he now after defeating the people of the west'.

A study some day might be made of the text which the adapters had before them: it contained, for example, *uiscera* in l. 633 (see *ibid.* p. 77).

I must gratefully acknowledge the kind permission of the Editors of the Loeb Classical Library to illustrate my Explanatory Notes with occasional citations from Mr J. D. Duff's translation, of the Delegates of the Clarendon Press to quote extracts from Bywater's translation of Aristotle's *Poetics* (pp. xxv–xxviii), and of the Editors of the *American Journal of Philology* to reprint observations made by B. L. Gildersleeve (pp. xliv–xlvi). My best thanks are also due to the scholars and friends who have assisted me in various ways: *i.e.* to Professor W. B. Anderson for suggesting the aim and scope of Introduction I (i); to Mr J. M. Wyllie, Assistant Editor of the Oxford Latin Dictionary, for discussing with me line 128; to my former colleagues Mr S. F. Bonner and Dr R. W. Hunt of the University of Liverpool for useful hints regarding Introduction V; to Professor J. F. Mountford of the same University and Professor A. Souter, Editor of the Oxford Latin Dictionary, who have made at various times many valuable suggestions in matters of detail, and, with my wife, have shared the task of proof-reading; and to the care and skill of all at the University Press who have co-operated in the production of this book.

R. J. GETTY

St John's College,
   October 2, 1939

I am indebted to Miss Audrey M. Grove, Westcliff High School for Girls, and to Professors G. Bagnani, R. T. Bruère, G. B. A. Fletcher, and M. T. Smiley for calling my attention to certain *corrigenda* which I have adopted in the reprint of 1955.

University College, Toronto, July 15, 1954

CONTENTS

INTRODUCTION

I. LUCAN'S LIFE AND WORK

Lucan's life and work have been discussed so frequently and
so capably in recent years that there is little need to repeat all
the details of a well-known story in a volume of this compass.
In the essays of Professor H. E. Butler[1] and Professor J. Wight
Duff[2] the student who approaches the poet for the first time
will find accounts which are interesting and comprehensive,
while Heitland's *Introduction* to the large edition by Haskins[3]
is still invaluable. At the beginning of this work the ancient
authorities are set forth and discussed with an attention to
detail rivalled only by Lejay in the *Introduction* to his edition.[4]
Another modern account of Lucan which should be consulted
is that of M. Plessis,[5] who has given more attention than writers
in this country to two interesting questions, one concerning
the personal reputation of the poet, the other of special importance for the reader of the First Book of his poem.[6] For
the convenience of English readers these will be considered
now.

[1] *Post-Augustan Poetry from Seneca to Juvenal*, Oxford, 1909,
pp. 97–124.
[2] *A Literary History of Rome in the Silver Age*, London, 1927,
pp. 296–329.
[3] London, 1887.
[4] Paris, 1894. The ancient *Lives* are also reprinted (from Weber's
Vitae Lucani collectae, progr. Marb. 1856–8) in the editions of
Francken (Leiden, 1897, pp. 257–62) and of M. Bourgery (Paris,
1926, pp. xxi–xxv), as well as in those of Hosius.
[5] *La Poésie Latine*, Paris, 1909, pp. 543–77.
[6] Only in recent years, and since Hosius's first edition, has the
true title *De Bello Ciuili* permanently superseded the false *Pharsalia*
with editors (except Francken), though historians of Latin literature in this country still display a perversity for which there is no
excuse, at any rate since Housman reinterpreted 9. 985. The title *De
Bello Ciuili* has, however, appeared sporadically on editions since
1520.

(i) DID LUCAN ACCUSE ACILIA?

On the disclosure of the conspiracy which goes by the name of
C. Calpurnius Piso and was formed in A.D. 65 for the purpose
of killing Nero at the feast of Ceres, it was found that Lucan
was implicated. The hostile tone, which is apparent all through
the *Life* ascribed to the authorship of Suetonius, is stressed
nowhere more than in the words with which his part therein
and his subsequent actions are described. These are as
follows: *ad extremum paene signifer Pisonianae coniurationis
exstitit, multus in gloria tyrannicidarum palam praedicanda ac
plenus minarum, usque eo intemperans ut Caesaris caput proximo
cuique iactaret. uerum detecta coniuratione nequaquam parem
animi constantiam praestitit; facile enim confessus et ad humilli-
mas deuolutus preces matrem quoque innoxiam inter socios nomi-
nauit, sperans inpietatem sibi apud parricidam principem pro-
futuram.* ('In the end he appeared as practically the standard-
bearer in the conspiracy of Piso. Often he spoke openly of the
glory which awaited the slayers of tyrants, and was profuse in
his threats, with so little restraint that he talked freely to
everybody near him about the Emperor's life. However,
when the conspiracy was revealed, he was far from displaying
the same amount of resolution, for he promptly confessed,
and, stooping to the most abject entreaties, he named among
his fellow conspirators his innocent mother as well, in the hope
that his unfilial conduct would stand him in good stead with a
ruler who had murdered his own mother.')[1] The *Life* by
Vacca, which is generally favourable to the poet, is silent about
this accusation of his mother, but Tacitus alludes to it as
follows: *ex quibus Lucanus Quintianusque et Senecio diu ab-
nuere: post promissa inpunitate corrupti, quo tarditatem excu-
sarent, Lucanus Aciliam matrem suam, Quintianus Glitium
Gallum, Senecio Annium Pollionem, amicorum praecipuos, nomi-
nauere.* ('Of these Lucan, Quintianus, and Senecio kept
pleading not guilty for a long time, but afterwards they were
bribed by a promise that they would not be punished. So, to

[1] 6–8.

obtain pardon for their delay in confessing, Lucan named his
mother Acilia, and Quintianus and Senecio accused their.
special friends Glitius Gallus and Annius Pollio respectively.')[1]
In a subsequent chapter[2] we hear that she suffered no harm:
*Acilia mater Annaei Lucani sine absolutione sine supplicio dissi-
mulata.* ('No attention was paid to Acilia, the mother of
Lucan, and she was neither pardoned nor punished.') The
usual view of historians, who are not unnaturally shocked at
such conduct, may be summed up in Heitland's words[3]:
'Lucan however did not escape by means of an act almost
worthy of the matricide Emperor himself.' Such is the ger-
mination of the mischievous seed sown by Suetonius, who
suppresses, and indeed contradicts with his *facile confessus*, the
information given by Tacitus. According to the latter, Lucan,
Quintianus, and Senecio resisted until their reluctance to confess
was overcome by a promise that they would not be punished.[4]
On the other hand there is no mention in Tacitus of the basely
abject entreaties which Lucan is alleged by Suetonius to have
made in the hope that Nero, who had been responsible for the
death of his own mother, should experience a fellow feeling for
him.

Regarding the denunciation of Acilia, which led neither to
acquittal nor to conviction, Lejay remarks[5]: 'Cette formule
ambiguë pourrait même donner lieu de croire que la dénon-
ciation n'a jamais été portée et que Tacite s'est fait l'écho d'un

---

[1] *Ann.* 15. 56. Tacitus goes on to say (*ibid.* 57) that these three
continued to lay information against other fellow conspirators: *non
enim omittebant Lucanus quoque et Senecio et Quintianus passim
conscios edere.*   [2] *Ibid.* 71.   [3] *Op. cit.* p. xxx.

[4] Professor W. B. Anderson has drawn my attention to the not
dissimilar circumstances surrounding the mutilation of the Hermae
at Athens in 415 B.C., when Teukros under a promise of impunity
gave information which led to the conviction of eighteen people.
Afterwards one Diokleides laid charges against forty-two more, including the orator Andokides and his father. To save the latter
Andokides was induced to tell what he knew, and so not merely to
confirm the original story of Teukros, but also to accuse four more
conspirators. See the *De Mysteriis* of Andokides *passim.*

[5] *Op. cit.* p. xii, n. 8.

mauvais bruit, d'origine officielle.' M. Plessis does well to
raise the question of the fate of Lucan's father, M. Annaeus
Mela, as recounted by Tacitus.[1] Apparently he had not been
denounced by the poet, but lived until the following year,
when Nero coveted his wealth and he felt obliged to commit
suicide. Tacitus's words are: *quo* (i.e. *Lucano*) *interfecto dum
rem familiarem eius acriter requirit, accusatorem conciuit Fabium
Romanum, ex intimis Lucani amicis. mixta inter patrem filiumque
coniurationis scientia fingitur, adsimilatis Lucani litteris, quas
inspectas Nero ferri ad eum iussit, opibus eius inhians.* ('In
prosecuting a keen search for Lucan's personal estate after the
latter's death, Mela provoked an accusation against himself on
the part of Fabius Romanus, one of his son's intimate friends.
It was falsely alleged that the father and the son shared in the
knowledge of the conspiracy, and letters purporting to have
been written by Lucan were forged. Nero examined these,
and ordered them to be taken to Mela, for he coveted his
wealth with wide open jaws.')

M. Plessis suggests that Nero may well have had recourse to
a similar scheme after Lucan's death, and that he trumped up
the story that the poet had denounced his mother. If in his
lifetime Lucan had placed himself on an equality with the
Emperor as a poet, why should they not appear before posterity as rival matricides? The cunning brain of the man who
said on his deathbed *qualis artifex pereo*[2] was capable of con-
ceiving plans no less tortuous and treacherous.

Such is the reasoning of M. Plessis. Tacitus makes a plain
and unvarnished statement about Lucan's accusation of his
mother without adverse comment. Indeed the historian can
have had no ill opinion of the poet when he could say that the
latter was *grande adiumentum claritudinis*[3] of his father and
mention him in the same breath as Vergil and Horace[4] as an
author who merited study by those who wished to beautify
their rhetorical style. Nor is it likely that Statius, if he had
been familiar with such a story then current, would have suggested in the poem addressed on Lucan's birthday to the

[1] *Ann.* 16. 17. [2] Suet. *Ner.* 49.
[3] *Ann.* 16. 17. [4] *Dial.* 20.

latter's widow, Argentaria Polla, the idea of her husband's
ghost listening to the tortures of the damned and beholding
the matricide Nero pale at the sight of his mother's torch:

> *tu magna sacer et superbus umbra*
> *noscis Tartaron et procul nocentum*
> *audis uerbera pallidumque uisa*
> *matris lampade respicis Neronem.*[1]

In any case the unpleasant story, which is so heavily under-
lined by Suetonius, may have been due to slanderous reports
spread by Lucan's enemies after his death.

(ii) THE FIRST SEVEN LINES OF THE POEM

Another matter which is generally passed over in silence by
British scholars, but which has received careful treatment by
Lejay[2] and M. Plessis,[3] is the attribution of the first seven lines
of the *De Bello Ciuili* to Lucan's uncle, the younger Seneca.
In the *Life* of the poet which is found in the Leidensis Vossianus Secundus Lat. xix, f. 63 (U) and is derived in the main
from Suetonius,[4] the following words occur: *unde morte prae-
occupatus quaedam quae inchoauerat inperfecta reliquit...
libellos etiam suos inemendatos auunculo suo Senecae ut eos
emendaret tradidit. sciendum quia primo iste liber a Lucano non
ita est inchoatus, sed taliter:* 'quis furor, o ciues, quae tanta
licentia ferri.' *Seneca autem, qui fuit auunculus eius, quia ex
abrupto inchoabat, hos vii uersus addidit:* 'bella per Emathios'
usque 'et pila minantia pilis'. ('Being cut off in this way by a
premature death, he left unfinished some works which he had
begun.... He also handed over his notebooks, which had not
been revised, to be corrected by his uncle Seneca. It should
be realized that originally Lucan did not make this Book
begin as it does now, but as follows: *quis furor, o ciues,* etc. But
Seneca, who was Lucan's uncle, on account of the abrupt
beginning added the following seven lines: *bella per Emathios...et pila minantia pilis.*')[5]

[1] *Silu.* 2. 7. 116–19.   [2] *Op. cit.* pp. xxi–xxiii, n. 8–9.
[3] *Op. cit.* pp. 553–7.   [4] Lejay, *op. cit.* p. vii.
[5] 6–9.

The origin of this story seems to be in the sentence of the Suetonian *Life*: *inpetrato autem mortis arbitrio libero codicillos ad patrem corrigendis quibusdam uersibus suis exarauit*. ('When he had requested and obtained permission to choose freely how he should die, he wrote out final instructions to his father for the correction of some of his lines.')[1] The story itself, however, has been affected by the source of the scholiast's remark: *hos vii uersus primos dicitur Seneca ex suo addidisse, ut quidam uolunt auunculus Lucani, ut quidam uolunt frater, ne uideretur liber ex abrupto inchoare dicendo 'quis furor'*. ('The story is that Seneca, who according to some was Lucan's uncle but according to others his brother, added the first seven lines of his own composition, so that the work should not seem to begin abruptly with the words *quis furor*.')[2] Lucan, then, according to this account sent his poem in an unrevised condition before his death to Seneca so that the latter might revise it before publication.

Now there are three objections to the story. First, if the account of Vacca[3] is to be believed, Lucan had already published three books of the *De Bello Ciuili*. Though there is some divergence of opinion as to which these were,[4] it is probable that they were the first three, on account of the comparatively impartial tone in dealing with the two sides, as contrasted with the highly unfavourable portrait of Caesar and the sympathetic treatment of Pompey in the rest of the poem.[5] Second, Seneca was neither the *auunculus* or mother's brother nor the *frater*, but the *patruus* or father's brother, of Lucan. Third, the uncle's suicide preceded the nephew's.[6]

Such extremely cogent considerations as these preclude any possibility of Senecan authorship of lines 1-7, but M. Plessis, following Weber,[7] is determined to assign them to Lucan's father. Weber's assumption is that the words, which were the origin of the scholiast's remark, were in the first place: *hos vii*

---

[1] 9.   [2] *Comm. Bern.* ed. Usener (1869) n. 1. 1.

[3] *Vita* 13: *ediderat:...tres libros quales uidemus.*

[4] Wight Duff, *op. cit.* p. 317.   [5] Plessis, *op. cit.* p. 569.

[6] Tac. *Ann.* 15. 63, 70.

[7] *De dupl. Phars. exordio*, Marburg, 1860.

uersus primos pater Lucani addidit, and that *auunculus*, which in later Latin tended to become the sole word for 'uncle', ousted *patruus*, which, like the scholiast's *frater*, was itself a corruption of the original *pater*. The best known of Lucan's relations was Seneca, who was his uncle; therefore his name entered the story to explain *auunculus*.

Weber's theory is, then, that the poem as first conceived began with the words of line 8 (*quis furor*, etc.), but that Lucan left instructions that, after his death, his father should see to the substitution of lines 1–7, which are genuinely Lucanic,[1] for lines 8–66, with their fulsome adulation of Nero. This circumstance is contrary to the usual view of the *ille ego...at nunc horrentia Martis* lines at the beginning of the *Aeneid*, namely that Vergil wrote them, but left some indication that he did not intend them to be the opening lines of his poem.

To Weber's view there is the objection that the First Book was probably already published. Besides, the difference in tone and outlook alleged by M. Plessis[2] between the 'first' (1–7) and the 'second' (8–66) introduction does not seem obvious.[3] The other Roman epics do not begin with a question like line 8. On the other hand, there is a strong resemblance between the commencement of the *De Bello Ciuili* and that of the *Aeneid*.[4] There is in the latter poem also an exordium of seven lines, followed by an invocation and a dependent question, *Musa, mihi causas memora, quo numine laeso*, etc., to correspond with Lucan's independent *quis furor, o ciues, quae tanta licentia ferri?* Valerius Flaccus, like Lucan, follows the example set by Vergil, except that he has an exordium of four lines, and then invokes Phoebus. Silius before invoking the

---

[1] They are attested by Seru. ad Verg. *Aen.* 1. 1, Aug. *Ciu. Dei* 3. 13, Prisc. II. 348 (*G.L.K.*) and Isid. *Orig.* 18. 3. 2, and in particular by Fronto (Naber, p. 157; Loeb, ii, pp. 104–6).

[2] *Op. cit.* p. 554.

[3] In fact the verbal echoes, which Plessis lists (p. 553), between the two passages argue in favour of these having stood side by side from the first. For the ubiquity of repetition in Lucan see 25 n., Heitland, *op. cit.* p. lxxxi and Plessis, *op. cit.* p. 553.

[4] This is noted also by Bourgery, *op. cit.* p. ix.

Muse has an exordium of two lines and a word, and the beginning of Statius's *Thebais* is similar; but of the poets mentioned Lucan is the nearest to Vergil in the method of introducing his poem.

II. WHO IS THE HERO OF THE POEM?

The student of Latin literature who consults modern historians of the subject as well as editors of Lucan, cannot but feel baffled as he confronts the diversity of answers to this question. Caesar is nominated by some (*e.g.* Professor H. E. Butler)[1] for the position, Pompey by others (*e.g.* M. Plessis).[2] Suggestions are also made in favour of Cato,[3] the Roman people,[4] the Senate,[5] and even Freedom (*Libertas*).[6] Professor Wight Duff tries to reconcile the views which concern the three principal characters of the poem, in the following words:[7]

Some have submitted that the *Pharsalia* is an epic without a hero, or alternatively an epic with three. Perhaps it is truer to argue that Lucan in a real degree rose to the inherent greatness of his theme by so portraying Caesar that, while Pompey was his formal hero and Cato his spiritual hero, Caesar, however much disliked and maligned by the author, was and still is

[1] *Op. cit.* p. 105: 'Whoever was intended by the poet for his hero, the fact remains that Caesar dominates the poem as none save the hero should do. He is the hero of the *Pharsalia* as Satan is the hero of *Paradise Lost*.' In the same vein Teuffel chooses Caesar, and is followed by Heitland (*op. cit.* pp. lxii–lxiii), who says 'he is a hero not in virtue of the poet's efforts, but in spite of them'.

[2] At any rate for Books IV–VIII, *vid. op. cit.* p. 560.

[3] Johnson, *Life of Milton* and *Life of Rowe*; Pichon, *Hist. de la litt. lat.* p. 567; E. E. Sikes, *Roman Poetry*, pp. 194–202. Butler (*loc. cit.*) and Plessis (*loc. cit.*) deny this, and the latter remarks 'Caton n'est qu'un personnage épisodique'.

[4] Plessis (*loc. cit.*), for the complete poem.

[5] Merivale, *History of the Romans under the Empire*, c. 54, à propos of 3. 104 *turba patrum*.

[6] Nutting in *Am. Journ. Phil.* liii, 1932, pp. 41–52.

[7] *Op. cit.* p. 329.

the practical hero of the poem in virtue of the defiant egoism
and the untiring energy summarized in the line,

'Thinking naught done while aught remained to do,
   (*Nil actum credens cum quid superesset agendum*, ii. 657).'

The appropriate comment on this opinion is made by Professor Eva Matthews Sanford as follows:[1] 'This is surely a
triumvirate from which the Muse of Epic Unity would have
averted her face in very shame.'

The mention of the Muse of Epic Unity is timely, and should
prompt the reader to consider what epic unity is and what it
demands. The answer is supplied by Aristotle, who based his
arguments upon the practice of the Greek poets, but did not
necessarily lay down laws for posterity to follow. In the
Poetics[2] he states that epic unity requires not a single hero, but
a single theme. The translation which follows is Bywater's:

The construction of its (*i.e.* of the epic) stories should
clearly be like that in a drama; they should be based on a single
action, one that is a complete whole in itself, with a beginning,
middle, and end.[3]...Nor should one suppose that there is
anything like them in our usual histories. A history has to
deal not with one action, but with one period and all that
happened in that to one or more persons, however discon-
nected the several events may have been. Just as two events
may take place at the same time, e.g. the sea-fight off Salamis
and the battle with the Carthaginians in Sicily, without con-
verging to the same end, so too of two consecutive events one
may sometimes come after the other with no one end as their
common issue. Nevertheless most of our epic poets, one may
say, ignore the distinction.

Herein...we have a further proof of Homer's marvellous
superiority to the rest. He did not attempt to deal even with the
Trojan war in its entirety, though it was a whole with a definite
beginning and end—through a feeling that it was too long a
story to be taken in in one view,[4] or if not that, too complicated
from the variety of incident in it. As it is, he has singled out
one section of the whole; many of the other incidents, how-

[1] 'Lucan and Civil War', *Class. Phil.* xxviii, 1933, p. 121.

[2] C. 23.

[3] δεῖ τοὺς μύθους καθάπερ ἐν ταῖς τραγῳδίαις συνιστάναι δραματικοὺς καὶ
περὶ μίαν πρᾶξιν ὅλην καὶ τελείαν ἔχουσαν ἀρχὴν καὶ μέσα καὶ τέλος.

[4] λίαν γὰρ ἂν μέγας καὶ οὐκ εὐσύνοπτος ἔμελλεν ἔσεσθαι.

ever, he brings in as episodes....As for the other epic poets, they treat of one man, or one period; or else of an action, which, although one, has a multiplicity of parts in it. This last is what the authors of the *Cypria* and *Little Iliad* have done. And the result is that, whereas the *Iliad* or *Odyssey* supplies materials for only one, or at most two tragedies, the *Cypria* does that for several, and the *Little Iliad* for more than eight....[1]

Now the centre round which the *Iliad* revolves is not Achilles but the wrath of Achilles (μῆνιν ἄειδε, θεά, Πηληϊάδεω Ἀχιλῆος), while the theme of the *Odyssey* is not merely Odysseus himself (ἄνδρα) but his wandering and his efforts to return home (ἄνδρα μοι ἔννεπε, Μοῦσα, πολύτροπον, ὃς μάλα πολλὰ | πλάγχθη...ἀρνύμενος ἥν τε ψυχὴν καὶ νόστον ἑταίρων). Other Greek epics, like those of the *Epic Cycle* or the *Thebais* of Antimachus of Colophon, violated the unity of action in at least one of the three ways which Aristotle specifies.

The Roman tradition cannot be said to conform with the example set by the *Iliad* and *Odyssey*. As in their buildings, so in their epics the Romans tended to vast and even unwieldy construction. In order to see the native method of writing an epic one has to turn to the two earliest specimens, the *Bellum Punicum* of Naevius and the *Annales* of Ennius. To use the language of Aristotle, they ignored the distinction between epic poetry and history, and to them, with one outstanding exception who had indeed one imitator, the unity of action in a poem revolving around one theme meant nothing. That exception was Vergil, the central theme of whose *Aeneid* was not the life of Aeneas, but the fulfilment by Aeneas of his own destiny in founding the nation which was to become Rome; and his imitator was Valerius Flaccus in the *Argonautica*. Vergil as the Roman Homer was careful to observe the canons which Aristotle inferred from the *Iliad* and *Odyssey*. If Aeneas is the 'hero' of the *Aeneid*, it is not the modern sense of the word that must be understood. He is the 'hero' because he is the most important person in the poem, and he is the most important person in the poem because it revolves around one phase or rather purpose in his life. Therefore much of the criticism levelled against Aeneas as if he were the hero of a

[1] He goes on to enumerate them.

modern work falls flat. In the same way Achilles is the 'hero' of the *Iliad* and Odysseus of the *Odyssey*. So it is exceedingly dangerous to ask who the 'hero' of any ancient epic is; and if it is dangerous in the case of Homer, Vergil, or Valerius Flaccus, it is futile in that of any other poet, Greek or Roman.

Marmontel in the preface to his translation of Lucan[1] says: '(Lucain) semble avoir oublié ce grand principe d'Aristote, que l'Epopée ne doit être qu'une tragédie en récit.' The *De Bello Ciuili* is but an annalistic poem in the Roman tradition. Just as the *Bellum Punicum* of Naevius is a history in verse of the First Punic War, or the *Annales* of Ennius of Rome down to the author's own day, or the *Punica* of Silius Italicus of the Second Punic War, so Lucan's poem is a history in verse of the Civil War. This fact, though sometimes disputed, was clearly recognized in antiquity, as well as during and since the Middle Ages.

Such, for instance, is the criticism brought against it by Petronius, who says: *ecce belli ciuilis ingens opus quisquis attigerit, nisi plenus litteris, sub onere labetur. non enim res gestae uersibus comprehendendae sunt, quod longe melius historici faciunt.* ('Now the man who sets his hand to the immense task of writing a *Civil War* will sink beneath the burden, unless he is full of the spirit of literature. He must not clothe historical facts in verse, because this is far inferior to what historians [*i.e.* those who write in prose] do.')[2] The same objection seems to have been felt in Martial's[3] day, and later writers allude to Lucan as a historian rather than a poet.[4]

[1] Paris, 1766. [2] *Sat.* 118.

[3] 14. 194 *sunt quidam qui me dicant non esse poetam.*

[4] *E.g.* Seru. ad Verg. *Aen.* 1. 382 *Lucanus...ideo in numero poetarum esse non meruit quia uidetur historiam composuisse, non poema*; Iord. *Getica* 5. 43 *Lucano plus storico quam poeta*; Isid. *Orig.* 8. 7. 10 *Lucanus ideo in numero poetarum non ponitur, quia uidetur historiam composuisse, non poema.* Cf. John of Salisbury, *Policraticus* 441 a, b (Webb, i, p. 109) *poeta doctissimus (si tamen poeta dicendus est, qui uera narratione rerum ad historicos magis accedit)*, and G. J. Vossius, *De Historicis Latinis* (i, c. 26) *inter historicos etiam locum damus M. Annaeo Lucano Cordubensi.* The matter is carefully discussed in an important article by Professor Sanford, entitled 'Lucan and his Roman Critics' (*Class. Phil.* xxvi, 1931, pp. 233–57).

Accordingly there can be no question of a hero amid any of the great characters depicted in the *De Bello Ciuili*, either in the sense in which Aeneas is the hero of the *Aeneid*, or still less in the modern meaning of the word. Lejay alone, perhaps, of recent commentators realizes the truth, though his reasons for stating it are not as fully set forth as was possible for him. He remarks:

On se pose d'ordinaire une question au sujet des person-
nages: Quel est le héros de la *Pharsale*? Mais il faut d'abord
se demander s'il y a lieu de se poser cette question. Le système
de Lucain ne suppose pas nécessairement un héros. La matière
choisie doit se découper en un certain nombre de 'lectures'....
Il suffit qu'il y ait unité de sujet, d'intérêt et de héros dans
chaque partie....Une autre preuve qu'il n'y a pas de héros,
c'est qu'avec les 8000 vers que nous avons, il nous est impossible de conjecturer l'étendue normale du poème. Il n'y a
donc aucune unité d'aucune sorte, aucun personnage éminent
dont le sort mis en question au début, puisse servir de
dénouement.[1]

Of the other extant epics of the Silver Age, the unfinished *Achilleis* of Statius is open to the objection of Aristotle, which is also stated in the *Poetics* as follows: 'The Unity of a Plot does not consist, as some suppose, in its having one man as its subject. An infinity of things befall that one man, some of which it is impossible to reduce to unity; and in like manner there are many actions of one man which cannot be made to form one action. One sees, therefore, the mistake of all the poets who have written a *Heracleid*, a *Theseid*, or similar poems; they suppose that, because Heracles was one man, the story also of Heracles must be one story.'[2] The same author's *Thebais* treats 'of an action, which, although one, has a multiplicity of parts in it'.[3] However, as has already been hinted, the case of the *Argonautica* of Valerius Flaccus is different, for in its theme epic unity is attainable. Valerius, who is nearer in most respects to the Vergilian model, follows his master also in composing a poem which revolves around one purpose of its

[1] *Op. cit.* pp. xxxvii–xxxviii.
[2] C. 8, tr. Bywater.   [3] *Ibid.* C. 23 (*cit. supr.*).

principal character, *i.e.* the quest of the Golden Fleece by Jason.

Those who have persisted in trying to find heroes for Latin epics in the annalistic tradition have failed to pay due attention to Statius's testimony against the theory that an epic should display a unity of hero. At the beginning of the *Thebais* he admits that he is unable to choose what hero he should celebrate first, as so many claim his attention:

> *quem prius heroum, Clio, dabis? inmodicum irae*
> *Tydea? laurigeri subitos an uatis hiatus?*
> *urguet et hostilem propellens caedibus amnem*
> *turbidus Hippomedon, plorandaque bella proterui*
> *Arcados atque alio Capaneus horrore canendus.*[1]

III. LUCAN'S HISTORICAL AUTHORITIES FOR THE EVENTS DESCRIBED IN THE FIRST BOOK

There can be little doubt that Lucan throughout must have relied mainly upon his most obvious source—the lost books of Livy (109–116) which dealt with the Civil War. The main arguments in support of this belief have been collected and concisely set forth by Postgate,[2] who incidentally notes the existence of a *color Liuianus* in the Eighth Book; and in the First it is possible also to trace some Livian influence on the language. In 5 n. the fondness of Livy for the neuter of the perfect participle passive used substantivally is mentioned, and other Livian words or usages are *semirutis* (24), *decretum est* with the infinitive (290), *et ipsi* (291), *in bellum prono* (292), and *Romani nominis* (359–60). Of these passages 289–92 certainly is imbued with the *color Liuianus*.

[1] 1. 41–5.
[2] See his editions of Book VII, pp. xii–xiii and of Book VIII, pp. xi–xii, as well as Pichon, *Les Sources de Lucain*, Paris, 1912, pp. 51 sqq. It is known that Livy, whom Augustus called a Pompeian, was a favourite author also of Lucan's grandfather and uncle, the elder and the younger Seneca (*Suas.* 6. 22; *Contr.* 10, *praef.* 2; *Epist.* 100. 9).

Postgate, however, goes on to say 'no evidence is forth-coming that Lucan did actually draw from any other source'. Pichon, who holds the same view,[1] points out that Caesar, in spite of the tribute paid to him by Cicero in the *Brutus*,[2] was not a favourite with Roman readers, and that Lucan would have ignored him for political reasons. On the other hand, if Caesar was one of Livy's sources, as Ussani[3] remarks, did his influence merely exert itself indirectly upon Lucan through the medium of Livy, or did the poet go back to him directly? Ussani observes the similarity between Caes. *B.C.* 1. 54. 1–2 and Luc. 4. 134–6. Attention also should be drawn to the striking passage 1. 409–11, where Lucan's interest in the tides of the Atlantic may possibly have been inspired by the descrip-tion of the coast of the Veneti in the Third Book of the *De Bello Gallico*. This argument, it must be admitted, cannot be pressed, as the movements of the Atlantic never failed to excite the attention of the Romans, who were accustomed to their own tideless sea; and accordingly allusions to tides were commonplaces in their literature. However, one would not expect a writer, who displays practically no poetic colour in his own work, to suggest many verbal parallels to Lucan, and it is perhaps an unprofitable undertaking to search for them.

The observation has already been made[4] that Lucan was often thought of as a historian rather than a poet, and his account in the First Book of the events in the early stages of the Civil War must now be considered side by side with those of other historians.

When anchor is finally weighed at 183, Caesar appears on the banks of the Rubicon, having previously[5] crossed the Alps from Transalpine into Cisalpine Gaul. Before he left Trans-alpine Gaul, he sent the 13th legion into Italy (*i.e.* Cisalpine

[1] *Op. cit.* p. 107: 'la Pharsale dérive exclusivement du récit de Tite-Live.'   [2] 262.

[3] *Sul valore storico del poema lucaneo* (Rome, 1903), quoted by Pichon, *op. cit.* p. 97.   [4] P. xxvii.

[5] In November or early in December of 50 B.C. See Hirtius, *B.G.* 8. 54 and Rice Holmes, *The Roman Republic*, Oxford, 1923, ii, pp. 323–7.

Gaul) to take the place of the 15th,[1] which he had been ordered
by a senatorial decree of the previous May to hand back to
Pompey. His other legions had been left in winter quarters.
Four were under the command of C. Trebonius in the country
of the Belgae, and four with C. Fabius among the Aedui.[1] By
Dec. 13 or 14 he reached Ravenna.[2] He had previously heard
of the commission[3] with which the consul Marcellus had
charged Pompey on Dec. 2, and forthwith must have ordered
the scattered detachments of the 13th legion to assemble at
Ravenna.[4] Rice Holmes[5] assumes that he also sent for the 8th
and 12th legions from the four which had been left with
Fabius. This assumption appears to be necessary on account
of Caesar's silence in his *De Bello Ciuili*, for his intention was
perhaps to suggest that he committed no hostile act until
forced by the news of what had happened at Rome, *i.e.* the
flight of the tribunes on the night of Jan. 7, or even the
meeting of the Senate and the preparations for war on the
following day.

On Jan. 11 Caesar crossed the Rubicon with the 13th legion
only and entered Ariminum. Plutarch and Appian,[6] who here
as elsewhere may be deriving their accounts from Asinius
Pollio[7] rather than from Livy, state that he had sent a detachment under Hortensius the younger on the previous day to seize
that town, but of this there is no mention in Caesar or Lucan.
Even if this story was in Livy, it is not surprising to find Lucan
ignoring it, as he must have seen that the sudden entry of the
troops into Ariminum and the consternation of the inhabitants
would enhance the drama of the invasion of Italy.

In the meantime the tribunes Antony and Cassius, accompanied by Curio and Caelius, had left Rome. Lucan agrees

[1] Hirt. *loc. cit.*   [2] Rice Holmes, *op. cit.* p. 326.
[3] Marcellus placed a drawn sword in Pompey's hand, and requested him to raise levies against Caesar. See Hirt. *op. cit.* 55.
[4] The date is not certain. See Rice Holmes, *op. cit.* pp. 254-5.
[5] *Op. cit.* pp. 322 and 324.
[6] Plut. *Caes.* 32. 1, App. 2. 35.
[7] See Pichon, *op. cit.* pp. 93-4. According to Plutarch, Asinius
Pollio was actually with Caesar when he entered Italy.

with Caesar himself, Livy, Plutarch, Appian, and Dio[1] that they were expelled, or at any rate that they felt obliged to flee on account of the hostile attitude of the Pompeians. Cicero, however, in a letter written on Jan. 12,[2] suggests that they were not forcibly ejected.

Caesar states[3] that he met the tribunes at Ariminum, and this is the account of Lucan, as well as of Suetonius and Dio.[4] There is a rival story that they joined him while he was still at Ravenna, and those who, like Professor Tenney Frank,[5] uphold it, invoke the authority of Plutarch and Appian. Their view is that, as the crossing of the Rubicon is to these two writers, as to Lucan, a significant fact,[6] while on the other hand Dio, Florus, and Orosius ignore even the name of the river, Plutarch and Appian are both again following Asinius Pollio. Professor Frank has to assume that Antony later falsified Caesar's original account by inserting the words *ibique tribunos plebis...conuenit*, but this is not all. In fact Plutarch, in his *Life* of Caesar, and Appian,[7] as Rice Holmes[8] points out, do not say that the tribunes came to Ravenna. They do not make it clear where the meeting took place, but observe only that Caesar showed the tribunes, who were worn and travel-stained, to the soldiers to excite their compassion. Only in his *Life* of Antony[9] does Plutarch say definitely that Caesar met the tribunes before he crossed the Rubicon, but this may well be a mistake typical of the biographer.[10] It is most likely, then, that Rice Holmes is right in following Caesar's statement that the place of meeting was Ariminum, and it is equally probable that Livy reported the same story, while Asinius Pollio was vague.

[1] Caes. *B.C.* 1. 5, Liu. *Perioch.* 109, Plut. *Caes.* 31 and *Ant.* 5, App. 2. 33, Dio 41. 3. 2.
[2] *Fam.* 16. 11. 2: *nulla ui expulsi.*
[3] *B.C.* 1. 8. 1.   [4] Suet. *Iul.* 33, Dio 41. 4. 1.
[5] *Class. Quart.* i, 1907, pp. 223–5.
[6] Compare also Plut. *Pomp.* 60. 2.
[7] Plut. *Caes.* 31, App. 2. 33.   [8] *Op. cit.* p. 335.
[9] 5.
[10] Sihler, *Annals of Caesar*, New York, 1911, p. 302, remarks: 'He (Plutarch) confuses various data as to sequence.'

If there are any grounds for believing that what Plutarch says in his *Life* of Antony represents a different tradition, it may well go back to a misunderstanding of Caesar's words: *profugiunt statim ex urbe tribuni plebis seseque ad Caesarem conferunt. is eo tempore erat Rauennae.*[1] Here *sese...conferunt*, etc., may have been taken as 'reached Caesar who was then at Ravenna' instead of 'made their way towards Caesar', etc. Such a mistake is not improbable in the case of Plutarch with his uncertain knowledge of Latin.

It was at Ariminum that Caesar, according to his own account,[2] sent for the rest of his legions from winter quarters in Transalpine Gaul. If Rice Holmes is correct in his inferences, the 8th and 12th legions had already been summoned.[3] The 12th joined Caesar at the beginning of February, between Auximum and Cingulum in Picenum,[4] and the 8th came with new levies from Gaul to him at Corfinium on the 17th of that month.[5] There is no real reason for believing that Livy had a different version from that of Caesar, for Dio probably means that the general began to send for his soldiers at Ariminum, when he says συναγαγὼν τοὺς στρατιώτας.[6] On the other hand, Plutarch and Appian[7] assert that Caesar summoned his army before crossing the Rubicon, though here again their account may go back to Asinius Pollio rather than to Livy.

So far Lucan's source may have been either Caesar or Livy, and the only event described in the First Book which draws attention to possible disagreement between these two authorities is the delivery of Caesar's speech to his troops. According to Caesar himself,[8] it was made to the 13th legion at Ravenna before he crossed the Rubicon and after he heard what had been happening at Rome;[9] but Suetonius, Dio, and Orosius all agree with Lucan that it took place at Ariminum.[10]

[1] *B.C.* 1. 5.   [2] *B.C.* 1. 8. 1.   [3] See above, p. xxxi.
[4] *B.C.* 1. 15.   [5] Rice Holmes, *op. cit.* iii, p. 19.
[6] 41. 4. 1. The aorist seems to be ingressive.
[7] Plut. *Caes.* 32. 1, App. 2. 34.   [8] *B.C.* 1. 7.
[9] Including the expulsion of the tribunes.
[10] Suet. *Iul.* 33, Dio 41. 4. 1, Oros. 6. 15. 3.

Dio gives the additional information that it followed a speech made by Curio. Plutarch and Appian[1] again merely imply that it was pronounced after the arrival of the tribunes. Here it does seem that Lucan is following Livy rather than Caesar. Indeed Pichon[2] risks the suggestion that Livy, and after him Lucan, wished to depreciate Caesar's initiative by refusing to allow him to do anything decisive until he had been encouraged by Curio. Against this is the fact that he had by now crossed the Rubicon and *moras soluit belli*[3]—like a lion too!

If Caesar's own account is correct, and he delivered a speech at Ravenna and there only, it is still not surprising to find the dramatic sense of both Livy and Lucan prompting them to make Caesar appeal to his soldiers *after* the arrival of the tribunes, when they could see for themselves the miserable plight of these men. To Lucan the arrival of the refugees on the scene opened the way for a display of rhetoric, for Caesar's speech could be introduced by the persuasive words of Curio, and rounded off afterwards by the encouragement of Laelius.[4]

Rice Holmes, however, in order to reconcile the two accounts and answer Professor Frank, suggests[5] that there were probably two speeches, one at Ravenna and the other at Ariminum, the first before 'the vital step was taken',[6] the second when the soldiers could believe the sight of their own eyes so that their resolution was confirmed. In any case, the truth seems to be that Lucan is following Livy, who supplied him with the most trustworthy and likely account, that Caesar crossed the Rubicon and entered Ariminum, where he met Curio and the tribunes, exhorted his soldiers of the 13th legion, and summoned the rest of his forces from Transalpine Gaul. Even in this detail, the Livian and Lucanic version does not necessarily conflict with Caesar's story. If there is no strong reason for supposing that Lucan was indebted to Caesar directly without the medium of Livy, there are equally no sufficient grounds in the First Book for believing that he followed only

[1] *Loc. cit.*   [2] *Op. cit.* p. 100.
[3] 204.   [4] Laelius's speech may be unhistorical.
[5] *Op. cit.* ii, pp. 334–7.   [6] Frank.

Livy, and had either omitted to read Caesar, or disregarded him because he himself was a partisan of the Pompeian side.

How far was Lucan affected by Cicero's correspondence? Ussani and Pichon[1] have both discussed this question, the former arguing that Lucan was an admirer of Cicero and pointing to some resemblances, the latter replying that the poet really speaks coldly of the orator[2] and casting doubt upon the alleged parallels.

In 277 Lucan is obviously thinking of the famous phrase which Cicero used in the *Pro Milone*, namely *silent enim leges inter arma*,[3] especially as Curio is expressing his grievance too against the conduct of the Pompeians. Did the language of Cic. *Att.* 6. 6. 4 *Pompeius eo robore uir, eis radicibus* suggest the simile of 136–43? At 303–5 Lucan says that, from the point of view of the senatorial party, it might well have been Hannibal who had crossed the Alps instead of Caesar. The latter is also compared with Hannibal by Cicero writing in January 49 of the advance into Italy: *utrum de imperatore populi Romani an de Hannibale loquimur?*[4] It is possible, however, that such parallels with the great Carthaginian may be only a commonplace of rhetoric. No other passage can be adduced from Lucan's First Book to show any more marked resemblance to any part of Cicero's letters, and accordingly it cannot be asserted that the poet made much use of them, if indeed he employed them as a source at all. In fact, a possible disagreement has already been noted between Cicero, who was probably biased, and some of the other authorities about the expulsion of the tribunes.

At lines 466–8 Lucan leaves Caesar with a general statement that, after Ariminum, his forces began to spread all over Italy, and the poet does not return to a particular description of the advance southwards until 2. 439. The rest of the First Book is occupied with a description of the panic in Rome, the portents, and the measures taken to learn the will of heaven. The terror felt at the news of Caesar's approach is mentioned more than

[1] See the latter, *op. cit.* pp. 101–5.   [2] In the passage 7. 62–7.
[3] Cf. 321 *insolita...corona* and see note. These words may also be a reminiscence of the *Pro Milone*.   [4] *Att.* 7. 11. 1.

once by Cicero,[1] but Livy, with his love of narrating prodigies
and expiations, seems again to have been the real source of the
second half of this Book. Plutarch[2] vividly describes the flight
of the citizens of the smaller towns to Rome, the confusion
there, and the departure of Pompey and the Senate. His
description closes with a simile comparing the city with a ship
abandoned by her helmsman in a storm, and Lucan introduces
the same picture at 498–504. Appian's[3] interest in the prodigies
is probably derived from Livy rather than from Asinius Pollio.[4]
He mentions *inter alia* portents and signs in the sky (cf. Luc.
524–5), the lightning which struck the temples (534–5), the
sweat which issued from the statues of the gods (557), and a
mule foaling (590–1 n.). Dio's description[5] of the feelings of
those who fled from Rome and of those who were left is vivid.
The latter feared pillage and plunder (cf. Luc. 483–4),
especially because so large a part of Caesar's army was composed of barbarians.[6] The prodigies, however, are ignored.

Lucan himself as a historical authority must be employed
with caution. His political bias does not permit him to be
thought of as an objective historian, and his main utility consists in the fact that 'his work throws more light on the inter-
pretations of Roman history current in his circle than on the
events themselves'.[7] Fortunately, his proved indebtedness to

---

[1] *E.g. Att.* 7. 12. 2 (written on Jan. 22) *plena timoris et erroris
omnia.*   [2] *Caes.* 33–4, *Pomp.* 60–1.

[3] 2. 36. Ussani (*op. cit.* p. 9) has attempted to show that Appian
as well as Dio and Orosius have borrowed from Lucan, but Pichon
(*op. cit.* pp. 81 sqq.) asserts that the evidence is weak. It is more
likely that both Lucan and Appian derived their accounts from
Livy than that Appian was directly indebted to Lucan. See Postgate's edition of Book VIII, p. xvi n.

[4] The prodigies described by Appian (2. 68) and Plutarch (*Caes.*
43, *Pomp.* 68) as occurring before Pharsalia 'definitely point to Livy
as the common source' (Sihler, *op. cit.* p. 305).   [5] 41. 7–9.

[6] *Ibid.* 8. 6: πολὺ πλείω καὶ δεινότερα, ἅτε καὶ βαρβαρικοῦ τὸ πλεῖστον
τοῦ στρατοῦ αὐτοῦ ὄντος, πείσεσθαι προσεδόκων.

[7] Sanford, 'The Eastern Question in Lucan's *Bellum Ciuile*'
(*Classical and Mediaeval Studies in Honor of Edward Kennard Rand*,
New York, 1938, p. 264).

Livy makes him a useful, though by no means the most important, witness in the reconstruction of that historian's account of the Civil War.

IV. LUCAN'S GEOGRAPHICAL KNOW-LEDGE AS SHOWN BY BOOK I

The well-to-do Romans of the age in which Lucan lived had a keen interest in geography. While the poet was yet a child, Pomponius Mela, who was also a Spaniard and may have been a relation, published the first systematic treatise which is extant in Latin on the subject. The larger works of Strabo and the Elder Pliny are, of course, respectively earlier and later than Lucan, and the latter's uncle, Seneca the Younger, dealt more than once with geography and cosmology in essays which have not been preserved (*e.g.* the *De Situ Indiae, De Ritu et Sacris Aegyptiorum, De Motu Terrarum,* and *De Forma Mundi*), as well as in the *Naturales Quaestiones.* As for Lucan himself, scarcely any other Roman poet attempts to satisfy his readers with such a wealth of learning in the fields of history, astronomy, and geography,[1] though 'unfortunately this learning was of a loose and inaccurate kind'.[2]

Even the prose writers like Curtius, Mela, and Pliny are notoriously careless, and it is not surprising to find the poets as inaccurate. The student of Vergil's *Eclogues* on reaching I. 62 *aut Ararim Parthus bibet aut Germania Tigrim* discovers that the poet apparently thought the Arar to be in Germany. Proceeding for three more lines he comes to *pars Scythiam et rapidum Cretae ueniemus Oaxen,* where all the ink

---

[1] Also natural philosophy of all kinds, religious observance, and divination, as will be apparent to the reader of Book I.

[2] Heitland, *op. cit.* p. lii, where he gives several examples. See also Plessis, *op. cit.* pp. 566–7 and Housman's Astronomical Appendix (*Edition*, pp. 325–37). A particularly gross astronomical error is the placing of the sun in Libra on the occasion of Pompey's departure from Brundisium on Jan. 26 of the reformed calendar (2. 692).

that has been wasted on this verse does not alter the fact that Vergil believed the Oaxes, which was thought to flow into the Caspian, to be in Crete. Turning to the Second Eclogue he sees at line 24 *Amphion Dircaeus in Actaeo Aracyntho*, where, if he is wise, he will not credit the various views of many ancient and modern scholars,[1] but will conclude that Vergil places Mt. Aracynthus in Attica, though it is really in Aetolia. Then, skipping the rest of the *Eclogues* he comes to *Georg.* 1. 489–92:

> *ergo inter sese paribus concurrere telis*
> *Romanas acies iterum uidere Philippi;*
> *nec fuit indignum superis bis sanguine nostro*
> *Emathiam et latos Haemi pinguescere campos,*

where he exclaims at once '*Iterum! Bis!* But there was no previous battle at Philippi—it was at Pharsalia six years before'.

The best comment on this passage is Postgate's note on *Philippos* in his edition of Lucan's Seventh Book. Its conclusion must be quoted:

It may however be doubted whether the confusion is due to sheer mistake. Rhetoric and flattery probably had a hand in its production. How effective was it to make the two great battles fought on the same ground! How dexterous to suggest to a ruler who wished to bring his own fortunes into the closest connexion with the career of his 'parent' that here too he followed him '*perque patris* pater Augustus *uestigia* uicit!'[2]

In any case Vergil's lines perpetuated the confusion between Pharsalia and Philippi, so that later poets[3] use one name instead of the other,[4] or place Philippi in Thessaly or Pharsalia

---

[1] *E.g.* Servius, La Cerda, Fairclough (*Class. Phil.* xxv, 1930, pp. 37 sqq.), and L. P. Wilkinson (*Class. Rev.* l, 1936, pp. 120–1). Vergil's influence is seen in Propertius's similar mistake (3. 15. 42) despite Butler and Barber *ad loc.*

[2] Manil. 1. 913. Postgate's note (*op. cit.* p. 88) should be consulted in its entirety. See also Plessis, *op. cit.* pp. 566–7.

[3] To the passages mentioned by Postgate add Sidon. *Carm.* 9. 242 (*Lucanus*) *dans lacrimas suis Philippis.* Florus 2. 13 (4. 2) 43 speaking of Pharsalia calls it Philippi: *proelio sumpta Thessalia est, et Philippicis campis urbis imperii generis humani fata commissa sunt.*

[4] This is the case at 680, and is probably so at 694, though the priestess may mean 'I have seen a (battle like) Philippi already'.

in Macedonia, as Lucan may be doing at 1. 1, if he is not speaking τροπικῶς. It is, of course, frequently difficult to decide whether a poet is using a trope or committing a mistake in his geography. Philippi for Pharsalia or *vice versa* may be simply an instance of metonymy,[1] and it is always possible to explain, for example, *Germania* in Verg. *Ecl.* 1. 62 as a metonymy for *Gallia*.[2] This possibility is recognized by Postgate when, in the Introduction to his edition of Lucan's Eighth Book,[3] he discusses the poet's geographical inaccuracies; and an argument in its favour is that Thessaly was part of the province of Macedonia, so that the names of the two places Pharsalia and Philippi in the same province were the more easily interchangeable.

Another passage where Vergil seems undoubtedly to have caused Lucan to err is *Aen.* 4. 480–2:

> *Oceani finem iuxta solemque cadentem*
> *ultimus Aethiopum locus est, ubi maximus Atlas*
> *axem umero torquet stellis ardentibus aptum.*

The words *Oceani finem iuxta* seem to have made Lucan believe that Atlas was beside the sea (554–5),[4] but this, of course, is not the case.

However, the great majority of Lucan's errors cannot be laid for certain at the door of Vergil or of his other predecessors. A historical slip occurs at 254–6, where the people of Ariminum complain that their town, on account of its geographical position, was always the first to be exposed to the violence of any hostile force invading Italy. The enemies who are specifically mentioned are the Senones, Cimbri, Carthaginians, and Teutones. It is true that the Senones threatened

---

[1] See pp. lvi–lvii.

[2] Metonymies are not always recognized even where they are genuine, *e.g.* Mackail does not see that in Verg. *Aen.* 8. 677 *Leucaten = Actium* (see his note on *id.* 3. 268–76).

[3] P. lxxviii. See *ibid.* pp. lxxxix sqq. for a discussion of Lucan's use of *Thessalia* and *Pharsalia*.

[4] See note and *Class. Quart.* xxx, 1936, p. 62. In extenuation of Vergil it should be noted that Strabo (17. 3. 2) mentions a similar belief, which may have been the common one in antiquity.

Ariminum in 236 B.C.,[1] and Hasdrubal's route into Italy in 207
passed it, but it was never in immediate danger[2] from the Cimbri
and Teutones, the latter of whom indeed never entered even
Cisalpine Gaul, while the former were checked near Vercellae
by Marius and Catulus.[3] But the immediate concern of this
part of the *Introduction* is to speak of the poet's geographical
mistakes in his First Book.

The matter has been discussed not only by Heitland and
Plessis, who have been mentioned already, but also by Pichon,[4]
by M. Bourgery,[5] and by the present writer.[6] The most important part of the First Book in this connexion is the passage
which serves as a catalogue and purports to describe the Gallic
tribes from whom Caesar withdrew his legions. It is likely
that here Lucan's ultimate source was Posidonius, the Stoic
philosopher, who was also the authority upon whom Diodorus
Siculus[7] and Strabo[8] drew for their descriptions of Gaul.[9] The
similarities between these authors and the poet will be mentioned in the commentary. Lejay's opinion,[10] however, is that
Lucan had immediately before him a list or perhaps a map of
the peoples of Gaul, with the names of some rivers and mountains, some information about their religion, and a little knowledge about their general characteristics, *i.e.* that they were

[1] *Camb. Anc. Hist.* vii, p. 807.

[2] Lucan may, of course, mean that the inhabitants of Ariminum
were in a state of terror while the Cimbri and Teutones were
moving to and fro on the other side of the Alps.

[3] Plessis (*op. cit.* p. 566) calls attention to a further alleged error
which concerns the date of the *feriae Latinae* (550). According to
some authorities, this festival was normally held in March or April,
but Pease on Cic. *Diu.* 1. 18 (*Edition*, p. 104) mentions January as a
possible month for its occurrence.

[4] *Op. cit.* pp. 1–49.

[5] 'La Géographie de Lucain' (*Rev. de Philologie*, 1928, pp. 25–40).

[6] *Class. Quart.* xxx, 1936, especially pp. 59–60.

[7] 5. 25–40.   [8] 4. 1–5.

[9] Hosius, 'Lucanus und Seneca' (*Neue Jahrbücher*, 1892, p. 347),
N. Pinter, *Lucanus in tradendis rebus geographicis quibus usus sit
auctoribus*, Münster, 1902, p. 15. Posidonius may also have influenced Caesar, according to Müllenhoff, *Deutsche Alterth.* ii,
pp. 307–8.   [10] *Op. cit.* pp. xlix–l.

fair-haired and lightly armed, that they wore trousers, etc. All
that he did then was to apply certain characteristics at random
to particular peoples, whom he not infrequently assigned to
incorrect geographical positions. Then he threw in pell-mell
notes on the gods and druids, with the banal transition *et
quibus* (444), in no proper order.

Lejay's view seemed too harsh to scholars like Salomon
Reinach, Jullian, and Pichon, but it is difficult for the dis-
cerning reader to arrive at any other conclusion,[1] coming to the
Gallic passage, as he does, with the preliminary information
that the Rubicon rises in the Alps (219).[2] Place-names etc.
which seem to be used incorrectly will be discussed in order.

397 *Vogesi* is attested by the MSS and *Vosegi* is a correction, which, nevertheless, is not necessarily what Lucan wrote.
He seems to have thought the name to be that of a river and
not of a mountain, so that Grotius's correction of *ripam* to
rupem in the same context is unwarranted.

398 *Lingonas.* In fact, the territory of the Lingones lay
considerably to the West of the Vosges, which rather domi-
nated the Leuci. The error may go back to Caes. *B.G.* 4. 10. 1
(or to the source of this passage) *Mosa profluit ex monte
Vosego, qui est in finibus Lingonum.* Has Lucan a confused recollection of this passage, which, according to Meusel and
Klotz, is spurious, and by *Vogesi* does he mean the Meuse?
For the situation of the Lingones, see Rice Holmes, *Caesar's
Conquest of Gaul,* 2nd ed. 1911, p. 692, n. 2.

399 *Isarae.* For reasons why it may be thought that Lucan
really had the Saône (Arar) and not the Isère in mind, the
notes should be consulted. In the same way M. Bourgery
suggests[3] that the Cinga (432), which is a Spanish and not a

[1] In *Rhein. Mus.* N.F. lxxxviii, 1939, pp. 164–79, Mr R. Samse
tries to find an orderly plan in this catalogue, and consequently has
to resort to three improbable emendations at 419, 432, and 442.

[2] At 2. 429 Lucan distinguishes the Alps and the Apennines, and
here he may be employing the one name for the other.

[3] *Op. cit.* p. 32: 'Lucain aurait mis par exemple *Cinga* pour
Sequana, fleuve dont les sinuosités justifieraient admirablement le
verbe *pererrat.*'

Gallic river (as Lucan well knew at 4. 20-3), is a mistake for Sequana (the Seine).

419 *Nemetis*. As the Nemetes are coupled with the Aturus (Adour), Lucan seems to believe that they were situated between the Gironde and the Pyrenees, whereas in fact they dwelt beside the Rhine.

427 *Aruernique ausi Latio se fingere fratres* ('and the Aruerni who dared to pretend that they are brethren of the Romans'). Since 123 B.C. the Aedui were recognized as Friends and Allies of the Roman People,[1] as is attested by Caes. *B.G.* 1. 33. 2, Cic. *Att.* 1. 19. 2, Tac. *Ann.* 11. 25, and Plut. *Caes.* 26. 3. On the other hand, the Aruerni in Caesar's day were hostile to the Aedui and, consequently, to the Romans.[2] Oudendorp defends Lucan's veracity by interpreting the line to mean that the Aruerni dared to claim kinship with the Romans when only the Aedui had that right, and Cortius quotes Sidon. *Ep.* 7. 7. 2[3] for the story that they claimed their descent from Antenor. But Sidonius is a much later authority, and in quoting Lucan here is almost certainly influenced by his mistake. That *Aruerni* in Lucan is a metonymy for *Aedui* seems barely possible.

429 *Neruius et caesi pollutus foedere Cottae*. Cotta was slain in fact by the Eburones, not by the Nervii (see note *ad loc.*). Is this also a metonymy?

448-9 *uates...Bardi*. Lucan seems to confuse the *uates* with the *Bardi*, whereas, according to Strabo (see note), the Bards, Vates, and Druids were distinct classes.

Because of Lucan's proved inaccuracy, it is dangerous to emend his text to make it agree with fact, and for this reason emendations like the spelling *Vosegi* (397), Bentley's *Belgis* for *bellis* (463),[4] or Van Jever's *Albim* for *Alpem* (481) should not be accepted readily. The two last passages should be considered.

463-4 *uos, crinigeros bellis arcere Caycos | oppositi*, etc. The

---

[1] Rice Holmes, *op. cit.* p. 3.   [2] Caes. *B.G.* 1. 31. 3-4.

[3] *Aruernorum, pro dolor, seruitus, qui, si prisca replicarentur, audebant se quondam fratres Latio dicere et sanguine ab Iliaco populos computare.*

[4] Cf. the same critic's *Aeolii* for *Aegaei* at 2. 665.

Chauci, however, did not dwell near the Rhine,[1] but occupied
the territory close to the sea between the Visurgis (Weser) and
the Albis (Elbe), *i.e.* between Bremen and Hamburg. It is
possible to say that *Caycos = Germanos* by synecdoche (*i.e.* part
for the whole), and that Lucan has in mind such German tribes
as the *feroces Sygambros*,[2] who, because of their geographical
position immediately across the Rhine, were always liable to
invade Gaul.[3] For a defence of *bellis* see p. xlix.

481 *tunc inter Rhenum populos Alpemque iacentes* (*Caesarem
sequi*). Van Jever's emendation *Albimque* makes Lucan assert
that there were Germans in Caesar's train. It would indeed be
a tribute to the exactness of the poet's attention to Caesar as a
historian if, on the assumption that *Albim* is the true reading,
it were argued seriously that these Germans are those whom
Caesar enlisted in 52 B.C.[4] But Lucan elsewhere does not speak
of Caesar as bringing them into Italy either in fact or according
to rumour. On the other hand, at 2. 570 *Rheni gelidis quod*
(*Caesar*) *fugit ab undis* he implies that they were still un-
conquered. Housman in defending *Albim* quotes 2. 52, which
in reality proves the emendation wrong. With the preceding
line, Lucan's words there are *fundat ab extremo flauos aquilone
Suebos | Albis et indomitum Rheni caput*, and are made part of
the prayers of the distracted Romans to the gods, that the
barbarians may attack the city (so far, of course, there is no
question of their doing so), if only the peril of civil war be
avoided. In other words, there had been no German invasion;
and the feat of imagination, which those who read *Albim* wish
to foist upon the disordered minds of the citizens, is greater
than even Lucan intended. In his conception of the geography
of Gaul, the Rhine was in the North (see 371 and 2. 51 *cit.
supr.*), and the Alps formed the southern boundary of Transalpine Gaul, which was a northern country;[5] so that a traveller

[1] Only Tacitus, in a passage which has caused some difficulty
(*Germ.* 35), implies that they extended as far South as the Chatti,
i.e. near the right bank of the Rhine.
[2] Hor. *Carm.* 4. 2. 34–6.   [3] Caes. *B.G.* 4. 16.
[4] Caes. *B.G.* 7. 65.
[5] Cf. 3. 74 *Gallorum tantum populis Arctoque subacta.*

entering Italy or even Cisalpine Gaul was thought of as coming South. Therefore the nations living between the Rhine and the Alps were the peoples of Transalpine Gaul. Compare also Pompey's words in 2. 535 *Gallica per gelidas rabies effunditur Alpes*.

The confusion in 555 between Calpe, Abyla, Ampelusia, and Atlas on account of the connexion of Heracles with all these places is discussed in the note on that line. But from the First Book alone sufficient instances have been given 'to prove how shallow was the erudition so ostentatiously displayed'.[1]

V. A NEGLECTED ASPECT OF LUCAN'S RHETORIC

The great American scholar B. L. Gildersleeve in a review[2] of Rhys Roberts's *Demetrius on Style*[3] once expressed sympathy with those who in his day were deploring the decline of rhetoric in France. Such was d'Haussonville, who in a critique of George Sand pleaded that the rhetorical precepts of modern times are the same as those which were taught in Greece and Rome, and that the student who fails to discern their eternal truth when it is hidden beneath arid formulas is like an architect who embellishes the exterior of his building without having due regard to the firmness of the base on geometric principles.

'No one', remarked Gildersleeve, 'can be surprised at these pleas, these warnings, who knows how much the sanity of French prose is due to rhetorical studies. With the new era the old charm will disappear. On the one hand, we shall have, nay, we have, utter carelessness, on the other, sublimated symbolism. And if rhetoric is neglected in France, what shall we say of the scant attention it has received in Anglo-Saxon countries?'

[1] Heitland, *op. cit.* p. lii.

[2] *Am. Journ. Phil.* xxiv, 1903, pp. 101–11, reprinted in *Selections from the Brief Mention of B. L. Gildersleeve*, Baltimore, 1930, pp. 90–4.   [3] Cambridge, 1902.

There has been, indeed, a feeling abroad for many years that literature is killed by attention to its scientific study, and essays which talk in vague but pleasant generalities are more popular with an easy-going public than works which invite precise application to details. The ancient grammarians have been discarded long ago as so much useless lumber, and modern writers on the same subject are also beginning to suffer. If the disastrous effects of this neglect are seen everywhere now in the English language and in ephemeral works produced in it, they have been obvious long ago in the study of Greek and Latin literature. The folly of interpreting ancient languages by the standards (or lack of them) of the present age may be illustrated from modern editions of the authors of Greece and Rome.

A frequent remark of historians of ancient literature is the vague suggestion that so-and-so was influenced by his rhetorical training, but few writers on the subject take the trouble to explain how this rhetorical training manifests itself in a particular work, or how important a knowledge of it is for the interpretation of a given oration or poem. Of no ancient author is this statement made more frequently without amplification than of Lucan,[1] the reason being that Quintilian observes, in the one part of the *Institutio Oratoria* which no one fails to read, that this poet was *magis oratoribus quam poetis imitandus*.[2]

The student, then, is usually told that Lucan had been trained in a school of rhetoric and consequently displays all the characteristics of this system of education. To find out what this system of education was is a task which fortunately has been made easy by Quintilian, who was the poet's contemporary. Gildersleeve[3] complained: 'And sometimes I cannot help thinking that it would be better if our classical scholars themselves had read something more of Quintilian than the first chapter of the Tenth Book, to which most of them seem

[1] Wight Duff (*op. cit.* pp. 323–9) in considering 'the action of rhetoric on Lucan's genius' pays more attention to detailed explanation than the majority of writers on the subject, and is consequently more helpful to beginners than most of those who pretend to cater for them. [2] 10. 1. 90. [3] *Loc. cit.*

to confine their attention.' The whole of the *Institutio Oratoria* is extremely important, but the beginner who wishes to study the framework upon which style and language were built in the ancient schools of rhetoric must turn his attention particularly to the neglected Eighth and Ninth Books. Here he will find a discussion of the theory of style, which is the most difficult part of the orator's task,[1] and of the rules for the cultivation of *eloquentia*, to which Cicero had previously devoted great care.[2] Among these rules are those governing the use of tropes and figures, which were of prime importance in the instruction given in Quintilian's day.

Of the various features of rhetorical theory none is less popular to-day than the ancient view that language is divided into two compartments, the familiar and the unfamiliar,[3] and that excursions from the former into the latter constitute tropes and figures of speech, which should be catalogued carefully and taught to students in order that they may learn how to adorn their style. True, this is an artificial method and savours of hard work, so that the wit even of serious writers on the subject finds ready acceptance,[4] and the whole matter is contemptuously brushed aside, because it is not in accordance with modern taste. This is bad policy in scholarship. Whether this manner of rhetorical instruction finds approval or not is of little moment; for what does matter is that it was inculcated in the ancient orators and poèts (of whom Lucan is a supremely good example) from the moment when their training began,[5] and if it be ignored, their interpretation and translation will

[1] 8. *pr.* 13 *elocutionis rationem tractabimus, partem operis, ut inter omnes oratores conuenit, difficillimam.*

[2] *Ibid.* 15. [3] See *infr.* p. l.

[4] *E.g.* Saintsbury (*History of Criticism*, i, p. 53): 'drugs or simples, existing independently, acting automatically, and to be "thrown in", as the physician exhibits his pharmacopoeia, to produce this or that effect'. Cf. *ibid.* p. 102 'the famous, or infamous, Figures', p. 166 'these idols', etc.

[5] E. E. Sikes (*Roman Poetry*, 1923, p. 17) observes: 'The marks of this training are apparent in every form of the literature. Except Martial, no Augustan or post-Augustan poet was wholly free from the influence of rhetoric, whether—like Virgil—he might try to

suffer inevitably. It is all very well to pray with Paul-Louis
Courier[1] 'Dieu, délivre nous du malin et du langage figuré', or
to gibe with Samuel Butler[2] 'All a rhetorician's rules Teach
nothing but to name his tools', but this attitude will not help
the student of Roman poetry, for whom it is better to face the
matter squarely, even though he grudges doing so. Mr E. E.
Sikes[3] remarks:

Style depended on the successful employment of the Figures,
regarded as touchstones of literary excellence. Here, at least,
the Greeks were 'always children', holding the ingenuous
belief that the art of writing could be taught by attention to
apostrophe, asyndeton, periphrasis and the rest. Of course
the Figures had—and may still have—a certain value as convenient labels of virtues (or vices) in style. The danger of
analysing literature in figurative terms is due, not so much to
the recognition that language *is* largely figurative, as to the
misuse of the method by the rhetorical teachers, who seem
always to suggest that Homer or Demosthenes may be suc-
cessfully imitated by borrowing or plundering their tropes.

The sad results of Bentley's disregard of Horace's use of
figurative language are alluded to in Bell's *The Latin Dual and
Poetic Diction*,[4] a work which displays some faults of arrangement and a tendency to exaggerate, but which has met in many
quarters with a reception by no means worthy of its utility.
But Bentley is by no means the only scholar who has fallen
foul of passages which he has misunderstood because of in-
sufficient knowledge of rhetorical and poetical usage.

Hor. *Carm.* 1. 6 begins with the lines:

> *scriberis Vario fortis et hostium*
> *uictor, Maeonii carminis alite*

---

escape, or—like Lucan—gloried in his "eloquence".' It is, however, by no means certain that Vergil tried to escape from it; cf.
Macrob. *Sat.* 5. 1. 1–20, where it is agreed that he was an orator as
much as a poet. Florus wrote a work entitled *Vergilius orator an
poeta?* and Servius (on *Aen.* 10. 18) says that Titianus and Calvus
used to teach rhetoric from him.

[1] Quoted by Gildersleeve, *loc. cit.*
[2] Quoted by Saintsbury, *op. cit.* i, p. 43.
[3] *The Greek View of Poetry*, 1931, pp. 212–13.
[4] Oxford, 1923.

('your victorious exploits will be described by Varius, a bird of Homeric song'). Modern commentators explain *Vario...
alite* either as an ablative absolute or as an ablative of the personal agent without *ab*, or else they see that *Vario* must be a dative of the agent, and then proceed to alter *alite* to *aliti* in defiance of the testimony of the MSS and the ancient authorities. No attention is paid to Servius when he remarks[1] that *Vario* is the dative of the agent; but this is the usual fate of ancient grammarians when, in teaching the grammar of their own language, they conflict with modern preconceptions.[2] *Alite* is the ablative for the dative, in other words the figure *antiptosis* or use of one case for another, which is mentioned by Servius elsewhere. A good instance also is Sil. 13. 409 *cetera, quae poscis, maiori uate canentur*, where *uate = uati*.

Another example is from Lucan's First Book. Lines 427–8 are:

> *Aruernique ausi Latio se fingere fratres*
> *sanguine ab Iliaco populi.*

Here, on account of a passage in Sidonius, who, if his text is sound, seems not to have understood the figure, Bentley alters *populi* to *populos*;[3] and Housman embodies the general misinterpretation in his note, where he follows Haskins, who takes *populi* as nominative plural.[4] No better illustration is required of Postgate's dictum regarding hypallage: 'a figure which, wherever there is an opening, the modern annotator is prone to misunderstand',[5] and here the pit gapes for the unwary who have forgotten Verg. *Aen.* 8. 526 *Tyrrhenus tubae...clangor*, Hor. *Carm.* 1. 12. 34 *superbos Tarquini fasces*, and similar expressions.[6]

[1] Ad *Ecl.* 9. 35, *Georg.* 3. 6, *Aen.* 1. 440.

[2] Among those who overrule the testimony of Servius may be mentioned Housman, whose view of the passage was heard by the writer during a lecture in 1930.

[3] This emendation is as bad as his change of *uarius* to *uarios* in Hor. *Carm.* 2. 5. 12, and as unnecessary as Gronovius's alteration of *Tyrios* to *Tyriis* in Stat. *Theb.* 1. 10.

[4] So Duff translates 'The Arvernian clan'.

[5] 'Flaws in Classical Research' (*Proc. Brit. Acad.* iii, 1908), p. 9.

[6] For one to the contrary, cf. Verg. *Aen.* 2. 713–14 *templum desertae Cereris.*

Yet a third instance may be considered in lines 463–4 of this Book. They are:

> uos, crinigeros bellis arcere Caycos
> oppositi.

The inadvisability on historical grounds of Bentley's emendation *Belgis* for *bellis* is discussed in the explanatory note to 463, but uncertainty as to the meaning of *bellis* has contributed in large measure to the frequent acceptance of *Belgis* by later scholars. The opinion that the word is equivalent to *a bellis gerendis* is negatived, not so much by what Tacitus says[1] of other German tribes in ch. 33 of his *Germania*, as by his precise statement two chapters later[2] about the Chauci. But Housman shows his complete misunderstanding of the meaning by his remark in rejecting the instrumental ablative: 'neque bellorum ope Romani, sed castrorum praesidiorumque, Caycos arcebant'. *Bella* are precisely *castra praesidiaque*, or *arma* generally, by a metonymy which is of the most frequent occurrence in Latin poetry, and of which line 277 (see the explanatory note) contains not the only instance in Lucan.[3] The translation is, then: 'you (soldiers) who have been stationed opposite the Chauci (Germans) in order to keep them at a distance by force of arms'. Varro's definition of *arma*, which is as follows: *arma ab arcendo, quod his arcemus hostem (Ling. Lat. 5. 115)*, excellently illuminates the use of *bellis arcere*, as does Tac. *Hist.* 4. 74 *exercitus quibus Germani Britannique arceantur.*

Such examples might be developed to the advantage of the student, but with little credit to modern annotation. The history of the attention paid to tropes and figures must be outlined briefly before Quintilian's teaching of the subject is discussed in detail.

The practice of basing a valuation of literature in terms of figures upon prose and poetry already in existence seems to go

---

[1] Which Housman mentions in attempting to refute this explanation.   [2] See the explanatory note on 463.

[3] *E.g.* 3. 64 *bellaque Sardoas etiam sparguntur in oras*, which Duff translates 'other troops were detached for the borders (!) of Sardinia', and 6. 191–2 *bellum atque uirum, i.e.* 'an army and a man'.

back to Gorgias and the sophists in the fifth century B.C.,
though the nucleus of figurative criticism, as it was known later
to the Alexandrians and Romans, appears first in Aristotle.
One of his greatest contributions to the study of literature is
his distinction in the twenty-first and twenty-second chapters
of the *Poetics* between words which are ' ordinary ' or ' proper '
(κύρια) and those which are 'unfamiliar' (ξενικά); and in the
same context he goes on to discuss metaphor (μεταφορά) and
some of its varieties. In the second and subsequent chapters
of the Third Book of the *Rhetoric* he also deals with metaphor
(including simile), as well as with epithets and compound
words.[1]

After Aristotle had laid the foundation of this study, it is
likely that the grammarians of Alexandria, with their usual
fondness for cataloguing, compiled lists of tropes and figures.
The most important work in Greek on the subject between
Aristotle and ' Longinus ' is probably Tryphon's περὶ τρόπων,
which was written in the Augustan age. An abridgement of
this treatise is published in the third volume of Spengel's
Rhetores Graeci,[2] which contains also various writings[3] by
other grammarians of a later date on the same subject. Before
Tryphon's time, Cicero mentions a number of figures in the
De Oratore and *Orator*; and Cornificius, if he was the author
of the *Rhetorica ad Herennium*, handles these instruments of
rhetoric exhaustively in his Fourth Book. The Augustan
rhetoricians, Dionysius of Halicarnassus and Caecilius of
Calacte, also produced special works περὶ σχημάτων which
were known to Quintilian,[4] but which were subsequently lost.
Either in the Augustan age or somewhat later P. Rutilius
Lupus published a treatise on the same subject. This work
was used and quoted by Quintilian, and an abridgement is
published in Halm's *Rhetores Latini Minores*,[5] which, like

[1] The influence of Aristotle's teaching on this matter is seen
clearly in Demetrius's περὶ ἑρμηνείας, sections 77–127.
[2] Leipzig, Teubner, 1856.
[3] These are both περὶ τρόπων and περὶ σχημάτων. The volume also
contains the περὶ ἑρμηνείας of Demetrius. See Saintsbury, *op. cit.* i,
pp. 102–3.   [4] 9. 3. 89.   [5] Leipzig, 1863.

Keil's *Grammatici Latini*, contains also the teaching of later grammarians on the matter. 'Longinus'[1] deals at length with figures and says of them: 'if dealt with in the fitting manner, they contribute not a little to elevation',[2] but his treatment is that of the essayist instead of that of the cataloguer. No later grammarian is more illuminating than Servius in his commentary on Vergil. It is of interest to find the polymath Bede compiling a tract on the tropes and figures of the Holy Scriptures.[3]

In modern times the use of tropes and figures is fully and learnedly discussed after the example of Quintilian by G. J. Vossius in the Fourth and Fifth Books of his treatise on Rhetoric, which first appeared at Leiden in 1606. Earlier, in 1553, Thomas Wilson, of King's College, Cambridge, published *The Arte of Rhetorique*,[4] and in 1589 George Puttenham *The Arte of English Poesie*.[5] In the latter work a formidable list appears at the end of the Third Book (chs. xix–xxii). The *Lexicon Technologiae Latinorum Rhetoricae*[6] of Johann Christian Gottlieb Ernesti is of considerable service to students, while the most complete modern work on formal rhetoric is Volkmann's *Die Rhetorik der Griechen und Römer*,[7] where tropes and figures are adequately discussed. Two dissertations may be mentioned also, H. Gross's *Die Tropen und Figuren*[8] and R. Bonnet's *De tropis graecis capita selecta*.[9] A useful treatment will be found in Chaignet's *La Rhétorique et son Histoire*.[10] In English, an important book is Rutherford's *A Chapter in the History of Annotation*,[11] especially Part II, which is entitled *Interpretation Determined by the Poetical Tropes*, and C. S.

[1] 16–29 and 38.   [2] *Ibid.* 16.
[3] *De Schematis et Tropis Sacrae Scripturae*, Migne, *P.L.* xc, pp. 175–86; Halm, *op. cit.* pp. 607–18.
[4] Ed. G. H. Mair (Tudor and Stuart Library), Oxford, 1909. See pp. 170 sqq.   [5] Ed. Willcock and Walker, Cambridge, 1936.
[6] Leipzig, 1797.
[7] Berlin, 1872–4, 2te Aufl. 1885. There is a summary in Iwan von Müller's *Handbuch*, ii, 3 (1901), where see especially pp. 40–9.
[8] Diss. Leipzig, 1888.   [9] Diss. Marburg, 1920.
[10] Paris, 1888, pp. 467–507.
[11] Being *Scholia Aristophanica*, vol. iii.

Baldwin's *Ancient Rhetoric and Poetic*[1] should be consulted.
The student of Latin poetry, however, who wishes to under-
stand the ancient point of view must be referred to two highly
instructive articles by J. L. Moore entitled *Servius on the
Tropes and Figures of Vergil*.[2] Bell's *The Latin Dual and
Poetic Diction* has been mentioned already.

If, however, the rhetorical training which Lucan underwent
in his youth is to be comprehended, recourse must be had
in primis to Quintilian. The task of understanding the principles of ancient rhetoric must be shirked no more by the
conscientious reader of to-day than by the pupils of that great
teacher. *Via tamen opus est incipientibus*, says he at the outset of
his introduction to the principles of 'eloquence', *sed ea plana
et cum ad ingrediendum tum ad demonstrandum expedita* ('beginners, however, must be shown the way, but it must be level
and suitable, not merely for them to walk in it, but for their
teachers as well to indicate it to them').

In Book VIII of the *Institutio Oratoria*, chapter 1 advises
that style should be correct and idiomatic, 2 contrasts clearness
and obscurity, 3 is concerned with ornament (*ornatus*), which
cannot be attained until the faults of style are discarded,
4 discusses amplification and its opposite quality, attenuation
(*amplificandi uel minuendi species*), and 5 deals with *sententiae*
or striking reflections which are such a feature of the age.[3]

TROPES

In chapter 6 Quintilian handles the subject of tropes (τρόποι).
At the beginning a trope is defined as the artistic alteration of a
word or a phrase from its proper meaning to another (*tropus*

[1] New York, 1924.
[2] *Am. Journ. Phil.* xii, 1891, pp. 157–92 and 267–92.
[3] Quintilian (10. 1. 90) describes Lucan as *sententiis clarissimus*,
and Heitland (*op. cit.* pp. lxv–lxvii), after discussing the *sententiae*
of the whole poem (he selects from the First Book those in lines 32,
81, 92, 281, 331–2, and 348–9), comes to the conclusion that their
'matter is for the most part trite and commonplace' and that
'Quintilian is judging by a low standard, and...Lucan has not
attained a high one'.

est uerbi uel sermonis a propria significatione in aliam cum uirtute mutatio), and the author goes on to discuss metaphor, synecdoche, metonymy, antonomasia, onomatopoeia, catachresis, metalepsis, epithet, allegory, periphrasis, hyperbaton, and hyperbole. These may be illustrated from the First Book of Lucan's poem as follows.

(i) METAPHOR is, of course, distinguished from simile by the statement that not only is it shorter, but in the latter some object is compared with what we wish to describe, while in the former this object is actually substituted for it.[1] Simile, for instance, consists in saying that a man acts like a lion,[2] while metaphor is the statement that he is a lion. A list of Lucan's similes will be found in Heitland's *Introduction*[3] (he lists fourteen from the First Book), where the conclusion is reached that one grave defect is the over-description of the object which is to be illustrated by the simile. 'Then', says Heitland, 'when the simile does come, it falls flat.' An instance is seen in the contexts before the similes contained in 136–43 and 151–7, where Pompey and Caesar respectively are described so fully that the similes, when they come, add more to the general interest than to the clarity of the descriptions.[4] Heitland also discusses the metaphors of Lucan,[4] remarking that in the First Book they are mainly drawn from gladiators (7, 97, and 348), law (128), and the balance (57). Examples of mixed metaphors, against which Quintilian utters the warning sentence (8. 6. 50) *nam id quoque in primis est custodiendum ut, quo ex genere coeperis translationis, hoc desinas*, may be seen at 159 *semina...mersere* and 262–4 *faces...stimulos...moras*.

(ii) SYNECDOCHE is the use of a part for the whole or the whole for a part.[5] An instance of the part for the whole is *Emathia = Macedonia* (see 1 n.), while the whole is used for a part at 398 and 423, where *armis* in the former line refers specifically to shields and in the latter to swords.[6] Quintilian also mentions the employment of the singular for the plural

[1] Quint. 8. 6. 8–9.   [2] Cf. 205–12.   [3] Pp. lxxxiv–lxxxix.
[4] See for all this *op. cit.* pp. lxxxix–xc.   [5] Quint. 8. 6. 19.
[6] See the notes *ad loc.* These really belong to the class *e genere species*, while an instance of *e specie genus* is 165 *muribus = feminis*.

and the plural for the singular,[1] of which there are many
instances in Lucan's First Book, *e.g.* 236 *miles* = *milites*,[2] 254
Cimbrum = *Cimbros*,[3] and 602 *septemuir* = *septemuiri*, as well as
169 *Curiorum* = *Curii*,[4] 519 *bellorum* = *belli*, and 594 *pomeria* =
pomerium. Sometimes, as with other tropes, this interchange
of number may be explained on metrical grounds,[5] *e.g.* at 351
dominos, where the singular *dominum* (= *Pompeium*) would not
scan, or at 610, where *molas* = *molam*, or where one number
must be used because the other is metrically inconvenient, as
in the examples cited from 594 and 602. A form of synecdoche which is not stressed by writers on style is the attribution to a part of characteristics common to the whole, or *vice
versa*; *e.g.* at 402 the Ruthenians are called *flaui*, which is an
epithet applicable to the Gauls generally, at 423 the Suessones
are similarly described as *leues* ('lightly-armed', see note),
at 430 the Vangiones, like other Gallic tribes, appear wearing a
trousered dress, and at 463 the Cayci or Chauci are termed
crinigeri.

The use of the simple verb for the compound[6] may be
regarded as a division of synecdoche. Though Quintilian does
not mention it, Servius Danielis (on *Aen.* 4. 116) classifies it
in this way. Examples in Lucan's First Book are: 13 *parari* =

[1] He also lists this trope among the figures (9. 3. 20). Cf. Longin.
περὶ ὕψους 23–4.

[2] Cf. 305 *tirone*, 345 *ueteranus*, 3. 622 *uolnere multo*, 3. 687 *hic*
(= *hi*), and 4. 254 *milite multo*.

[3] This is very common with the names of nations or tribes, cf.
419 sqq. Quintilian (8. 6. 20) alludes to Livy's fondness for *Romanus*
= *Romani*, and this frequent synecdoche has led to misunderstanding
of 484 on the part of commentators (see note).

[4] The usual rendering of such plurals (*e.g.* 'men like Curius') is
inexact (cf. 313 *Catones*, there being only one Cato in question), and
the translation should be simply 'of Curius'. Cf. 3. 402–3 *Panes*...
Siluani.

[5] Or because of cacophony which would otherwise result. See
481 n., where *Alpesque iacentes* would be objectionable, even to
Lucan, because *iacentes* does not even qualify *Alpes*.

[6] Bell (*op. cit.* p. 330) observes that the trope occurs sometimes in
English poetry, *e.g.* Marvell's 'And does in the pomegranate *close*
Jewels more rich than Ormus shews'. With *close* cf. 323 *clauserunt*.

comparari, 86 *missi=emissi*, 147 *ferre=conferre*, 372 *sequi*
=exsequi, and 609 *fundere=infundere*. The simple for the compound may be found also in the case of nouns derived from
verbs, such as 255 *cursum=incursum*, or with adjectives, *e.g.*
354 *feras=efferas*. Of less frequent occurrence is the compound verb for the simple, but 357 *emeriti=meriti* and 505
eualuit=ualuit should be noted, while a similar use of the
adjective occurs at 105 *Assyrias=Syrias* (see note).

Another division of synecdoche is *e praecedentibus sequentia*,
which includes its opposite *e sequentibus praecedentia*.[1] In fact,
ignorance of this trope, whereby it is recognized that the
meaning of words may be inferred from what follows, has
caused Housman, who follows Guyet, to bracket 282 *par
labor atque metus pretio maiore petuntur*. He objects that
Curio wishes to say that the toil and danger in the case of the
Civil War are not equal to, but less than, the toil and danger of
the Gallic War. But the meaning of *par* must be understood
from the subsequent *proelia pauca* (284) to be not so much
'equal' as 'no greater' (Duff), *i.e.* 'probably less'. Conversely
in 446 *Scythicae non mitior ara Dianae* the meiosis *non mitior*
='no more gentle', *i.e.* 'just as cruel', if Ussani's punctua-
tion is adopted. Another interesting passage is 240-1 *arma |
quae pax longa dabat*, which is both misunderstood and mistranslated by Mr Duff as 'such arms as the long peace
supplied', as if *dabat* were *dedit*. That the meaning of *dabat*
(with *longa*) is 'had been ruining' (*i.e. perdebat*) is manifest
from the description which follows of the neglected condition
of the arms. It is also possible to explain this synecdoche as an
instance of the simple for the compound verb, for *dabat* is
possibly from **do* ('I put, place'), which survives in the
compounds *abdo, condo, perdo, subdo*, etc., and which, though
originally quite distinct from *do* ('I give') is often confused
with it and is of comparatively common occurrence.[2] That
dabat has the meaning of *perdebat* is clear, (*a*) from the descrip-

[1] This is included by Quintilian in his definition of synecdoche
(see p. liii, n. 5). Cf. also Seru. ad Verg. *Aen.* 1. 209.
[2] Cf. Ouid. *Trist.* 2. 476, where Mr S. G. Owen's note is important, and see also Munro on Lucr. 4. 41.

tion, which follows in 311, of Pompey as being in a condition similar to that of the arms on account of the long years of peace (*longa pace solutus*), and (*b*) from the fact that lengthy duration of time naturally has the effect of wasting or destroying (*perdere*). Compare Ouid. *Pont.* 4. 10. 7 *tempus edax omnia perdit*.

Other examples of *e sequentibus praecedentia* may be seen at 291, where *duci* must be understood with *et ipsi* from *ducem* in 293; at 301, where *hoc* is explained by the content of 302, just as at 341 *his* is taken up in 342 by *miles iste*; at 327, where *tigres* = 'tiger cubs' on account of *matrum* in 328; at 405, where *portus* = *portus Herculis Monoeci*, though the reader must wait until he comes to 408; and at 618, where the *color* is specified by the description which follows.

(iii) METONYMY is related closely to synecdoche in that it is the use of one name for another when there is some connexion between them.[1] When *Emathia* = *Thessalia* (see 1 n.), this is metonymy, as the two regions are geographically adjacent.[2] Of course the practice is not confined to proper names, as is shown by 267 and 487, where *curia* = *senatus*; 463, where *bellis* = *armis* (see also p. xlix); and 467, where *fidem* = *fiduciam*, which is metrically inconvenient. A frequent variety of metonymy is the use of the concrete for the abstract, *e.g.* 131 *ducem* = *esse ducem* ('leadership'), with which Verg. *Aen.* 2. 591 *confessa deam* = *confessa se esse deam* may be compared; 178 *fasces* = *honos*; 667 *manu* = *ui*; or of the abstract for the concrete, *e.g.* 343 *exsanguis senectus* = *milites exsangues ac senes*; 4. 660 *Romana uictoria* = *Romanus uictor*. Such a common metonymy as 299 *Martis* = *belli* would fall into Quintilian's classification of the Inventor for the Invention.[3]

One begins to see why, according to Cicero,[4] the rhetoricians called metonymy *hypallage*,[5] when such an example as that in

[1] Quint. 8. 6. 23.

[2] See p. xxxix, and cf. 10 *Babylon* = *Parthia*, 64 *Cirrhaea* = *Delphica*, 403 *Latias* = *Romanas*, and also 544 and 7. 452, where *Mycenae* and *Argos* appear as interchangeable place-names.

[3] *Loc. cit.*   [4] *Orat.* 27. 93.

[5] Quint. 8. 6. 23. For the difference between metonymy and hypallage see Vossius, *op. cit.* 4. 7. 1.

19 is considered. Here *barbarus Araxes = barbari qui iuxta Araxen incolunt*, where the epithet is transferred from the people to the place. Hypallage (*mutatio*) is not merely transference of epithet, but may also involve interchange of cases (*mutua casuum permutatio*). Of the former kind instances may be seen at 137 *ueteris = ueteres*, 220 *obliquum = obliquus*, 371 *arctoo spumantem = arctoum spumanti*, 428 *Iliaco = Iliaci* (see above p. xlviii), 464 *feroces* (acc.) = *feroces* (nom.), 603 *laeto = laetus*, 605 *effusam = effusi*, and 676 *attonitam = attonita* (though this last is doubtful, and may at most be an example of amphibole). Lines 258–9 (see note) provide a good specimen of the latter kind. An extreme instance of hypallage occurs at 212,[1] and another interesting line is 282, which has been partly discussed already on p. lv. Here *par labor atque metus pretio maiore petuntur = pari labore atque metu maius petitur pretium*. This is rejected by Housman, who is as unconscious of the hypallage as he is of the trope involved in *par*.

(iv) ANTONOMASIA is the use of (*a*) an epithet or (*b*) a description for a proper name,[2] *e.g.* (*a*) 35 *Tonanti = Ioui*, 484 *Romano = Caesare*, 662 *Cyllenius = Mercurius*; (*b*) 92 *regni sociis* = Pompey and Caesar, 95 *fraterno sanguine* = the blood of Remus which his brother Romulus shed.

(v) ONOMATOPOEIA, or the coinage of a new word, is, as Quintilian remarks,[3] much rarer in Latin than in Greek. The term is usually extended to include the representation in speech of inarticulate sounds. Perhaps the best example in Lucan's First Book of this accommodation of sound to sense is contained in 569–70.

(vi) CATACHRESIS ('abuse')[4] is the use of a word out of its usual denotation. Quintilian remarks that poets employ the 'abuse' of words even where there are proper terms available.[5] Examples in this Book are 314 *extremi* (= *infimi*) *clientes*, 553 *iugis nutantibus* (= *labantibus*), and 555 *summum* (= *ultimum*) *Atlanta*.

(vii) METALEPSIS ('transumption')[6] is an intermediate stage between the expression which is transferred, and that to

---

[1] Cf. Bell, *op. cit.* p. 324.   [2] Quint. 8. 6. 29.
[3] 8. 6. 31.   [4] Quint. 8. 6. 34.
[5] 8. 6. 35.   [6] Quint. S. 6. 37.

which it is transferred,[1] but Quintilian observes that it is rare
in Latin, except in comedy, where, and where only, he sees any
advantage in it.[2] He remarks that the commonest example is
cano as a synonym for *dico* (cf. 2 *canimus*) through the intermediate stage of *canto*.[3]

(viii) EPITHET like the other tropes which now follow
serves only the purpose of adornment.[4] Quintilian states that
poets use it with special frequency and freedom, because it is
enough for them if it suits the word to which it *is* applied.[5]
A good example occurs at 622 *pulmonis anheli*. Epithet be-
comes a trope if it adds anything to the meaning;[6] but in Latin
poetry there are many instances of ekes, or adjectives which
are inserted primarily for the purpose of completing the line,[7]
but which make no real contribution to the sense. Such an
otiose epithet occurs at 322 in the *medias* of *medias perrumpere
leges*. Quintilian also observes that, when two epithets are
attached to one noun, the result is unbecoming even in verse;[8]
whence the remark of Bentley that the double epithet in 655
saeuum...Nemeaeum...leonem is worthy of Accius or Pacu-
vius, but not of Lucan.[9] The last-mentioned poet, however,
like Vergil,[10] occasionally permits the double epithet, as may
be seen in a remark of the excursus[11] on 74–7 about *omnis* with
another adjective, and from 218.

(ix) ALLEGORY ('inversion')[12] is achieved either by a succession of metaphors, as in Hor. *Carm*. 1. 14 (the ode which
concerns the 'ship of state') or without them, as in Verg.
Ecl. 9. 7 sqq.[13] The picture of Rome as a huge pile which cannot
but fall by its own weight (70–2) is an example from Lucan's
First Book. Quintilian's main subdivision of allegory is *irony*

[1] Quint. 8. 6. 38.   [2] *Ibid.* 39.
[3] *Ibid.* 38.   [4] *Ibid.* 40.
[5] *Ibid.*   [6] *Ibid.* 41.
[7] Compare what Servius says on *Aen*. 3. 691: *INFELICIS
VLIXI: epitheton ad inplendum uersum positum more Graeco, sine
respectu negotii.*   [8] 8. 6. 43.
[9] Accordingly he emended *saeuum* to *tergum*.
[10] In whom one of the epithets is often a present participle, *e.g.*
Aen. 3. 70.   [11] P. 142.
[12] Quint. 8. 6. 44.   [13] Quintilian's examples.

('illusion'),[1] which may mean blame under the pretence of praise or praise under the pretence of blame. A good example is 305 *inplentur ualidae tirone cohortes* (see note *ad loc.*).

(x) PERIPHRASIS ('circuitous speech',[2] 'circumlocution'[3]) is so called when its effect is decorative; and it thereby differs from *perissology*,[4] for this trope is a fault. The example of periphrasis which Quintilian quotes (Verg. *Aen.* 2. 268–9) shows the characteristic which Henry calls *theme and variation*,[5] or the repetition of the same thought in different language. Frequent as is its occurrence in poetry and prose of all periods, it is a conspicuous feature in the Latin poets, and in none more than in Lucan. Examples may be seen at 28–9, 58–9, 162, 171–2, 184, 221–2 etc.; and of course lines 1–7 contain an extreme instance of the theme (*bella...canimus*) followed by a sevenfold variation (including *iusque datum sceleri*) like the shield of Ajax.[6] Perhaps the best specimen of perissology in the First Book occurs at 352–3, where *dubium, non claro murmure*, and *secum incerta fremit* convey an impression of redundancy. Compare also 3. 658 *eiectat saniem sanguis*.

(xi) HYPERBATON ('transposition of a word')[7] is, according to Quintilian, deservedly reckoned among the qualities of a good style,[8] though he criticizes it elsewhere[9] as frequently causing obscurity.[10] The poets of the Silver Age, including Lucan, are guilty of some extremely distorted expressions

---

[1] 8. 6. 54.   [2] *Ibid.* 59.
[3] *Ibid.* 61.   [4] *Ibid.* 61.
[5] On Verg. *Aen.* 1. 546 (*Aeneidea* I, pp. 745–51).
[6] Fronto (Naber, p. 157, *Loeb*, ii, pp. 104–6) ...*de Aiacis scuto corium. Annaee, quis finis erit?* This is an interesting context for its criticism of the practice of theme and variation. For another theme and sevenfold variation see 72–80 and Appendix B, p. 142. The practice, indeed, proves the reading *numina* to be right as against *lumina* at 452.
[7] Quint. 8. 6. 62. The trope is discussed by Postgate ('Flaws in Classical Research', pp. 7–8).   [8] *Ibid.*
[9] 8. 2. 14.
[10] His example is taken from Verg. *Aen.* 1. 109 *saxa uocant Itali, mediis quae in fluctibus, Aras.*

which may be classified under hyperbaton, and Heitland[1] mentions several passages, including the unnatural insertion of the antecedent within the relative clause in 14.[2] Other postpositions, which are by no means uncommon in Latin poetry generally, are those of *et* 224, *quo* 343, and *cum* 612. If the transposition takes place in the case of two words only, it is then called *anastrophe* ('reversal of order'),[3] *e.g.* 4. 159 *quos inter* and 5. 250 *non e stabili* tremulo sed *culmine*.

(xii) HYPERBOLE or 'exaggeration' (*exaggeratio*) is a bold trope.[4] According to Quintilian,[5] who mentions the fact with approval, Pindar in a lost Hymn describes the attack of Hercules upon the Meropes, and compares the hero with the thunderbolt. The same comparison is used of Caesar by Lucan at 151–7. Heitland[6] gives numerous examples of the poet's hyperbole, some of which are dangerously near to the ridiculous. Such is the example in 53–9, where Nero is requested to sit in the zodiac and thereby to maintain the equal poise of heaven.

FIGURES

In Book IX Quintilian comes to figures (σχήματα), which he distinguishes from tropes by saying that the latter term is applied to the transference of expressions from their natural and proper meaning to another which is not properly theirs, while a figure is the name used when the language is shaped after a manner removed from the obvious and ordinary.[7] He distinguishes figures of thought (διανοίας) from figures · of speech (λέξεως). Under the former heading he quotes Cic. *De Oratore* 3. 201–7 and *Orator* 39. 134–9 at length, and discusses[8] emphasis, questions, anticipation (πρόληψις), hesitation, communication, suspension, exclamation, licence (παρρησία), impersonation (πρυσωποποιία), apostrophe, ocular de-

---

[1] *Op. cit.* p. cvii.

[2] At 385 it is furthermore attracted to the case of the relative.

[3] Quint. 8. 6. 65.

[4] *Ibid.* 67. The term *exaggeratio* is not Quintilian's, but is used by Servius on *Aen.* 1. 727, and by Gellius (13. 25. 9 and 16).

[5] *Ibid.* 71.   [6] *Op. cit.* pp. lxxvii–lxxviii.

[7] 9. 1. 4.   [8] 9. 2.

monstration (*sub oculos subiectio*, ὑπυτύπωσις), irony as a figure
rather than as a trope, aposiopesis (*reticentia*), imitation of the
characteristics of others (ἠθοποιία or μίμησις), and comparison.
These are some of the Ciceronian figures, but there are others
to which Quintilian alludes on the authority of Gorgias,
Rutilius, and Celsus. Of those mentioned, a few may be illustrated from Lucan's First Book.

Question is of frequent occurrence in Caesar's famous speech
(299–351). *Anticipation* is shown when Curio forestalls possible
objections on the part of Caesar (279–85), and Caesar employs
licence in his denunciation of Pompey all through his speech.
As a famous instance of *impersonation* or *personification* Quintilian cites two passages from Cicero's First Catiline,[1] where
Rome, the *patria*, is spoken of as appealing to Cicero and
Catiline. This is exactly what happens at 185–203, when
Caesar sees the vision of *Roma*. *Apostrophe* especially is common in Lucan,[2] and Mr J. D. Duff,[3] after calling attention to
it, sensibly decides to ignore it generally in his translation.

In chapter 3 Quintilian goes on to discuss figures of speech,
and divides them into two classes. One is grammatical and
consists in the form of the language, the other is rhetorical and
is attained by the arrangement of the words.[4] In the former
class he mentions *inter alia* the verb used for the participle
(a category which may include the noun or adjective used for
the participle, or *vice versa*), the present for the past tense,
ἑτεροίωσις or alteration of the normal idiom, Grecisms (including the so-called accusative of respect after adjectives or
passive perfect participles), and the comparative for the positive adjective (or *vice versa*). These can be illustrated from
Lucan's First Book as follows:

(i) VERB FOR PARTICIPLE (or rather gerundive): 251–3
dedisses...claustra tueri (*tuenda*).[5] Noun for participle: 454
auctoribus. Participle for noun: 5 *certatum* (= *certamen*,
possibly, but see note), 70 *negatum*.

---

[1] 7. 18 and 11. 27.   [2] Heitland, *op. cit.* p. lxxi.
[3] *Op. cit. Preface*, p. vi.   [4] 9. 3. 2.
[5] Cf. Verg. *Aen.* 5. 248 *magnum dat ferre talentum*, which Quin
tilian cites.

(ii) PRESENT FOR PAST. This figure is very common in Latin poetry, and present tenses generally should be rendered by pasts in an English prose translation.

(iii) ʹΕΤΕΡΟΙΩΣΙΣ[1]: 267 and 329 (see the notes *ad loc.*).

(iv) ACCUSATIVE OF RESPECT[2]: 587 *edoctus motus uenasque* (but see the note *ad loc.*).

(v) POSITIVE FOR COMPARATIVE: 479 *ferus* in the phrase *maiorque ferusque... uictoque inmanior hoste.*

Among rhetorical figures of speech, which depend upon the arrangement of words, Quintilian[3] includes addition, especially when it is used for the sake of emotional effect, as well as asyndeton, zeugma, homoeoteleuton, amphibole, and antithesis.

(i) ADDITION (*adiectio*) is used properly for the sake of amplification or emphasis, *e.g.* 156 *magnamque cadens magnamque reuertens,* 203 *ille...ille,* 347 *tollite...tollite,* and 521 *danda...danda.* One variety comprises clauses which begin with the same words for the sake of force and emphasis,[4] *e.g.* 190–1 and 344–5.

(ii) ASYNDETON (*dissolutio*), which means the absence of connecting particles,[5] occurs at 259–60 and 664–5. Compare also 4. 440–1 and 510.

(iii) ZEUGMA ʻoccurs when a word expressed in one clause is supplied with another clause in order to complete the sense ʼ.[6] Quintilian,[7] in discussing this figure under the name of ἐπεζευγμένον, includes in it cases where several clauses are completed by the same verb, or where genders and numbers are interchanged or taken comprehensively (*e.g. filii* in the sense of male and female children). Modern writers and commentators, however, prefer to reserve the term *zeugma* for instances when two or more different constructions are combined,[8] and when, as is often the case, parts of speech (especially

---

[1] Quintilian's example is Sallust's *neque ea res falsum me habuit* (*Iug.* 10. 1).   [2] Heitland, *op. cit.* p. ciii.   [3] 9. 3. 28sqq.
[4] *Ibid.* 30. *Adiectio* is mentioned previously among the grammatical figures also (*ibid.* 18).   [5] *Ibid.* 50.
[6] Moore, *op. cit.* p. 279.   [7] 9. 3. 62–4.
[8] *Ibid.* 64. An example may be seen at 251–3, where in the first clause *dedisses* governs nouns in the accusative case, and in the second the infinitive *tueri.*

verbs) have to be taken accordingly in two or more different
senses. The favourite example of the grammarians is Verg.
Aen. 3. 359–60 *qui numina Phoebi, | qui tripodas, Clarii laurus,
qui sidera sentis*, which is paraphrased by Bell[1] as follows: *qui
numina Phoebi suscipis, qui oracula Pythii nosti, qui astrologiae
peritus es.*

Indeed, often an entirely different verb must be supplied
mentally to make the threefold expression fourfold. Nor is
this form of the figure even confined to verbs, as two remarkable examples from Lucan's First Book show, where in each
case the missing word should be provided from another, which
naturally suggests it, in the same context. At 504 *natum* must
be supplied with *nullum* (and *parens*) to balance *coniunxue
maritum*,[2] and at 549 *Scyllae* must be understood with *canes*
from *Charybdis* in 547. Zeugma also may mean the understanding not merely of a missing word, but of a missing clause
in a threefold expression, as may be seen from Housman's note
on 7. 323–5.

The variety of zeugma which some grammarians call
syllepsis is of frequent occurrence, and includes cases where
'a word expressed in one clause is supplied in a modified form
with another',[3] *e.g.* when a singular verb like *auxerat* (217) has
to be understood with the plural noun *Alpes*, as well as with
its own nearer subject *Cynthia.*

When the same expression or part of speech is understood
in more than one context without a change of meaning, the
construction is called ἀπὸ κοινοῦ. Examples are 72–3, where
mundi qualifies both *conpage* and *hora*; 638, where *ambage* is
qualified by both *flexa* and *multa*, and 4. 23 *qui praestat terris
aufert tibi nomen Hiberus*, where *nomen* must be supplied with
praestat as well as taken with *aufert.*

(iv) HOMOEOTELEUTON or similarity in the ending of
different words is often a defect on account of the cacophony,[4]
as at 123 *times...series* and 521 *tantorum...pauorum* (a line

[1] *Op. cit.* p. 312.
[2] For a similar example see 8. 610 and Postgate's note *ad loc.*
[3] Moore, *op. cit.* p. 280.
[4] Seru. ad Verg. *Aen.* 4. 504; cf. Quint. 9. 3. 77.

which also contains the 'addition' of *danda...danda*). This figure extends to the like ending of adjacent lines,[1] as at 115–16.

(v) AMPHIBOLE is discussed previously by Quintilian,[2] from whom it is learnt that the Latin term is *ambiguitas*. The term is applied most frequently to words or expressions which can be taken more than once in different meanings from those which they possessed in the first instance. A good example is the amphibole of *male* at 87 and 248.[3] In 87 *male* with *concordes = perniciose* ('dangerously'), and with both *concordes* and *caeci* = 'unfortunately' (see note *ad loc.*); and in 248 the word with *uicinis = perniciose*, and with *condita* = 'unfortunately'. The scholiast on 87 aptly compares Verg. *Aen.* 4. 8 *cum sic unanimam adloquitur male sana sororem*, where Servius observes that *male* may be for *minus* or for *perniciose*.[4]

(vi) ANTITHESIS (*contrapositum* or *contentio*).[5] Lucan's fondness for this figure, which includes oxymoron, is discussed by Heitland,[6] who instances 504 *in bellum fugitur*.

Among other figures which are recognized as such by Servius and the later grammarians are hendiadys, antiptosis and hysteron proteron.

(i) HENDIADYS, or 'the resolution of a complex expression into its parts',[7] is very rare in Lucan according to Heitland,[8] though it is of frequent occurrence in Vergil. A good instance occurs at 163: *auro tectisue = auro tectorum*. Compare 2. 676 *uela ratesque* = 'ships under sail', and see 123 n.

(ii) ANTIPTOSIS[9] is the use of one grammatical case for another, and is frequently determined by the exigencies of metre.

---

[1] See Heitland, *op. cit.* pp. xcvii–xcviii.

[2] 7. 9.

[3] Also at 6. 177–8 *ac male defensum fragili conpage cerebrum | dissipat.*   [4] Bell, *op. cit.* p. 293.

[5] Quint. 9. 3. 81.   [6] *Op. cit.* pp. lxxix–lxxx.

[7] Moore, *op. cit.* p. 273. He quotes Servius's definition, which is at *Aen.* 1. 61 *MOLEMQUE ET MONTES: i.e. molem montis. et est figura, ut una res in duas diuidatur, metri causa interposita coniunctione*, etc.   [8] *Op. cit.* p. lxxxi.

[9] The term is used by Servius on *Aen.* 1. 120, and by some of the grammarians (Donatus, Priscian, etc.). See p. xlviii.

(a) *Ablative for dative* occurs at 392 *milite = militi* and 513 *Caesare = Caesari*. Perhaps the most striking of the Vergilian passages quoted by Servius is *Aen.* 11. 56–7 *nec sospite dirum | optabis nato funus pater*, where *sospite = sospiti*. Cf. p. xlviii.

(b) *Dative for genitive* occurs at 30 *tantis cladibus auctor*, and 374 *signa decem castris*. Compare 3. 553 *Grais pinus*.

(c) *Ablative for genitive* occurs at 3. 414–15 *ipse situs putrique facit iam robore pallor | attonitos*, where *putri robore = putris roboris*.

[*DIGRESSION*. At this point it may be remarked that the exigencies of metre may determine certain poetical devices other than synecdoche, metonymy, and antiptosis. Of these the following are examples, which do not by any means exhaust the substitutions found elsewhere in Latin poetry:

(a) *One adjective for another*: 206 *aestiferae = aestuosae*.

(b) *One verb for another*: 275 *traximus = prorogauimus* (see note).

(c) *Adjective for adverb*: 267 *minax = minaciter* (see note, and compare the discussion of ἑτεροίωσις). Here the balance of the line is ensured by the adjective, as the two nouns in it (*iure* and *Gracchis*) are qualified respectively by two participles. (*uicto* and *iactatis*). Compare 329 *altus = alte* (see note).

(d) *Adverb for adjective*: 346 *melius = meliores*.

(e) *One preposition for another*: 543 *per ortus = in ortus;* conversely 588 *in aere = per aera*.]

(iii) HYSTERON PROTERON is a figure[1] which apparently inverts the normal order of a narrative or description, *e.g.* 464–5 *petitis Romam Rheniqne feroces | deseritis ripas*, where the modern habit of thought would consider that the departure from the Rhine is prior to the journey towards Rome. It is, however, erroneous to imagine that the semblance of putting the cart before the horse is an example of ancient caprice. Postgate[2] observes: 'The modern sentence, to put it roughly, is an arrangement in line, the ancient one within a circle', and goes on to say of hysteron proteron: 'To the lineal mind these "inversions" are nonsense; to the circular but legitimate

---

[1] Moore lists it among tropes (*op. cit.* pp. 189–90).

[2] 'Flaws in Classical Research', p. 7.

variations.' Such differences of order are, as he points out, absolutely without significance, and are often only metrical devices.[1] Earlier than Postgate, T. E. Page[2] made sensible observations of a similar nature about hysteron proteron, which, after all, is a practice analogous to that of 'theme and variation'.

Only the most important figures which Quintilian mentions have been discussed. In his time and earlier, there was a craze among certain rhetoricians for the addition and classification of more and more figures among the recognized lists.[3] Of this practice he disapproves, and remarks in conclusion that, when true figures are placed in a suitable context, they are an ornament to style, but that they are completely inept when the orator seeks to employ them to excess.[4] This, apparently, was one of the weaknesses of the age, and it is significant that, even in one book of the *De Bello Ciuili*, illustrations of practically every trope and figure mentioned in the *Institutio Oratoria* can be found.[5] Even in the framework of his style it is abundantly clear to one who considers this aspect of his technique, why Lucan according to Quintilian should be imitated by orators rather than by poets.

[1] See his note on 8. 324.

[2] *Class. Rev.* viii, 1894, pp. 203–4; cf. his edition of the *Aeneid*, 6. 361 n.   [3] 9. 3. 99.

[4] *Ibid.* 100: *ego illud de iis etiam, quae uere sunt, adiciam breuiter, sicut ornent orationem opportune positae, ita ineptissimas esse, cum inmodice petantur.*

[5] A useful commentary on Quintilian's *Institutio Oratoria* is Jean Cousin's *Etudes sur Quintilien* (Paris, 1936). See Tome i, pp. 437–57 for tropes and figures, as well as Tome ii (Vocabulaire grec de la terminologie rhétorique), *passim.*

M. ANNAEI LVCANI

BELLI CIVILIS

LIBER PRIMVS

The subject of the poem

Bella per Emathios plus quam ciuilia campos
iusque datum sceleri canimus, populumque potentem
in sua uictrici conuersum uiscera dextra,
cognatasque acies, et rupto foedere regni
certatum totis concussi uiribus orbis   5
in commune nefas, infestisque obuia signis
signa, pares aquilas et pila minantia pilis.

The poet's rebuke of the citizens of Rome

  quis furor, o ciues, quae tanta licentia ferri?
gentibus inuisis Latium praebere cruorem,
cumque superba foret Babylon spolianda tropaeis   10
Ausoniis umbraque erraret Crassus inulta,
bella geri placuit nullos habitura triumphos?
heu, quantum terrae potuit pelagique parari
hoc quem ciuiles hauserunt sanguine dextrae,
unde uenit Titan et nox ubi sidera condit   15
quaque dies medius flagrantibus aestuat horis
et qua bruma rigens ac nescia uere remitti
astringit Scythicum glaciali frigore Pontum!
sub iuga iam Seres, iam barbarus isset Araxes
et gens siqua iacet nascenti conscia Nilo.   20
tum, si tantus amor belli tibi, Roma, nefandi,

totum sub Latias leges cum miseris orbem,
in te uerte manus: nondum tibi defuit hostis.
at nunc semirutis pendent quod moenia tectis
urbibus Italiae lapsisque ingentia muris   25
saxa iacent nulloque domus custode tenentur
rarus et antiquis habitator in urbibus errat,
horrida quod dumis multosque inarata per annos
Hesperia est desuntque manus poscentibus aruis,
non tu, Pyrrhe ferox, nec tantis cladibus auctor   30
Poenus erit: nulli penitus descendere ferro
contigit; alta sedent ciuilis uolnera dextrae.

The flattering address to Nero

quod si non aliam uenturo fata Neroni
inuenere uiam, magnoque aeterna parantur
regna deis caelumque suo seruire Tonanti   35
non nisi saeuorum potuit post bella Gigantum,
iam nihil, o superi, querimur; scelera ipsa nefasque
hac mercede placent. diros Pharsalia campos
inpleat, et Poeni saturentur sanguine manes,
ultima funesta concurrant proelia Munda,   40
his, Caesar, Perusina fames Mutinaeque labores
accedant fatis et quas premit aspera classes
Leucas et ardenti seruilia bella sub Aetna,
multum Roma tamen debet ciuilibus armis
quod tibi res acta est. te, cum statione peracta   45
astra petes serus, praelati regia caeli
excipiet gaudente polo. seu sceptra tenere
seu te flammigeros Phoebi conscendere currus
telluremque nihil mutato sole timentem
igne uago lustrare iuuet, tibi numine ab omni   50
cedetur, iurisque tui natura relinquet

quis deus esse uelis, ubi regnum ponere mundi.
sed neque in Arctoo sedem tibi legeris orbe
(nec polus aduersi calidus qua uergitur Austri),
unde tuam uideas obliquo sidere Romam.   55
aetheris inmensi partem si presseris unam,
sentiet axis onus. librati pondera caeli
orbe tene medio; pars aetheris illa sereni
tota uacet nullaeque obstent a Caesare nubes.
tum genus humanum positis sibi consulat armis,   60
inque uicem gens omnis amet; pax missa per orbem
ferrea belligeri conpescat limina Iani.
sed mihi iam numen; nec, si te pectore uates
accipio, Cirrhaea uelim secreta mouentem
sollicitare deum Bacchumque auertere Nysa.   65
tu satis ad uires Romana in carmina dandas.

The causes of the civil war

fert animus causas tantarum expromere rerum,
inmensumque aperitur opus, quid in arma furentem
inpulerit populum, quid pacem excusserit orbi.
inuida fatorum series summisque negatum   70
stare diu nimioque graues sub pondere lapsus
nec se Roma ferens. sic, cum conpage soluta
saecula tot mundi suprema coegerit hora
antiquum repetens iterum chaos, omnia mixtis
sidera sideribus concurrent ignea, pontum   75
astra petent, tellus extendere litora nolet
excutietque fretum, fratri contraria Phoebe
ibit et obliquum bigas agitare per orbem
indignata diem poscet sibi, totaque discors
machina diuolsi turbabit foedera mundi.   80
in se magna ruunt: laetis hunc numina rebus

crescendi posuere modum. nec gentibus ullis
commodat in populum terrae pelagique potentem
inuidiam Fortuna suam. tu causa malorum
facta tribus dominis communis Roma, nec umquam 85
in turbam missi feralia foedera regni.
o male concordes nimiaque cupidine caeci,
quid miscere iuuat uires orbemque tenere
in medium? dum terra fretum terramque leuabit
aer et longi uoluent Titana labores   90
noxque diem caelo totidem per signa sequetur,
nulla fides regni sociis, omnisque potestas
inpatiens consortis erit. nec gentibus ullis
credite, nec longe fatorum exempla petantur:
fraterno primi maduerunt sanguine muri.   95
nec pretium tanti tellus pontusque furoris
tunc erat: exiguum dominos commisit asylum.

Reasons for the rivalry between Pompey and Caesar

temporis angusti mansit concordia discors,
paxque fuit non sponte ducum; nam sola futuri
Crassus erat belli medius mora. qualiter undas   100
qui secat et geminum gracilis male separat Isthmos,
nec patitur conferre fretum (si terra recedat,
Ionium Aegaeo frangat mare); sic, ubi saeua
arma ducum dirimens miserando funere Crassus
Assyrias Latio maculauit sanguine Carrhas,   105
Parthica Romanos soluerunt damna furores.
plus illa uobis acie, quam creditis, actum est,
Arsacidae: bellum uictis ciuile dedistis.
diuiditur ferro regnum, populique potentis,
quae mare, quae terras, quae totum possidet orbem, 110
non cepit fortuna duos. nam pignora iuncti

sanguinis et diro ferales omine taedas
abstulit ad manes Parcarum Iulia saeua
intercepta manu. quod si tibi fata dedissent
maiores in luce moras, tu sola furentem   115
inde uirum poteras atque hinc retinere parentem
armatasque manus excusso iungere ferro,
ut generos soceris mediae iunxere Sabinae.
morte tua discussa fides bellumque mouere
permissum ducibus. stimulos dedit aemula uirtus. 120
tu, noua ne ueteres obscurent acta triumphos
et uictis cedat piratica laurea Gallis,
Magne, times. te iam series ususque laborum
erigit inpatiensque loci fortuna secundi.
nec quemquam iam ferre potest Caesarue priorem   125
Pompeiusue parem. quis iustius induit arma
scire nefas: magno se iudice quisque tuetur;
uictrix causa deis placuit sed uicta Catoni.

A comparison of the two leaders

nec coiere pares. alter uergentibus annis
in senium longoque togae tranquillior usu   130
dedidicit iam pace ducem, famaeque petitor
multa dare in uolgus, totus popularibus auris
inpelli plausuque sui gaudere theatri,
nec reparare nouas uires, multumque priori
credere fortunae. stat magni nominis umbra,   135
qualis frugifero quercus sublimis in agro
exuuias ueteris populi sacrataque gestans
dona ducum nec iam ualidis radicibus haerens
pondere fixa suo est, nudosque per aera ramos
effundens trunco, non frondibus efficit umbram,   140
et quamuis primo nutet casura sub Euro,

tot circum siluae firmo se robore tollant,
sola tamen colitur. sed non in Caesare tantum
nomen erat nec fama ducis, sed nescia uirtus
stare loco, solusque pudor non uincere bello.   145
acer et indomitus, quo spes quoque ira uocasset,
ferre manum et numquam temerando parcere ferro,
successus urguere suos, instare fauori
numinis, inpellens quidquid sibi summa petenti
obstaret gaudensque uiam fecisse ruina,   150
qualiter expressum uentis per nubila fulmen
aetheris inpulsi sonitu mundique fragore
emicuit rupitque diem populosque pauentes
terruit obliqua praestringens lumina flamma:
in sua templa furit, nullaque exire uetánte   155
materia magnamque cadens magnamque reuertens
dat stragem late sparsosque recolligit ignes.

Further latent causes of the war

     hae ducibus causae, suberant sed publica belli
semina, quae populos semper mersere potentes.
namque, ut opes nimias mundo fortuna subacto   160
intulit et rebus mores cessere secundis
praedaque et hostiles luxum suasere rapinae,
non auro tectisue modus, mensasque priores
aspernata fames; cultus gestare decoros
uix nuribus rapuere mares; fecunda uirorum   165
paupertas fugitur totoque accersitur orbe
quo gens quaeque perit; tum longos iungere fines
agrorum, et quondam duro sulcata Camilli
uomere et antiquos Curiorum passa ligones
longa sub ignotis extendere rura colonis.   170
     non erat is populus quem pax tranquilla iuuaret,

quem sua libertas inmotis pasceret armis.
inde irae faciles et, quod suasisset egestas,
uile nefas, magnumque decus ferroque petendum
plus patria potuisse sua, mensuraque iuris   175
uis erat; hinc leges et plebis scita coactae
et cum consulibus turbantes iura tribuni;
hinc rapti fasces pretio sectorque fauoris
ipse sui populus letalisque ambitus urbi
annua uenali referens certamina Campo;   180
hinc usura uorax auidumque in tempora fenus
et concussa fides et multis utile bellum.

Caesar crosses the Rubicon after seeing
a vision of the goddess Roma

iam gelidas Caesar cursu superauerat Alpes,
ingentesque animo motus bellumque futurum
ceperat. ut uentum est parui Rubiconis ad undas,   185
ingens uisa duci patriae trepidantis imago
clara per obscuram uoltu maestissima noctem
turrigero canos effundens uertice crines
caesarie lacera nudisque adstare lacertis,
et gemitu permixta loqui: 'quo tenditis ultra?   190
quo fertis mea signa, uiri? si iure uenitis,
si ciues, huc usque licet.' tum perculit horror
membra ducis, riguere comae gressumque coercens
languor in extrema tenuit uestigia ripa.
mox ait: 'o magnae qui moenia prospicis urbis   195
Tarpeia de rupe Tonans Phrygiique penates
gentis Iuleae et rapti secreta Quirini
et residens celsa Latiaris Iuppiter Alba
Vestalesque foci summique o numinis instar
Roma, faue coeptis. non te furialibus armis   200

persequor. en, adsum uictor terraque marique,
Caesar, ubique tuus (liceat modo) nunc quoque miles.
ille erit ille nocens, qui me tibi fecerit hostem.'
inde moras soluit belli tumidumque per amnem
signa tulit propere: sicut squalentibus aruis   205
aestiferae Libyes uiso leo comminus hoste
subsedit dubius, totam dum colligit iram;
mox, ubi se saeuae stimulauit uerbere caudae
erexitque iubam et uasto graue murmur hiatu
infremuit, tum torta leuis si lancea Mauri   210
haereat aut latum subeant uenabula pectus,
per ferrum tanti securus uolneris exit.
fonte cadit modico paruisque inpellitur undis
puniceus Rubicon, cum feruida canduit aestas,
perque imas serpit ualles et Gallica certus   215
limes ab Ausoniis disterminat arua colonis.
tum uires praebebat hiemps atque auxerat undas
tertia iam grauido pluuialis Cynthia cornu
et madidis Euri resolutae flatibus Alpes.
primus in obliquum sonipes opponitur amnem   220
excepturus aquas, molli tum cetera rumpit
turba uado faciles iam fracti fluminis undas.
Caesar, ut aduersam superato gurgite ripam
attigit, Hesperiae uetitis et constitit aruis,
'hic' ait 'hic pacem temerataque iura relinquo.   225
te, Fortuna, sequor. procul hinc iam foedera sunto;
credidimus fatis, utendum est iudice bello.'

Caesar captures Ariminum

  sic fatus noctis tenebris rapit agmina ductor
inpiger. it torto Balearis uerbere fundae
ocior et missa Parthi post terga sagitta,   230

uicinumque minax inuadit Ariminum, et ignes
solis Lucifero fugiebant astra relicto.
iamque dies primos belli uisura tumultus
exoritur; seu sponte deum, seu turbidus Auster
inpulerat, maestam tenuerunt nubila lucem.   235
constitit ut capto iussus deponere miles
signa foro, stridor lituum clangorque tubarum
non pia concinuit cum rauco classica cornu;
rupta quies populi, stratisque excita iuuentus
deripuit sacris adfixa penatibus arma   240
quae pax longa dabat; nuda iam crate fluentes
inuadunt clipeos curuataque cuspide pila
et scabros nigrae morsu robiginis enses.
ut notae fulsere aquilae Romanaque signa
et celsus medio conspectus in agmine Caesar,   245
deriguere metu, gelidos pauor occupat artus,
et tacito mutos uoluunt in pectore questus:
'o male uicinis haec moenia condita Gallis,
o tristi damnata loco! pax alta per omnes
et tranquilla quies populos: nos praeda furentum   250
primaque castra sumus. melius, Fortuna, dedisses
orbe sub Eoo sedem gelidaque sub Arcto
errantesque domos, Latii quam claustra tueri.
nos primi Senonum motus Cimbrumque ruentem
uidimus et Martem Libyes cursumque furoris   255
Teutonici: quotiens Romam Fortuna lacessit,
hac iter est bellis.' gemitu sic quisque latenti,
non ausus timuisse palam. uox nulla dolori
credita, sed quantum, uolucres cum bruma coercet,
rura silent, mediusque tacet sine murmure pontus, 260
tanta quies.

*Caesar is met by the expelled tribunes and
Curio. Curio's speech*

         noctis gelidas lux soluerat umbras:
ecce, faces belli dubiaeque in proelia menti
urguentes addunt stimulos cunctasque pudoris
rumpunt fata moras: iustos Fortuna laborat
esse ducis motus et causas inuenit armis.   265
expulit ancipiti discordes urbe tribunos
uicto iure minax iactatis curia Gracchis.
hos iam mota ducis uicinaque signa petentes
audax uenali comitatur Curio lingua:
uox quondam populi, libertatemque tueri   270
ausus et armatos plebi miscere potentes.
utque ducem uarias uoluentem pectore curas
conspexit 'dum uoce tuae potuere iuuari,
Caesar,' ait 'partes, quamuis nolente senatu
traximus imperium, tum cum mihi rostra tenere   275
ius erat et dubios in te transferre Quirites.
at post quam leges bello siluere coactae
pellimur e patriis laribus patimurque uolentes
exsilium: tua nos faciet uictoria ciues.
dum trepidant nullo firmatae robore partes,   280
tolle moras: semper nocuit differre paratis:
par labor atque metus pretio maiore petuntur.
bellantem geminis tenuit te Gallia lustris,
pars quota terrarum! facili si proelia pauca
gesseris euentu, tibi Roma subegerit orbem.   285
nunc neque te longi remeantem pompa triumphi
excipit aut sacras poscunt Capitolia laurus.
liuor edax tibi cuncta negat, gentesque subactas

uix inpune feres. socerum depellere regno
decretum genero est. partiri non potes orbem,   290
solus habere potes.' sic post quam fatus, et ipsi
in bellum prono tantum tamen addidit irae
accenditque ducem, quantum clamore iuuatur
Eleus sonipes, quamuis iam carcere clauso
inmineat foribus pronusque repagula laxet.   295

Caesar addresses his soldiers

conuocat armatos extemplo ad signa maniplos,
utque satis trepidum turba coeunte tumultum
conposuit uoltu dextraque silentia iussit,
'bellorum o socii, qui mille pericula Martis
mecum' ait 'experti decimo iam uincitis anno,   300
hoc cruor Arctois meruit diffusus in aruis
uolneraque et mortes hiemesque sub Alpibus actae?
non secus ingenti bellorum Roma tumultu
concutitur, quam si Poenus transcenderet Alpes
Hannibal: inplentur ualidae tirone cohortes,   305
in classem cadit omne nemus, terraque marique
iussus Caesar agi. quid, si mihi signa iacerent
Marte sub aduerso ruerentque in terga feroces
Gallorum populi? nunc, cum Fortuna secundis
mecum rebus agat superique ad summa uocantes,   310
temptamur. ueniat longa dux pace solutus
milite cum subito partesque in bella togatae
Marcellusque loquax et nomina uana Catones.
scilicet extremi Pompeium emptique clientes
continuo per tot satiabunt tempora regno?   315
ille reget currus nondum patientibus annis,
ille semel raptos numquam dimittet honores?
quid iam rura querar totum suppressa per orbem

ac iussam seruire famem? quis castra timenti
nescit mixta foro, gladii cum triste micantes   320
iudicium insolita trepidum cinxere corona
atque auso medias perrumpere milite leges
Pompeiana reum clauserunt signa Milonem?
nunc quoque, ne lassum teneat priuata senectus,
bella nefanda parat suetus ciuilibus armis   325
et docilis Sullam scelerum uicisse magistrum.
utque ferae tigres numquam posuere furorem,
quas, nemore Hyrcano matrum dum lustra sequuntur,
altus caesorum pauit cruor armentorum,
sic et Sullanum solito tibi lambere ferrum   330
durat, Magne, sitis. nullus semel ore receptus
pollutas patitur sanguis mansuescere fauces.
quem tamen inueniet tam longa potentia finem?
quis scelerum modus est? ex hoc iam te, inprobe, regno
ille tuus saltem doceat descendere Sulla.   335
post Cilicasne uagos et lassi Pontica regis
proelia barbarico uix consummata ueneno
ultima Pompeio dabitur prouincia Caesar,
quod non uictrices aquilas deponere iussus
paruerim? mihi si merces erepta laborum est,   340
his saltem longi non cum duce praemia belli
reddantur; miles sub quolibet iste triumphet.
conferet exsanguis quo se post bella senectus?
quae sedes erit emeritis? quae rura dabuntur
quae noster ueteranus aret, quae moenia fessis?   345
an melius fient piratae, Magne, coloni?
tollite iam pridem uictricia tollite signa.
uiribus utendum est quas fecimus. arma tenenti
omnia dat, qui iusta negat. nec numina derunt;
nam neque praeda meis neque regnum quaeritur armis:

detrahimus dominos urbi seruire paratae.'   351

The speech of the centurion Laelius

dixerat; at dubium non claro murmure uolgus
secum incerta fremit. pietas patriique penates
quamquam caede feras mentes animosque tumentes
frangunt, sed diro ferri reuocantur amore   355
ductorisque metu. summi tum munera pili
Laelius emeritique gerens insignia doni,
seruati ciuis referentem praemia quercum,
'si licet', exclamat 'Romani maxime rector
nominis, et ius est ueras expromere uoces,   360
quod tam lenta tuas tenuit patientia uires
conquerimur. deratne tibi fiducia nostri?
dum mouet haec calidus spirantia corpora sanguis,
et dum pila ualent fortes torquere lacerti,
degenerem patiere togam regnumque senatus?   365
usque adeo miserum est ciuili uincere bello?
duc age per Scythiae populos, per inhospita Syrtis
litora, per calidas Libyes sitientis harenas:
haec manus, ut uictum post terga relinqueret orbem,
Oceani tumidas remo conpescuit undas   370
fregit et Arctoo spumantem uertice Rhenum:
iussa sequi tam posse mihi quam uelle necesse est.
nec ciuis meus est, in quem tua classica, Caesar,
audiero. per signa decem felicia castris,
perque tuos iuro quocumque ex hoste triumphos,   375
pectore si fratris gladium iuguloque parentis
condere me iubeas plenaeque in uiscera partu
coniugis, inuita peragam tamen omnia dextra;
si spoliare deos ignemque inmittere templis,
numina miscebit castrensis flamma monetae;   380

castra super Tusci si ponere Thybridis undas,
Hesperios audax ueniam metator in agros.
tu quoscumque uoles in planum effundere muros,
his aries actus disperget saxa lacertis,
illa licet, penitus tolli quam iusseris urbem,   385
Roma sit.' his cunctae simul adsensere cohortes
elatasque alte, quaecumque ad bella uocaret,
promisere manus. it tantus ad aethera clamor,
quantus, piniferae Boreas cum Thracius Ossae
rupibus incubuit, curuato robore pressae   390
fit sonus aut rursus redeuntis in aethera siluae.

Caesar summons his forces from Gaul

Caesar, ut acceptum tam prono milite bellum
fataque ferre uidet, ne quo languore moretur
Fortunam, sparsas per Gallica rura cohortes
euocat et Romam motis petit undique signis.   395
deseruere cauo tentoria fixa Lemanno
castraque quae Vogesi curuam super ardua ripam
pugnaces pictis cohibebant Lingonas armis.
hi uada liquerunt Isarae, qui, gurgite ductus
per tam multa suo, famae maioris in amnem   400
lapsus ad aequoreas nomen non pertulit undas.
soluuntur flaui longa statione Ruteni.
mitis Atax Latias gaudet non ferre carinas
finis et Hesperiae, promoto limite, Varus.
quaque sub Herculeo sacratus nomine poɪ‿ʌs   405
urguet rupe caua pelagus: non Corus in illum
ius habet aut Zephyrus, solus sua litora turbat
Circius et tuta prohibet statione Monoeci.
quaque iacet litus dubium quod terra fretumque
uindicat alternis uicibus, cum funditur ingens   410

Oceanus uel cum refugis se fluctibus aufert.
(uentus ab extremo pelagus sic axe uolutet
destituatque ferens, an sidere mota secundo
Tethyos unda uagae lunaribus aestuet horis,
flammiger an Titan, ut alentes hauriat undas,   415
erigat Oceanum fluctusque ad sidera ducat,
quaerite, quos agitat mundi labor; at mihi semper
tu, quaecumque moues tam crebros causa meatus,
ut superi uoluere, late.) tum rura Nemetis
qui tenet et ripas Aturi, qua litore curuo   420
molliter admissum claudit Tarbellicus aequor,
signa mouet, gaudetque amoto Santonus hoste
et Biturix longisque leues Suessones in armis,
optimus excusso Leucus Remusque lacerto,
optima gens flexis in gyrum Sequana frenis,   425
et docilis rector monstrati Belga couinni,
Aruernique ausi Latio se fingere fratres
sanguine ab Iliaco populi, nimiumque rebellis
Neruius et caesi pollutus foedere Cottae,
et qui te laxis imitantur, Sarmata, bracis   430
Vangiones, Batauique truces, quos aere recuruo
stridentes acuere tubae; qua Cinga pererrat
gurgite, qua Rhodanus raptum uelocibus undis
in mare fert Ararim, qua montibus ardua summis
gens habitat cana pendentes rupe Cebennas.   435
tu quoque laetatus conuerti proelia, Treuir,   441
et nunc tonse Ligur, quondam per colla decore
crinibus effusis toti praelate Comatae,
et quibus inmitis placatur sanguine diro
Teutates horrensque feris altaribus Esus   445
et Taranis: Scythicae *non*[1] mitior ara Dianae.

[1] *Fortasse* et Taranis, Scythicae quo mitior ara Dianae (*vid.* App. D.)

uos quoque, qui fortes animas belloque peremptas
laudibus in longum uates dimittitis aeuum,
plurima securi fudistis carmina, Bardi.
et uos barbaricos ritus moremque sinistrum   450
sacrorum, Dryadae, positis repetistis ab armis.
solis nosse deos et caeli numina uobis
aut solis nescire datum est; nemora alta remotis
incolitis lucis; uobis auctoribus umbrae
non tacitas Erebi sedes Ditisque profundi   455
pallida regna petunt: regit idem spiritus artus
orbe alio; longae, canitis si cognita, uitae
mors media est. certe populi quos despicit Arctos
felices errore suo, quos ille timorum
maximus haut urguet leti metus. inde ruendi   460
in ferrum mens prona uiris animaeque capaces
mortis, et ignauum rediturae parcere uitae.
et uos, crinigeros bellis arcere Caycos
oppositi, petitis Romam Rhenique feroces
deseritis ripas et apertum gentibus orbem.   465

The terror in Rome at Caesar's approach
and the flight of the Senate

Caesar, ut inmensae conlecto robore uires
audendi maiora fidem fecere, per omnem
spargitur Italiam uicinaque moenia conplet.
uana quoque ad ueros accessit fama timores
inrupitque animos populi clademque futuram   470
intulit et uelox properantis nuntia belli
innumeras soluit falsa in praeconia linguas.
est qui tauriferis ubi se Meuania campis
explicat audaces ruere in certamina turmas

adferat, et qua Nar Tiberino inlabitur amni   475
barbaricas saeui discurrere Caesaris alas;
ipsum omnes aquilas conlataque signa ferentem
agmine non uno densisque incedere castris
(nec qualem meminere uident: maiorque ferusque
mentibus occurrit uictoque inmanior hoste);   480
tunc inter Rhenum populos Alpemque iacentes
finibus Arctois patriaque a sede reuolsos
pone sequi, iussamque feris a gentibus urbem
Romano spectante rapi. sic quisque pauendo
dat uires famae; nulloque auctore malorum   485
quae finxere timent. nec solum uolgus inani
percussum terrore pauet, sed curia et ipsi
sedibus exsiluere patres, inuisaque belli
consulibus fugiens mandat decreta senatus.
tum, quae tuta petant et quae metuenda relinquant 490
incerti, quo quemque fugae tulit impetus urguent
praecipitem populum, serieque haerentia longa
agmina prorumpunt. credas aut tecta nefandas
corripuisse faces, aut iam quatiente ruina
nutantes pendere domos; sic turba per urbem   495
praecipiti lymphata gradu, uelut unica rebus
spes foret adflictis patrios excedere muros,
inconsulta ruit. qualis, cum turbidus Auster
reppulit a Libycis inmensum Syrtibus aequor
fractaque ueliferi sonuerunt pondera mali,   500
desilit in fluctus deserta puppe magister
nauitaque et nondum sparsa conpage carinae
naufragium sibi quisque facit, sic urbe relicta
in bellum fugitur. nullum iam languidus aeuo
eualuit reuocare parens coniunxue maritum   505
fletibus, aut patrii, dubiae dum uota salutis

conciperent, tenuere lares; nec limine quisquam
haesit et extremo tunc forsitan urbis amatae
plenus abit uisu: ruit inreuocabile uolgus.
o faciles dare summa deos eademque tueri   510
difficiles! urbem populis uictisque frequentem
gentibus et generis, coeat si turba, capacem
humani facilem uenturo Caesare praedam
ignauae liquere manus. cum pressus ab hoste
clauditur externis miles Romanus in oris,   515
effugit exiguo nocturna pericula uallo,
et subitus rapti munimine caespitis agger
praebet securos intra tentoria somnos:
tu tantum audito bellorum nomine, Roma,
desereris; nox una tuis non credita muris.   520
danda tamen uenia est tantorum danda pauorum:
Pompeio fugiente timent.

Prodigies

                        tum, nequa futuri
spes saltem trepidas mentes leuet, addita fati
peioris manifesta fides, superique minaces
prodigiis terras inplerunt, aethera, pontum.   525
ignota obscurae uiderunt sidera noctes
ardentemque polum flammis caeloque uolantes
obliquas per inane faces crinemque timendi
sideris et terris mutantem regna cometen.
fulgura fallaci micuerunt crebra sereno,   530
et uarias ignis denso dedit aere formas,
nunc iaculum longo, nunc sparso lumine lampas.
emicuit caelo tacitum sine nubibus ullis
fulmen et Arctois rapiens de partibus ignem
percussit Latiare caput, stellaeque minores   535

per uacuum solitae noctis decurrere tempus
in medium uenere diem, cornuque coacto
iam Phoebe toto fratrem cum redderet ore
terrarum subita percussa expalluit umbra.
ipse caput medio Titan cum ferret Olympo   540
condidit ardentes atra caligine currus
inuoluitque orbem tenebris gentesque coegit
desperare diem; qualem fugiente per ortus
sole Thyesteae noctem duxere Mycenae.
ora ferox Siculae laxauit Mulciber Aetnae,   545
nec tulit in caelum flammas sed uertice prono
ignis in Hesperium cecidit latus. atra Charybdis
sanguineum fundo torsit mare; flebile saeui
latrauere canes. Vestali raptus ab ara
ignis, et ostendens confectas flamma Latinas   550
scinditur in partes geminoque cacumine surgit
Thebanos imitata rogos. tum cardine tellus
subsedit, ueteremque iugis nutantibus Alpes
discussere niuem. Tethys maioribus undis
Hesperiam Calpen summumque inpleuit Atlanta.   555
indigetes fleuisse deos, urbisque laborem
testatos sudore Lares, delapsaque templis
dona suis, dirasque diem foedasse uolucres
accipimus, siluisque feras sub nocte relictis
audaces media posuisse cubilia Roma.   560
tum pecudum faciles humana ad murmura linguae,
monstrosique hominum partus numeroque modoque
membrorum, matremque suus conterruit infans;
diraque per populum Cumanae carmina uatis
uolgantur. tum, quos sectis Bellona lacertis   565
saeua mouet, cecinere deos, crinemque rotantes
sanguineum populis ululárunt tristia Galli.

conpositis plenae gemuerunt ossibus urnae.
tum fragor armorum, magnaeque per auia uoces
auditae nemorum et uenientes comminus umbrae.   570
quique colunt iunctos extremis moenibus agros
diffugiunt: ingens urbem cingebat Erinys
excutiens pronam flagranti uertice pinum
stridentesque comas, Thebanam qualis Agauen
inpulit aut saeui contorsit tela Lycurgi   575
Eumenis, aut qualem iussu Iunonis iniquae
horruit Alcides uiso iam Dite Megaeram.
insonuere tubae et, quanto clamore cohortes
miscentur, tantum nox atra silentibus auris
edidit. e medio uisi consurgere Campo   580
tristia Sullani cecinere oracula manes,
tollentemque caput gelidas Anienis ad undas
agricolae fracto Marium fugere sepulchro.

The expiatory rites and ill-omened sacrifice of Arruns

  haec propter placuit Tuscos de more uetusto
acciri uates. quorum qui maximus aeuo   585
Arruns incoluit desertae moenia Lucae,
fulminis edoctus motus uenasque calentes
fibrarum et monitus errantis in aere pinnae,
monstra iubet primum quae nullo semine discors
protulerat natura rapi sterilique nefandos   590
ex utero fetus infaustis urere flammis.
mox iubet et totam pauidis a ciuibus urbem
ambiri et festo purgantes moenia lustro
longa per extremos pomeria cingere fines
pontifices, sacri quibus est permissa potestas.   595
turba minor ritu sequitur succincta Gabino,
Vestalemque chorum ducit uittata sacerdos

Troianam soli cui fas uidisse Mineruam.
tum, qui fata deum secretaque carmina seruant
et lotam paruo reuocant Almone Cybeben,   600
et doctus uolucres augur seruare sinistras
septemuirque epulis festus Titiique sodales
et Salius laeto portans ancilia collo
et tollens apicem generoso uertice flamen.
dumque illi effusam longis anfractibus urbem   605
circumeunt, Arruns dispersos fulminis ignes
colligit et terrae maesto cum murmure condit
datque locis numen. sacris tunc admouet aris
electa ceruice marem. iam fundere Bacchum
coeperat obliquoque molas inducere cultro;   610
inpatiensque diu non grati uictima sacri,
cornua succincti premerent cum torua ministri,
deposito uictum praebebat poplite collum.
nec cruor emicuit solitus, sed uolnere laxo
diffusum rutilo nigrum pro sanguine uirus.   615
palluit attonitus sacris feralibus Arruns
atque iram superum raptis quaesiuit in extis.
terruit ipse color uatem; nam pallida taetris
uiscera tincta notis gelidoque infecta cruore
plurimus asperso uariabat sanguine liuor.   620
cernit tabe iecur madidum, uenasque minaces
hostili de parte uidet. pulmonis anheli
fibra iacet, paruusque secat uitalia limes.
cor latet, et saniem per hiantes uiscera rimas
emittunt, produntque suas omenta latebras.   625
quodque nefas nullis inpune apparuit extis,
ecce, uidet capiti fibrarum increscere molem
alterius capitis. pars aegra et marcida pendet,
pars micat et celeri uenas mouet inproba pulsu.

his ubi concepit magnorum fata malorum,   630
exclamat 'uix fas, superi, quaecumque monetis,
prodere me populis; nec enim tibi, summe, litaui,
Iuppiter, hoc sacrum, caesique in pectora tauri
inferni uenere dei. non fanda timemus,
sed uenient maiora metu. di uisa secundent,   635
et fibris sit nulla fides, sed conditor artis
finxerit ista Tages.' flexa sic omina Tuscus
inuoluens multaque tegens ambage canebat.

The astrological predictions of Figulus

at Figulus, cui cura deos secretaque caeli
nosse fuit, quem non stellarum Aegyptia Memphis 640
aequaret uisu numerisque sequentibus astra,
'aut hic errat' ait 'nulla cum lege per aeuum
mundus et incerto discurrunt sidera motu,
aut, si fata mouent, urbi generique paratur
humano matura lues. terraene dehiscent   645
subsidentque urbes, an tollet feruidus aer
temperiem? segetes tellus infida negabit,
omnis an infusis miscebitur unda uenenis?
quod cladis genus, o superi, qua peste paratis
saeuitiam? extremi multorum tempus in unum   650
conuenere dies. summo si frigida caelo
stella nocens nigros Saturni accenderet ignes,
Deucalioneos fudisset Aquarius imbres
totaque diffuso latuisset in aequore tellus.
si saeuum radiis Nemeaeum, Phoebe, Leonem   655
nunc premeres, toto fluerent incendia mundo
succensusque tuis flagrasset curribus aether.
hi cessant ignes. tu, qui flagrante minacem
Scorpion incendis cauda chelasque peruris,

quid tantum, Gradiue, paras? nam mitis in alto   660
Iuppiter occasu premitur, Venerisque salubre
sidus hebet, motuque celer Cyllenius haeret,
et caelum Mars solus habet. cur signa meatus
deseruere suos mundoque obscura feruntur,
ensiferi nimium fulget latus Orionis?   665
inminet armorum rabies, ferrique potestas
confundet ius omne manu, scelerique nefando
nomen erit uirtus, multosque exibit in annos
hic furor. et superos quid prodest poscere finem?
cum domino pax ista uenit. duc, Roma, malorum   670
continuam seriem clademque in tempora multa
extrahe ciuili tantum iam libera bello.'

Disasters are foretold by a frenzied matron

terruerant satis haec pauidam praesagia plebem,
sed maiora premunt. nam, qualis uertice Pindi
Edonis Ogygio decurrit plena Lyaeo,   675
talis et attonitam rapitur matrona per urbem
uocibus his prodens urguentem pectora Phoebum:
'quo feror, o Paean? qua me super aethera raptam
constituis terra? uideo Pangaea niuosis
cana iugis latosque Haemi sub rupe Philippos.   680
quis furor hic, o Phoebe, doce. quot tela manusque
Romanae miscent acies bellumque sine hoste est!
quo diuersa feror? primos me ducis in ortus,
qua mare Lagei mutatur gurgite Nili:
hunc ego, fluminea deformis truncus harena   685
qui iacet, agnosco. dubiam super aequora Syrtim
arentemque feror Libyen, quo tristis Enyo
transtulit Emathias acies. nunc desuper Alpis
nubiferae colles atque aeriam Pyrenen

abripimur. patriae sedes remeamus in urbis,   690
inpiaque in medio peraguntur bella senatu.
consurgunt partes iterum, totumque per orbem
rursus eo. noua da mihi cernere litora ponti
telluremque nouam: uidi iam, Phoebe, Philippos.'
haec ait, et lasso iacuit deserta furore.   695

EXPLANATORY NOTES

References given thus: 44, 667, are to lines elsewhere in this book; 44n., 667n., are to the explanatory notes on these lines as well as to the lines themselves; and 4.172, 5. 3, are to other books of Lucan.

An asterisk affixed to the number of a line, thus 16*, refers the reader to a note in the Critical Apparatus, in the absence of any other indication.

Abbreviations: *C.R.*=*Classical Review*, *C.Q.*=*Classical Quarterly*, *C.W.*=*Classical Weekly*, *A.J.P.*=*American Journal of Philology*.

1. **Emathios**. Emathia, in fact, is the district in Macedonia of which Pella is the centre, whereas Pharsalia is in Thessaly. Just as *Emathius*=*Macedonius* by synecdoche in Ouid. *Trist.* 3. 5. 39 *ducis Emathii* (Alexander), so here it=*Thessalus* by metonymy. See Introduction, pp. liii and lvi.

Emathios...campos. Cf. Ouid. *Met.* 5. 313–14 *Emathiis... campis*.

plus quam. The phrase is Ovidian rather than Vergilian: in *Georg.* 4. 207 Vergil omits the *quam*. Cf. *Am.* 3. 14. 33, *Met.* 1. 573, 13. 451, and other passages, especially *Met.* 12. 578 *exercet (Neptunus) memores plus quam ciuiliter iras* (not only had the god built the walls of Troy and was in a sense its citizen, but he was angry because of the death of his son Cycnus). Cf. also Tac. *Ann.* 1. 12 *plus quam ciuilia agitaret*.

The exaggeration implies that the war was waged not merely between citizens, but between relatives like Caesar and Pompey (cf. 289–90). Cf. Florus 2. 13 (4. 2. 3–4) *Caesaris furor atque Pompei urbem Italiam gentes nationes...corripuit, adeo ut non recte tantum ciuile dicatur,...sed...plus quam bellum* (the whole of this context, which deals with the *Bellum Ciuile Caesaris et Pompei*, shows marked indebtedness to Lucan), and Sen. *Phoen.* 354–5.

2. **iusque datum sceleri**: 'legality conferred on crime' (Duff). Lejay quotes Sen. *Ep.* 18. 1 *ius luxuriae publicae datum est. Sceleri* is the crime of civil war, cf. 325, 666–9, and especially Tac. *Hist.* 3. 25, where also civil war is called a *scelus* on the occasion of a son

causing his father's death. It was of course a crime to kill Roman citizens.

populumque potentem: cf. 83, 109–11 n., 159, Ouid. *Fast.* 1. 88, 5. 729.

3. For the alliteration cf. Verg. *Aen.* 6. 833 *neu patriae ualidas in uiscera uertite uires.* Lejay quotes Florus 1. 34 (2. 19. 4) *in se ipse conuersus (populus Romanus)...Pompei et Caesaris manibus...semet ipse lacerauit.* Compare also Manil. 4. 43–4.

4. **cognatasque acies**. Statius begins his *Thebais* with the words *fraternas acies.* Cf. Sen. *Oed.* 738–50.'

foedere: the bond which holds various elements together, cf. 80, 86.

regni: not the Roman *imperium*, as Lejay takes it, but the 'tyranny' of the First Triumvirate of 60–59 B.C., when Caesar, Pompey, and Crassus formed a coalition. The words *rex* and *regnum* assumed a meaning as sinister as that which we associate with 'tyrant', 'tyranny', though the Greek τύραννος like *rex* at first meant simply 'king', 'ruler'. For this, the wickedness of Tarquin the Proud, the last king of Rome, was responsible. Cf. Liu. 27. 19. 4 *regium nomen alibi magnum, Romae intolerabile esse.*

5. **certatum**: usually taken as a substantival employment of the neuter participle, cf. 70 *negatum.* This is a common construction in Livy (see Page on Verg. *Aen.* 5. 5). Here it is the forerunner of the noun *certatus* ('contention', 'conflict'), which is found not merely in Stat. *Silu.* 3. 1. 152–3 (Lejay's parallel) *nudosque uirorum | certatus*, but also in Iord. *Rom.* 219. The neuter *certatum* is used by Iosephus Iscanus, *Bell. Troian.* 1. 257.

concussi uiribus orbis: cf. Sen. *Oct.* 517–18 *suis |. concussus orbis uiribus, Epigr.* 19. 5 *uersis uiribus orbis.*

6. **in**: to be taken with *certatum*, cf. Sen. *Phoen.* 298 *certant in omne facinus*, so that *certatum...in commune nefas* = 'the contention productive of sin on both sides'. *Nefas* in Lucan often means the sin of the civil war (cf. 4. 172 *ciuile nefas*), and is again combined with *scelus* in 37. Manilius (1. 84) already uses the expression *in commune bonum.*

6–7. **infestis...signa**: cf. Sen. *Phoen.* 414–15. There is a reminiscence of Enn. *Ann.* 570 (Vahlen) *pila retunduntur uenientibus obuia pilis.*

7. **pares**: 'matched', 'pitted against' (*commissas*). Haskins quotes 4. 710, 5. 3, and 6. 3, and observes that the word is used of gladiators. Cf. Hor. *Serm.* 2. 6. 44 *Threx est Gallina Syro par?*

Lucan is fond of metaphors drawn from gladiators, see Heitland, *Introd.* p. xc.

pila: 'the special weapons of Romans; cf. 10. 47–8 where they are opposed to the Macedonian *sarisae*' (Haskins). H. also quotes the imitation by Dryden, *Hind and Panther*, 2. 160–1: 'That was but civil war, an equal set, Where piles with piles and eagles eagles met.'

8–9. The usual punctuation formerly was to place a mark of interrogation or exclamation after *cruorem*, without any stop between 8 and 9; but Housman adopts that of Cortius, which makes 8 a self-contained question, on the ground that *'quae tanta licentia!* is not Latin: the exclamatory *quis* or *qui* cannot consist with *tantus'*, and that 8–9 'cannot be linked' to 10–12 'by the conjunction *que* nor by any conjunction'. His view is supported by the fact that the imitation by Dracontius, *Rom.* 5. 1 *quis furor iste nouus, quae tanta licentia ferri?* is a question independent of what follows.

8. **quae tanta licentia ferri**: cf. Cic. *Fam.* 4. 9. 4 *magna gladiorum est licentia.*

9. **gentibus inuisis**: 'envious *barbarian* nations', cf. 20, 82–4, 465, 512, 2. 47–8, and see Löfstedt, *Synt.* ii, pp. 465–7.

10. **Babylon**: metonymy for Parthia. The Parthian empire was the successor to that of Persia, and, if we go back to a more remote age, to that of Babylon. **superba**: the name of Babylon is used conventionally for the capital of the gentile and pagan world ('that great city') in the major prophets and in the Book of Revelation (*Is.* 13. 19, 47. 1, *Jer.* 25. 12, 50. 1, *Rev.* 14. 8, 17. 18).

tropaeis: the standards of Crassus, who was defeated and killed by the Parthians at Carrhae in 53 B.C. They were recovered in 20 B.C. by negotiation on the part of Augustus (for the regret in Rome at their capture and joy on their return cf. Verg. *Aen.* 7. 606, 8. 726, Hor. *Carm.* 4. 15. 6–8 *signa...derepta Parthorum superbis | postibus*, Prop. 2. 10. 13–14, Ouid. *A.A.* 1. 179, *Fast.* 5. 579 sqq.). Lucan attaches great importance to the battle of Carrhae, cf. 105 and 2. 553. At the beginning of 50 B.C. there was alarm at Rome because a Parthian army had crossed the Euphrates, and the Senate in the following May decreed that Pompey and Caesar should each contribute a legion for a Parthian expedition, which Lucan apparently thinks should have materialized instead of the civil war.

11. **Ausoniis**: metonymy for *Italis* and so for *Romanis*. The Αὔσονες or Aurunci were a branch of the Oscans, and were among the first people whom the early Greek settlers of Magna Graecia

met. The name of their tribe and country, accordingly, often designates the Italians and Italy in poetry from the Alexandrine period onwards (cf. Ap. Rhod. 4. 553 and 660).

umbraque erraret Crassus: cf. Ouid. *Met.* 4. 443, 15. 797–8.

12. **placuit**: for the postponement of this word after its infinitive cf. the similar delay until *iuuet* in 50 is reached after *tenere* and *conscendere*.

nullos...triumphos: triumphs could be claimed only for victory over a foreign foe, cf. 6. 260–1 and Val. Max. 2. 8. 7. The triumphs granted to Caesar in 46 B.C. and to Octavian in 29 B.C. were, nominally at least, for victories over the barbarians. Lejay points out that a slight exception was the ovation and gold statue awarded to Octavian after the defeat of Sextus Pompeius.

13. Compare the reflexions of the more thoughtful combatants before Pharsalia, as recounted in Plut. *Pomp.* 70.

parari = *comparari* ('to be bought'), simple for compound verb. *Comparare* in this not uncommon meaning is the ancestor of the Ital. *comprare* and the Span. *comprar*. *Parari* occurs with the ablative of price at 34.

14. **sanguine** is divorced from *hoc* and brought into the relative clause. For such examples of hyperbaton see Introduction, p. lx.

sanguine dextrae: cf. 10. 338.

15–18. The four points of the compass are now named in the following order: East, West, South, and North.

15. **Titan**: the Sun. His father was Hyperion and his mother Terra. Hyperion's father also was called Titan, and he was the elder brother of Saturn and son of Caelus (or Caelum) and Vesta. Caelus himself was the son of Aether and Dies. It is possible that Nox should be thus printed and personified in the text, for she was the mother of Aether and Dies by Erebus her brother.

nox ubi sidera condit: 'where night *hides* the stars' (Duff) is a mistranslation, for night does not hide the stars. The criticism in *C.Q.* xxxi, 1937, pp. 16–17 of the discussion of this line in *C.Q.* xxx, 1936, pp. 55–6 does not produce a single instance from Latin poetry to support the idea of night hiding the stars or laying them to rest. The Sun may lay himself to rest (Verg. *Georg.* 1. 438–9), as may any heavenly body or bodies (Manil. 5. 722); but in the evening night drives away or hides the day, and brings the stars forth (Ouid. *Her.* 19. 33–4), *i.e.* she substitutes her own luminaries for the Sun after he has set (4. 282).

What *nox* does 'hide' or 'lay to rest' (*condit*) is the Sun and the light of day. Compare 4. 472–3 *nam condidit umbra | nox lucem du-biam* and Sen. *Med.* 874–8 *nunc*, *Phoebe, mittte currus | nullo morante loro, | nox condat alma lucem, | mergat diem timendum | dux noctis Hesperus.* Conversely, in the morning the Sun lays the stars to rest (hides them), cf. Plin. *H.N.* 2. 61 (*inferiores stellae) occasu matutino conduntur.* Haskins therefore was right in following Burman and Van Jever so far as to suggest that *sidera = solem* (see Appendix A). Translate 'where the Sun rises, and where night hides his orb'. With *sidera* may be understood *Titanis*, just as in Verg. *Georg.* 1. 217–18 *candidus auratis aperit cum cornibus annum | Taurus, et aduerso cedens Canis occidit astro,* the *astro* is that of *Taurus.*

16. **qua**: Lejay observes how fond Lucan, like Ovid, is of *qua* instead of *ubi* (which happens here to be used also in antithesis to it).

dies medius: 'the South', cf. 9. 606, Verg. *Georg.* 3. 303, Ouid. *A.A.* 3. 723, *Met.* 3. 144, 10. 126, and Sen. *H.F.* 236. Note the similar use of *meridies*, which is formed indirectly from *medius dies* through the form *medidies*.

horis: see Critical Apparatus.

17. **bruma rigens**: 'the rigour of winter' (Duff). In its primary sense *bruma* means the winter solstice, *i.e.* the shortest day (*breuima*, whence *breuma* and so *bruma*), but the poets use it of winter generally by synecdoche.

nescia uere remitti: 'incapable of being thawed by spring'. The use of *nescius* with the infinitive in poetry in the sense of 'unable to' is a step from that of *scio* ('I am able to') with inanimate as well as animate subjects. Compare the use of *savoir*, *sapere*, and *saber* in the Neo-Latin languages. For *uere remitti* cf. Tibull. 3. 5. 4 and Ouid. *Fast.* 4. 126.

18*. **astringit**: this verb, which denotes the contraction pro-duced by cold, occurs several times in Ovid in this sense. Cf. 5. 436 *sic stat iners Scythicas astringens Bosporos undas e.q.s.* for this verb, as well as for the reading *Scythicum…Pontum.*

Scythicum…Pontum: the Euxine, cf. 2. 420, 580 *Scythici… diuortia Ponti,* and 5. 436 (*cit. supr.*). To the Roman poets the Euxine was a frozen sea in the winter, cf. Val. Flacc. 4. 723, and was also in the North, cf. *id.* 5. 618–19, just as the Phasis was a northern river (2. 585–6).

The allusion to the Euxine is apt, because by 49 B.C. Caesar had been to Britain, which usually was thought of as being in the extreme North (cf. 301 and Hor. *Carm.* 1. 35. 29–30 *ultimos | orbis*

Britannos), while of the lands adjoining the Black Sea, only Bithynia and Pontus along the southern shore had become Roman (in 74 and 65 B.C. respectively).

19–20. In the same vein Professor A. D. Nock (*C.R.* xl, 1926, pp. 17–18) points out that Lucan is not merely selecting the Seres and the dwellers by the Araxes and the source of the Nile as types of distant people, as does Horace (*Carm.* 3. 29. 25–8). Nero sent a detachment of praetorians, who probably returned in the summer of A.D. 63, to explore the sources of the Nile (Sen. *N.Q.* 6. 8. 3); and in A.D. 66 he probably intended an expedition against the Axumite kings of Abyssinia. The mention of the Araxes (the modern Aras, which flows into the Caspian) recalls Corbulo's campaigns in Armenia, in the course of which he burnt Artaxata on this river in A.D. 58. W. Schur ('Die Orientpolitik des Kaisers Nero', *Klio*, xv, 1923, pp. 42–3) supposes that Nero's projected expedition to the Caspian Gates aimed at securing the great northern route for trade between the West and the Chinese (*Seres*). The project may have been contemplated before A.D. 66, and could have been magnified by Lucan into an attempt to reduce China into submission. He is trying to honour Nero, and ignores the fact that Armenia had already submitted to Pompey; this being not merely an inadvertence, as Lejay suggests. See also Professor Eva Matthews Sanford, 'Nero and the East' (*Harvard Studies in Classical Philology*, xlviii, 1937, pp. 75–103).

19. **Seres**: according to Probus, *Cathol.* p. 27 Keil (Nettleship, *C.R.* i, 1887, p. 295), the word here is singular rather than plural; but for the plural cf. Sen. *H.O.* 414–15.

20*. **iacet** almost = *est*, cf. the similar meaning of *stare* as noted by Servius on *Aen.* 3. 210 *Strophades Graio stant nomine dictae*, and as seen in the use of *stare* and *estar* in Italian and Spanish.

nascenti conscia Nilo: 'knowing where the Nile rises'. *Conscius* with the dative is as Ciceronian as with the genitive. For the unknown origin of the Nile cf. Hor. *Carm.* 4. 14. 45–6. The problem had a fascination for Lucan, who makes Acoreus reply at length to a question by Caesar about the source of this river (10. 172–331).

21. **tum** = *tum demum*, 'then and only then'.

22. **miseris**: this poetical use of *mittere* ('to put', 'to place') is anticipatory of *mettre*, *mettere*, *meter* in French, Italian, and Spanish. *Miseris* is fut. perf. because *uerte* virtually = *uertas licebit*. Cf. Verg. *Aen.* 4. 231 *totum sub leges mitteret orbem* (of Aeneas).

23. nondum: 'never yet'.

24. at nunc, as Lejay observes, indicates the return from an unrealized hypothesis to reality.

quod here and in 28 anticipates *auctor* (30). This type of *quod* clause, which denotes effect and not cause, is especially common in Cicero's letters.

25. urbibus is either the dative for the genitive (antiptosis, for which see 30n. and Introduction, p. lxv), *i.e.* the meaning is *moenia urbium*, or else the ablative of place without *in*, which preposition may be understood, however, from *in urbibus* (27).

Housman (p. xxxiii) observes that such repetitions as that of *urbibus* here and in 27 are commoner in Lucan than in any other poet. Horace is freest from them, then the order is Vergil, Ovid, Lucan. Cf. also the repetitions in 45 (*tibi*...*te*); 46 and 76; 53, 58, and 61 (*orbe*...*orbe*...*orbem*); 80 and 86; 82 and 93; etc. Milton displays this characteristic in a marked degree, see J. W. Mackail, *Studies in Humanism*, London, 1938, p. 205 for an extreme example in *Par. Lost*. 6. 578–81.

26. saxa: 'for the massive building of the old Italian towns cf. Verg. *Georg*. 2. 155–6 *adde*...*tot congesta manu praeruptis oppida saxis*' (Haskins).

27. Cf. Verg. *Ecl*. 6. 40 *rara per ignaros errent animalia montes* and *Aen*. 1. 578 *urbibus errat*.

habitator: a prose word before Lucan, but adopted later by Statius. Cf. 6. 341 *habitator Olympi*.

28. Cf. Verg. *Aen*. 9. 381–2 *silua fuit late dumis atque ilice nigra | horrida*. The phrases *horrida dumis* (*Aen*. 8. 348) and *multos*...*per annos* (*Georg*. 2. 208, *Aen*. 2. 363, 715) are Vergilian, as is the adjective *inaratus* (*Georg*. 1. 83).

29. Hesperia, when used as a noun, properly means 'Western Land', and is usually either Italy or Spain (as in Hor. *Carm*. 1. 36. 4), but in Lucan is always Italy. Cf. 382n.

manus poscentibus aruis: cf. Verg. *Aen*. 11. 379 *bella manus poscunt*, and the imitation by Ennodius, *Vita Epifani* 141, *sed quid demoror manus arua poscentia?* The idea is that of Verg. *Georg*. 1. 506–7.

30–2. The thought is similar to that of Hor. *Epod*. 16. Cf. Enn. *Ann*. 274–5 (Vahl.) *at non sic duplex fuit hostis | Aeacida Burrus*.

30. ferox: 'proud', 'spirited'. He was like his namesake and putative ancestor, the son of Achilles, cf. Ouid. *Her*. 8. 1 *Pyrrhus Achillides animosus imagine patris*.

tantis cladibus: resumptive of 24–9. The use of the dative instead of the genitive with *auctor* is originally colloquial (Ter. *Adelph.* 671, Cic. *Att.* 8. 3. 3), see *Thes. Ling. Lat.* ii, 1201. Lucan is the first poet to employ the expression, and is followed by Claud. *IV Cons. Hon.* 638.

31*. **Poenus**: Hannibal, cf. 39. Pyrrhus is coupled with Hannibal also by Hor. *Carm.* 3. 6. 35–6 and Florus 2. 6. (3. 18. 11), 2. 8 (3. 21. 22) among the most dangerous enemies who had previously threatened Rome. Cf. 303–5.

erit: 'will prove to be', cf. Verg. *Aen.* 6. 883 *tu Marcellus eris.*

nulli: 'no other', 'no alien'. For this use of *nullus* cf. *ullus* in 82 and 93 as well as 5. 249, and *nullus* itself in 626. Lejay quotes Cic. *Tusc. Disp.* 4. 4. 8 *si ista* (*aegritudo*) *perturbare animum sapientis non potest, nulla poterit.* See also 663 n.

descendere: cf. 6. 216, Ouid. *Met.* 3. 67 and Liu. 1. 41. 5.

32. **contigit**: Mayor on Iuu. 8. 28 observes that *contingere* is generally used of good and *accidere* of ill fortune. A more accurate distinction is that of Lejay, who shows that *contingere* is applied to a happening that is in accordance with one's thoughts or expectations, *accidere* to a chance occurrence, fortunate or unfortunate, *optingere* to 'meeting', or 'coming across', and *euenire* to the realization of an issue. He mentions that the unfavourable sense of *contingere* is Ciceronian (*Nat. Deor.* 1. 27, *Fam.* 5. 16. 5, *Phil.* 14. 24).

alta sedent: 'are deep-seated', cf. 31 *descendere* and Ouid. *Met.* 3. 87–9. Note the use of the adjective for the adverb (see Introduction, p. lxv and cf. 46 *serus*).

33–66. Vergil (*Georg.* 1. 24 sqq.) began the practice of eulogizing the reigning emperor and of alluding to his deification, and in this was followed by the epic poets of the Silver Age. Unless Lucan is sarcastic, especially in 45–59, his panegyric of Nero must seem absurd and grotesque to modern taste. See also 45 n. and 46 n.

33–8. The meaning is: 'If no other way could have been found for the advent of Nero, the crimes of the civil war were not too high a price for us to pay. Similarly Jupiter attained the dominion of the sky only after the war against the giants.' Cf. Plin. *Paneg.* 6. 1–2.

33–4. **fata...inuenere uiam**: a Vergilian phrase (*Aen.* 3. 395, 10. 113).

34. **magno**: ablative of price, cf. Verg. *Aen.* 2. 104 *magno mercentur Atridae* and Cic. *Cael.* 7. 18 *conduxit in Palatio non magno domum.*

parantur: see 13 n.

35. **deis**: dative of the agent after a passive verb. On account of the circumstances of his death Nero was not destined to receive the honour of deification, but Lucan, with the examples of the deified Augustus and Claudius in his mind, is hinting at the likelihood of the same distinction befalling him. For the thought that the civil war produced emperors who were due to receive divine honours cf. 7. 457.

36. **Gigantum**: the giants sprang from the blood of Uranus as it fell on the Earth, which was consequently regarded as their mother. They made an attack on Heaven, but were routed with the assistance of Hercules by the gods, who buried them beneath Aetna and other volcanoes.

38-43. These lines form the concessive protasis to the apodosis which is contained in 44.

38. **diros...campos**: cf. 4. 803 *dira...Pharsalia*.

Pharsalia: for this, the proper title of the battle, see Postgate in *C.R.* xix, 1905, pp. 257-60.

39. **saturentur**: *i.e.* at the battle of Thapsus (46 B.C.) in Tunisia, Hannibal's own country. Cf. 6. 309-11 and Hor. *Carm.* 2. 1. 25-8.

sanguine: to be taken with both verbs by the ἀπὸ κοινοῦ construction (see Introduction, p. lxiii).

40. **ultima...proelia**: the last battle of the civil war (cf. Florus 2. 13 [4. 2. 77] *omnium postrema certaminum Munda* and Oros. *Adu. Pag.* 6. 16. 7 *ultimum bellum apud Mundam flumen gestum est*) was fought at Munda (45 B.C.) in Spain, when Caesar defeated Labienus and Pompey's two sons. Another explanation of *ultima* is that it refers to the distant position of Munda. This would involve a double hypallage or transference of epithets, and is not so likely, especially as Perusia, Mutina, and Actium are alluded to as subsequent additions (42 *accedant*) to the civil war.

funesta: 'with its corpses' (*funera*).

concurrant: cf. Verg. *Georg.* 1. 318 *concurrere proelia uidi*.

Munda: ablative of place.

41. **Caesar**: *i.e.* Nero. The punctuation must make it clear that this word is vocative and anticipatory of *tibi* (45), else, if it is taken as nominative and the commas are removed, Lucan is made to reckon Julius Caesar among the disasters to Rome and the sense is spoiled.

Perusina fames: the blockade of Lucius Antonius and Fulvia, the brother and wife of Antony, in Perusia during the winter of 41-40 B.C. by Octavian.

Mutinaeque labores: the fighting around Mutina and its siege in 43 B.C., when Decimus Brutus was blockaded by Antony. During these events, the two consuls Hirtius and Pansa were killed within a few days of each other, but the result was a defeat for Antony.

42. **accedant fatis**: cf. Ouid. *Her*. 7. 135 and *Trist*. 1. 8. 47.

quas premit aspera classes: cf. Petr. *Bell. Ciu*. 16 *fames premit aduena classes*.

classes: *i.e. naues* by synecdoche.

43. **Leucas**: Actium, which is on the mainland of Acarnania, is meant, but the name *Leucas* is used by metonymy, as at 5. 479 and Verg. *Aen*. 8. 677, where the masculine form *Leucates* occurs (ὁ Λευκάτας as opposed to the feminine ἡ Λευκάς).

seruilia bella: the war which Agrippa waged on behalf of Octavian against Sextus Pompeius in Sicily during 36 B.C. The latter filled his army with slaves, cf. Hor. *Epod*. 4. 17–19, 9. 7–10, and Manil. 1. 917–19 (*seruilia...bella*).

ardenti...Aetna: cf. Hor. *A.P*. 465 *ardentem...Aetnam*, as well as Ouid. *Met*. 2. 220, 15. 340, and Sen. *H.O*. 286.

44. **ciuilibus armis**: 'civil war', *armis* being used as a metonymy for *bellis* or *bello*. Cf. 325 and see 60n., also Introduction, p. xlix.

45. **acta...peracta**: for the cacophony, which in this case is lessened by the elision before *est*, cf. 2. 160–1 *gestata...congesta* and 3. 348 *contingi...attingere*. Such repetitions in the same line are not uncommon in Latin poetry.

statione peracta: 'when your watch on earth is over', cf. Ouid. *Trist*. 2. 219 *scilicet imperii princeps statione relicta*.

For similar passages which predict the inclusion of emperors in the constellations cf. Verg. *Georg*. 1. 32 sqq., Hor. *Carm*. 3. 25. 5–6, Ouid. *Met*. 15. 839, Sen. *H.O*. 87 sqq., 1564 sqq., Val. Flacc. 1. 16 sqq., Stat. *Theb*. 1. 24 sqq., *Silu*. 5. 1. 241.

46. **astra petes**: an Ovidian phrase, cf. *Met*. 1. 316, *Fast*. 2. 496.

serus: for the wish that the reigning emperor should postpone the hour of his decease as long as possible cf. Hor. *Carm*. 1. 2. 45 *serus in caelum redeas*, Ouid. *Met*. 15. 868–70, *Trist*. 5. 2. 51–2, Vell. Pat. 2. 131, Sen. *Pol*. 12. 5, Calp. Sic. 4. 145–6, Sil. 3. 626–7, Stat. *Silu*. 1. 1. 105–7, 4. 2. 22.

praelati: 'preferred to earth', implying that death is a matter of choice to Nero (Haskins).

47. **polo**: 'sky' by synecdoche from the original meaning of 'pole', and so 'the inhabitants of the sky', 'the gods', cf. 50–1.

Similarly in 9. 655–6 *caeloque timente . . . Gigantas* = 'when the gods feared the giants'.

sceptra tenere: an Ovidian phrase, cf. *Met.* 3. 265, *Fast.* 6. 506.

48. flammigeros: a neologism, borrowed later by Valerius Flaccus and Statius among others. The earlier word is *flammifer*, which was as old as Ennius (Vahl. *Scaen.* 29). Cf. 415.

conscendere currus: cf. Lucr. 6. 47, Ouid. *Trist.* 3. 8. 1, Manil. 5. 10.

Nero, who was passionately fond of chariot driving, will be a better deputy for the Sun-god than the unfortunate Phaethon. Cf. Suet. *Ner.* 53 *quia Apollinem cantu, Solem aurigando aequiperare existimaretur.*

49. mutato sole: '*i.e.* with Nero instead of Apollo as driver of the Sun's chariot' (Haskins), because he used to pose as νέος ἥλιος.

50–1. See Critical Apparatus.

51. iurisque tui: 'within your jurisdiction'. For this phrase, which is mainly prosaic, cf. 7. 55, Liu. 38. 9. 10, Vell. Pat. 2. 40. 1, 2. 69. 2, Claud. *III Cons. Hon.* 209.

53. in Arctoo . . . orbe: 'within the circle described by the Bear'. The expression is loose, for the celestial Arctic circle contains the Little Bear, but not the Great Bear.

legeris: the polite future perfect, cf. Liu. 44. 36. 13 *rationes alias reposcito*; *nunc auctoritate ueteris imperatoris contentus eris.*

What follows may be a glance at Nero's well-known obesity, cf. Suet. *Ner.* 51 *ceruice obesa, uentre proiecto*; but weight was a regular attribute of divinity, cf. Ouid. *Met.* 15. 693–4 *numinis illa | sensit onus, pressa estque dei grauitate carina.*

54*. aduersi: 'opposite to (the North)'.

calidus: the ancients generally had no clear conception of the southern hemisphere, and thought that the climate becomes gradually hotter as the equator is passed and the antarctic regions are approached, while the South Pole seemed to them to be the hottest place of all. Cf. Porphyrio ad Hor. *Carm.* 3. 3. 54 *australem cardinem significat, qui est torrentissimus*, Dracontius, *Rom.* 6. 73–4 *parte poli, qua flammeus axis | uoluitur australis conlustrans cardinis oras*, but see also Macrob. *Somn. Scip.* 2. 5. 21. . Lucan follows Ovid (*Met.* 7. 532) in assigning to the word *Auster* itself the epithet *calidus* at 9. 781 and 10. 222.

uergitur: 'sinks'. 'The ancients regarded the earth (*sic*, a mistake for "sky") as rising towards the north and sinking towards the south; cf. Verg. *Georg.* 1. 240–1' (Haskins). For the slope of

the sky (ἔγκλισις) cf. 3. 250–1, 9. 867, Ps. Cens. *frg.* 2. 1 (*circulus*)
australis humillimus et aquilonius excelsissimus.

55. **obliquo sidere**: 'with slanting ray'. *Obliquo* may be both
literal and metaphorical ('askance'), cf. Ouid. *Met.* 2. 787 *illa deam
obliquo fugientem lumine cernens.* The imitation of this expression
by Statius in *Theb.* 1. 159–61 *quasque procul terras* (*Sol*) *obliquo
sidere tangit | auius aut Borea gelidas madidiue tepentes | igne Noti*
is well explained by Heuvel in his edition (Groningen, 1932) as
follows: '*obliquo sidere*=oblique cadentibus radiis (quo enim
remotiores sunt regiones septentrionales et meridianae a certa
Solis via, eo invalidioribus obliquioribusque radiis tanguntur)'.

This line, however, refers strictly to 53 and not to 54, for, if
Nero were in the Antarctic circle, he would not be able to see
Rome at all on account of the sphericity of the earth, of which
Lucan was not ignorant. Cf. 9. 877–8, where the soldiers, who
imagine themselves to be in the southern hemisphere, cry *nunc
forsitan ipsa est | sub pedibus iam Roma meis.*

57. **axis**: not 'the axle of the sphere' (Duff), but 'the pole',
i.e. either end of the axis (by synecdoche). This is a common
meaning of the word, cf. 7. 422 *te geminum Titan procedere uidit
in axem*, as well as 6. 481, 8. 175, and 9. 542. If Nero does not
maintain the equipoise of heaven, either pole, like the end of a
seesaw, will feel his weight and sink down.

librati: proleptic like 58 *sereni* and 80 *diuolsi.* Cf. Ouid. *Met.*
1. 12–13 *tellus | ponderibus librata suis*, *Fast.* 2. 490 *caeli pondera*
and *id.* 6. 271 *ipsa uolubilitas libratum sustinet orbem.* Lucan is fond
of metaphors taken from the balance, see Heitland, *Introd.* p. xc.

58. **orbe…medio**: 'in the Zodiac', the *medium signorum…
orbem* of 9. 532. Housman (*Ed.* p. 330) observes of the Zodiac that
'it is called *medius* because, though not, like the equator, equi-
distant from the two poles throughout all its length, it comes no
nearer to the one of them than to the other', and he compares
4. 109 and Manil. 1. 308–9. See 540n. Similarly Vergil (*Georg.*
1. 32–5) wishes to place Augustus in the part of the Zodiac which
was then vacant, but which was later supplied by Libra. Even in
the Zodiac, of course, Nero would not be directly above Rome,
and his light would be oblique, though not so oblique as if he were
within the Arctic circle.

59. **nullaeque…nubes**: 'and may no clouds obstruct our view
of Caesar' (Duff).

a: 'on the side of', literally 'with Caesar as the point of departure'; cf. such phrases as *a fronte, a latere, a medio,* and *a tergo.* Lejay compares Sall. *Cat.* 58. 6 *exercitus hostium duo, unus ab urbe, alter a Gallia obstant* and Stat. *Theb.* 4. 17, 564, *Silu.* 1. 2. 23.

60–2. For this spirit of humanity and mutual love, cf. Lucan's appeal to *Concordia* at 4. 189–92. These lines are echoed by Oros. *Adu. Pag.* 3. 8. 5.

60. **positis...armis**: cf. Verg. *Aen.* 1. 291 *aspera tum positis mitescent saecula bellis.*

61. **in uicem**: properly 'in turn', but here in the sense of *inter se,* which is not used by Lucan. Cf. 7. 177 *inque uicem uoltus tenebris mirantur opertos* and Tac. *Hist.* 3. 25 *rumor...exercitus in uicem salutasse.* Lejay points out that alternately in Verg. *Aen.* 8. 452 *illi inter sese multa ui bracchia tollunt* the expression *inter sese* is employed in the sense of *in uicem.*

missa = *emissa,* cf. Ouid. *Fast.* 1. 121 *cum libuit pacem placidis emittere tectis.*

62. This line is a reminiscence of a passage of Ennius (Vahl. *Ann.* 266–7) with the opposite meaning: *post quam discordia taetra | belli ferratos postes portasque refregit.* The temple of Janus was closed in Nero's reign, cf. Suet. *Ner.* 14. For a coin of this period with the figure of Nero on the obverse and the temple of Janus closed on the reverse, which also bears the legend IANVM CLVSIT PACE P(opulo) R(omano) TERRA MARIQ(ue) PARTA, see Mattingly and Sydenham. *The Roman Imperial Coinage,* London, 1923, i, p. 148 (Nero 44) and Plate x, 153.

63–4*. **pectore...accipio**: cf. Verg. *Aen.* 9. 275–7.

64. **Cirrhaea** = *Delphica* by metonymy. Cirrha was the port of Delphi on the *sinus Crissaeus.* In the same way *Cleonaeus* (4. 612) = *Nemeaeus,* as Cleone was a small village near Nemea. Cf. 5. 95.

mouentem: 'who brings to light' (= *promouentem*), cf. Verg. *Aen.* 1. 262 *fatorum arcana mouebo.*

65. **sollicitare deum**: cf. Ouid. *Met.* 4. 473 and Sen. *Med.* 271. **deum**: Apollo.

auertere: *i.e.* and thereby *ad me conuertere.* This was a usual way of invoking deities, cf. Verg. *Georg.* 1. 16–18.

Nysa: there were several cities or towns of this name which claimed the honour of being the birthplace of Bacchus. Mayor on Iuu. 7. 64 thinks that this Nysa was the village on Mt Helicon. Lejay on the other hand places it in Thrace, but there was also a Nysa in India as well as one in Caria.

66. Compare Ouid. *Fast.* 1. 17 *dederis in carmina uires* and

Manil. 1. 10 *das animum uiresque facis ad tanta canenda*. Lucan
shows here his consciousness that he is a Roman poet. Statius says
of him (*Silu.* 2. 7. 52–3) *tu carus Latio memorque gentis | carmen
fortior exseris togatum.*

67–182. Lucan now proceeds to give six reasons for the civil
war: (i) Fate (70–84), (ii) the formation of the Triumvirate (84–97),
(iii) the death of Crassus (98–111), (iv) the death of Julia (111–20),
(v) the rivalry between Caesar and Pompey (120–57), (vi) the
corruption of the Romans (158–82).

67. **fert animus**: an Ovidian phrase (*Her.* 13. 85, *A.A.* 3. 467,
Met. 1. 1, 775), also in Sall. *Iug.* 54. 4 and Hor. *Epist.* 1. 14. 8–9.
causas...expromere: cf. Ouid. *Fast.* 3. 725.

68. **inmensumque aperitur opus**: cf. Verg. *Aen.* 7. 44–5.

in arma furentem: parodied by Petron. *Bell. Ciu.* 86 *in damna
furentem.*

70. **inuida**: cf. Florus 2. 13 (4. 2. 1) *inuidens Fortuna principi
gentium populo, ipsum illum in exitium sui armauit.*

fatorum series: cf. Ouid. *Met.* 15. 152 *seriemque euoluere fati.*
Haskins quotes Cic. *Diu.* 1. 125, to which add Cic. *Acad.* 1. 29.

negatum: see 5n.

70–1. **summisque...lapsus**: cf. Sen. *Ag.* 88 and Petron.
Bell. Ciu. 84–5. The idea that the civil war is Rome's punishment
for having become too powerful, and that she had no right to
outstrip the limits ordained by Fate, is repeated in 81–2.

72. **nec se Roma ferens**: 'and Rome unable to support her
own greatness' (Duff), cf. Hor. *Epod.* 16. 2 and Liu. *Praef.* 4.

nec=*et non*, cf. 138.

72–3. **conpage...hora**: both *conpage* and *hora* must be taken
with *mundi*, cf. 80n. and see Introduction, p. lxiii for this ἀπὸ κοινοῦ
construction. Cf. Gell. 7. 1. 7 (*natura) conpagem hanc mundi...
fecit*, Sen. *N.Q.* 7. 9. 4 *dissiparetur et terrae solida fortisque conpages*
and 5. 181 *non prima dies, non ultima mundi.*

conpage soluta: cf. Pers. 3. 58 and Stat. *Theb.* 8. 31. Tacitus
applies *conpages* to the Roman empire in *Hist.* 4. 74 *octingentorum
annorum fortuna disciplinaque conpages haec coaluit.*

73. **coegerit**: 'will have brought together' and so 'will have
closed', being the *last* hour (cf. the phrase *agmen cogere*).

suprema...hora: cf. Tibull. 1. 1. 59.

74. **antiquum...chaos**: cf. Ouid. *Met.* 2. 299.

74–7. For a detailed discussion of these lines see Appendix B.

77. **fratri contraria Phoebe**: normally, of course, the moon

appears to traverse the ecliptic in the same direction as the sun, *i.e.* from west to east, though at a speed more than twelve times as fast. See Sen. *Thy.* 838–42 and *Aetna* 231–3.

78. **obliquum...per orbem**: the plane of the ecliptic or apparent path of the sun is *obliquus* or inclined at an angle of about 23° 28′ to the plane of the celestial equator. For the slant of the ecliptic and zodiac cf. Ouid. *Met.* 2. 130 and Plin. *H.N.* 2. 81. Housman thought that the reference is to the fact that the moon's orbit cuts the ecliptic at a small angle of 5° 9′, and that *obliquum* consequently is not 'slanting across the equator' but rather 'slanting across the ecliptic'. It is possible, though, that by *obliquum* Lucan means only the general obliquity of the zodiac along which both sun and moon appear to move.

bigas agitare: cf. Sen. *Phaedr.* 312–13. The poets represented the Moon as riding on a two-horsed (Tert. *De Spectac.* 9) and the Sun on a four-horsed chariot (Plaut. *Amphitr.* 422).

79. **diem poscet sibi**: 'she will claim the day (*i.e.* the task of the Sun) for herself'. She will give up her *bigae* to drive his chariot during the day, just as in Sen. *Phaedr.* 309–16 he drove her chariot when she went to court Endymion.

80. **diuolsi**: proleptic.

machina...mundi: a commonplace expression, cf. Lucr. 5. 96 (also Manil. 2. 807). For *foedera mundi* cf. Sen. *Med.* 605–6. These passages prove that here both *machina* and *foedera* must be taken with *mundi* (cf. 72–3 n.). *Foedera mundi* are the laws which govern the universe, cf. Verg. *Georg.* 1. 60–1. For the fluctuations in Lucan of the meaning of *foedus* see Heitland, *Introd.* p. cii.

81. **in se magna ruunt**: 'great accomplishments come to grief upon themselves', cf. Sen. *Breu. Vit.* 4. 1 *in se ipsa Fortuna ruit*, *Phaedr.* 480 *in semet ruet*.

magna: cf. Sen. *Ag.* 88.

laetis...rebus: 'prosperity', an Ovidian phrase (*Trist.* 5. 14. 32, *Pont.* 4. 4. 15).

82. **crescendi posuere modum**: cf. 10. 331.

ullis: see 31 n.

83. **populum terrae pelagique potentem**: cf. 4. 375, 9. 304, Verg. *Aen.* 3. 528, Hor. *Carm. Saec.* 53, Ouid. *Fast.* 1. 88.

84. **causa malorum**: cf. Verg. *Aen.* 11. 361.

85. **communis**: Rome's becoming the joint property of three masters is the *regnum* or 'tyranny' of the next line, as of 4 (where see note).

nec umquam: 'and never before', 'and never at any other time'; cf. the use of *ullis* in 82, 93 etc. For *numquam* in the same sense Haskins compares Iuu. 12. 74.

86. **in turbam missi**: the commentators, who doubtless assume that three make a crowd, take *turba* to mean the number of the triumvirs, and translate 'tyranny never before shared between so large a number', but make no attempt to parallel this sense of *missus*. The meaning is not this, however, but 'tyranny never before let loose against the populace'. For *turba* applied to the Roman people as opposed to a triumvir cf. 5. 333–4, 6. 592–3, 7. 656, and Hor. *Carm.* 1. 1. 7 *turba Quiritium*.

missi = *emissi*, see 61 n. and cf. 4. 161–2 *emitti terrarum in deuia Martem | inque feras gentes Caesar uidet*. Sulla had launched despotism before against the people, but his was not despotism in partnership with others (*foedera regni*).

87. **male**: for the amphibole see Introduction, p. lxiv. The meaning is: 'How unfortunate they were in their mischievous union and in their blindness caused by excessive ambition.'

cupidine caeci: cf. 7. 747. The phrase is Lucretian (4. 1153) and Sallustian (*Iug.* 25. 7, 37. 4).

88. **miscere...uires**: another verbal reminiscence of Manil. 4. 414–15 (see Appendix B) *namque omnia mixtis | uiribus...consurgunt sidera*, where *mixtis uiribus* = 'with a mixture of power' (Professor W. H. Semple in *C.Q.* xxxi, 1937, p. 18). This establishes the interpretation 'to unite their strength' (Duff).

89. **in medium**: 'for use in common' (Haskins), 'for the common advantage of the triumvirs'. Just as *miscere uires* repeats *concordes* in 87, so *in medium* explains *nimia cupidine*. See the Critical Apparatus.

89–90. **dum...aer**: cf. 5. 94 *aere libratum uacuo...orbem*, Ouid. *Met.* 1. 12 *circumfuso pendebat in aere tellus*, Plin. *H.N.* 2. 10–11, Stat. *Theb.* 8. 310–11. The belief that air supports the earth is older than Stoicism, and Haskins aptly compares Eur. *Troades* 884 ὦ γῆς ὄχημα κἀπὶ γῆς ἔχων ἕδραν, where Zeus, who is addressed, is identified with Air. Plut. *De Placit. Philos.* 3. 15 ascribes it to Anaximenes, and Aristot. *De Caelo* 2. 13 to Anaximenes, Anaxagoras, and Democritus (see Diels, *Die Fragmente der Vorsokratiker*, 5te Aufl. i, 92, 11–13). For the whole passage cf. Sen. *Med.* 401–4.

90. **longi...labores**: 'as long as his lengthy task compels the Sun to go round (the earth)'. *Labores* in Verg. *Aen.* 1. 742 does not mean 'eclipses' as many commentators think (this passage is,

however, correctly explained by Henry). The beginning of Ouid.
Met. 2 should be studied carefully for an understanding of the
labores of the sun.

91. **totidem per signa**: there are always six signs of the Zodiac
above the horizon and six beneath, no matter what the hour of
the day or night is, cf. Vitruvius 9. 1. 4. *sex signa numero supra
terram cum caelo peruagantur, cetera sub terram subeuntia ab eius
umbra obscurantur* and Manil. 3. 241–2 *cum tamen, in quocumque
dies deducitur· astro,* | *sex habeat supra terras, sex signa sub illis.*
Aratus (*Phaen.* 553–6) also vouches for the truth that 'between the
sunrise and sunset of every day, no matter how long or short,
there always rise 6 signs or 180 degrees, half of the zodiac' (Housman, *Ed. Manil.* 3, p. xiii); cf. *Aetna* 236 *sex (signa) cum nocte rapi,
totidem cum luce referri.* Lucan's language displays an interchange
of cases or hypallage, which must be resolved before his meaning
is understood clearly. That his thought could be expressed directly
in prose as *sex signa per diem caelum transeunt, quae sex deinde per
noctem sequuntur* is proved by Sen. *De Otio* 5. 4 *(natura) sena per
diem, sena per noctem signa perducens.* Translate, then, 'and day and
night display in succession each the same number of signs'.

92. **regni sociis**: 'partners in tyranny' (Haskins), see 4n. Cic.
De Off. 1. 8. 26 applies to Caesar the following verse of Ennius
(Vahl. *scaen.* 404–5) *nulla sancta societas* | *nec fides regni est.* Cf.
Liu. 1. 14. 3 *ob infidam societatem regni*, Phaedrus 1. 5. 1 *numquam
est fidelis cum potente societas*, Sen. *Ag.* 259 *nec regna socium ferre
nec taedae sciunt* for an idea which became a commonplace after
originating probably with Hom. *Il.* 2. 204 οὐκ ἀγαθὸν πολυκοιρανίη·
εἷς κοίρανος ἔστω. Even in the Middle Ages 92–3 *nulla fides...erit*
was quoted frequently, according to Professor Eva Matthews
Sanford (*A.J.P.* lv, 1934, p. 6).

93. **erit** must be taken with both *fides* and *potestas.*

93–4. **nec gentibus ullis credite**: possibly a condensed phrase
which may be expanded from what follows as *nec credite a gentibus
ullis fatorum exempla petenda esse.*

95. **fraterno...sanguine**: an allusion to the murder of Remus
by Romulus. They were the first Romans to attempt to share
power, and their story is alluded to with the same moral by Hor.
Epod. 7. 17–20, cf. Tibull. 2. 5. 23–4. Cf. also 2. 149–50 *nati
maduere paterno* | *sanguine* and Catull. 64. 399 *perfudere manus
fraterno sanguine fratres.*

97. **dominos**: because not only as the fathers of the Roman

race but also as the lords of Rome in their own day they merited this term of deference. Tiberius rejected the title of *Dominus* (Tac. *Ann*. 2. 87, Suet. *Tib*. 27) as Augustus had done before him (Suet. *Aug*. 53), Caligula desired it (Aurelius Victor *Epit. de Caesaribus* 3.13), and Domitian permitted it (Suet. *Dom*. 13), but until the time of Diocletian it did not become official.

commisit: cf. Hom. *Il*. 1. 8 ἔριδι ξυνέηκε μάχεσθαι.

asylum: for the *asylum* of Romulus see Liu. 1. 8. 5, Dio Cass. 47. 19 and Verg. *Aen*. 8. 342.

In similar language Statius (*Theb*. 1. 150–1) remarks that *nuda potestas* armed Eteocles and Polynices to fight a *pugna de paupere regno*.

98. **temporis angusti**: 'for a brief space' (Duff). For this detached genitive cf. 8. 158 *stantis...fati* and Postgate *ad loc. Angustus* denotes the brevity of respite from danger, cf. 4. 476–7.

concordia discors: the expression, which provides a good example of oxymoron, occurs previously in Hor. *Epist*. 1. 12. 19 (see also Ouid. *Met*. 1. 433). Manil. 1. 142 has *discordia concors*. Cf. Sen. _N.Q_. 7. 27. 4 *tota haec mundi concordia ex discordibus constat*.

99. **sponte**: Lejay observes that this is the first occurrence of the word with the genitive, but in prose this construction is found also in Q. Curtius, Pliny the Elder, and Tacitus. Cf. 234.

ducum: *i.e.* Caesar and Pompey.

100. **belli...mora**: cf. Verg. *Aen*. 10. 428 *pugnae nodumque moramque*, Sen. *Ag*. 211 *non sola Danais Hector et bello mora*, and the discussion of the phrase in Sen. *Suas*. 2. 19. For the part which Crassus played in providing an obstacle to the outbreak of hostilities as long as he lived cf. Plut. *Pomp*. 53 μετ᾽ οὐ πολὺ δὲ καὶ Κράσσος ἐν Πάρθοις ἀπολωλὼς ἠγγέλλετο· καὶ τοῦτο κώλυμα ὂν μέγα τοῦ συμπεσεῖν τὸν ἐμφύλιον πόλεμον ἐκποδὼν ἐγεγόνει.

100–3. **qualiter...frangat mare**: 'just as the slender Isthmus cleaves and scarcely separates the waves, and suffers them not to mingle the two gulfs, but, if it were withdrawn, would dash the Ionian against the Aegean sea,...'.

101*. **geminum...fretum**: singular for plural. The reference in *Isthmos* is to the Isthmus of Corinth, which separates the Corinthian gulf from the Saronic. This Isthmus was a favourite theme with Roman poets from the time of Ovid, and its comparative narrowness appealed to them as remarkable. See Heuvel on Stat. *Theb*. 1. 120 for a list of references.

gracilis: for this word and for *terra* in the next line cf. Sen. *Thy.* 113 (*Isthmos*) *uicina gracili diuidens terra uada.*

male = *uix*, as is remarked by Lejay; compare Stat. *Theb.* 1. 120 *geminis uix fluctibus obstitit Isthmos.* For this sense of *male* cf. 6. 177–8 *ac male defensum fragili conpage cerebrum* | *dissipat* and Sen. *Ag.* 901–2 *pendet exigua male* | *caput amputatum parte*; and for the juxtaposition of *gracilis* and *male* cf. Ouid. *Her.* 21. 15 *gracilem uix.* Cf. also Ouid. *A.A.* 2. 660 *sit gracilis, macie quae male uiua sua est.* Attention is drawn to the note on this word in the Critical Apparatus.

102. **si terra recedat**: an echo in a different sense of Verg. *Aen.* 3. 72 *terraeque urbesque recedunt* and Ouid. *Met.* 11. 466 *ubi terra recessit.* *Terra* is an example of the noun for the pronoun and refers to *Isthmos*; compare the frequent use of *uir* in poetry for *is* or *ille*.

103*. **Ionium**: i.e. the Corinthian gulf, and similarly *Aegaeo* represents the Saronic gulf by synecdoche.

frangat = *frangi patiatur.* Housman compares for this condensed expression Iuu. 7. 26 *positos tinea pertunde libellos*, where *pertunde* = *pertundi sine.* For *frangat mare* cf. 5. 606 (*Boreas*) *in fluctus Cori frangit mare.* Here the tenses in the conditional sentence denote the improbability of an event which is yet possible; but for a supposition which has not been and will not be fulfilled see Stat. *Silu.* 4. 3. 59–60 *his paruus, nisi di uia uetarent,* | *Inous freta miscuisset Isthmos.*

104. **dirimens**: (= *qui dirimebat*) an instance of the imperfect participle, cf. Val. Flacc. 8. 211 *tot modo regna tenens.*

miserando funere: ablative of attendant circumstance. See Postgate on 8. 686 for other examples and cf. 112 *diro omine.* Translate: 'when Crassus, who used to keep the generals from engaging in cruel war, died miserably and stained...'.

105. **Assyrias**: 'Syrian' rather than 'Assyrian' by synecdoche, *i.e.* the compound for the simple adjective. For *Assyrius* = *Syrius* cf. Hor. *Carm.* 2. 11. 16 *Assyria nardo.*

maculauit sanguine: cf. 4. 181 *nullo maculatus sanguine miles* and Catull. 63. 7 *sanguine maculans.*

Carrhas: see 10n. Carrhae (Charan) was in Osroene, which lay on the Syrian border.

106. **Parthica...damna**: 'the disasters inflicted by the Parthians'. For the adjective used in passive and locative senses cf. 294 *Eleus sonipes* = 'racehorse at Olympia', 688 *·Emathias acies* = 'the armies that fought in Thessaly', 2. 402 *Dalmaticis*

fluctibus = 'billows coming from Dalmatia', 5. 703–4 *Hesperii duces* = 'the generals in Italy', and 8. 25 *acta Sullana* = 'Pompey's exploits in Sulla's day'.

107. **plus...quam**: see 1 n.

108. **Arsacidae**: Lucan is the first Roman author to use this precise term for the Parthians, cf. Tac. *Hist.* 1. 40 *auito Arsacidarum solio*. Arsaces was the first king of Parthia, and his dynasty ruled from B.C. 250 until A.D. 226, when it was succeeded by the Sassanids who held sway until the Mohammedan conquest (A.D. 651).

109. **diuiditur ferro regnum**: cf. Sen. *N.Q. pr.* 8.

109–11. **populique potentis...fortuna**: cf. Ouid. *Fast.* 5. 729.

110. Compare Lucr. 1. 278 *quae mare, quae terras, quae denique nubila caeli* and Verg. *Aen.* 1. 280 *quae mare nunc terrasque metu caelumque fatigat*.

111. **non cepit...duos**: 'was not large enough for the two leaders'. Cf. Verg. *Aen.* 9. 644 *nec te Troia capit* and Sen. *Thy.* 444 *non capit regnum duos*. Lejay compares the words of Philip to Alexander in Plut. *Alex.* 6 ὦ παῖ, ζήτει σεαυτῷ βασιλείαν ἴσην· Μακεδονία γάρ σε οὐ χωρεῖ. Lucan is imitated by Florus 2. 13 (4. 2. 14) *sic de principatu laborabant, tamquam duos tanti imperii fortuna non caperet* and by Minucius Felix, *Oct.* 18. 6 *generi et soceri bella toto orbe diffusa sunt, et tam magni imperii duos fortuna non cepit*.

pignora: Julia, Caesar's daughter, had married Pompey, but died in 54 B.C. after giving birth to a child which survived her only by a few days. The word accordingly may include both Julia and the infant, or the plural may be used for the singular; cf. Vell. Pat. 2. 47. 2 *concordiae pignus Iulia uxor Magni decessit*. For her death cf. Val. Max. 4. 6. 4, Sen. *Marc.* 14. 3, Florus 2. 13 (4. 2. 13), Plut. *Pomp.* 53 and *Caes.* 23.

112. **diro...omine**: see 104 n. The sense is not 'marriage which the dread omen turned to mourning' (Duff), but 'marriage which turned to mourning and so became a dread omen'. There is in *ferales taedas* a pregnant meaning: when the marriage took place and the *taedae* were *iugales* the omen was good, but now that they were *ferales* on account of Julia's death, it became *dirum*; cf. Sil. 2. 184 (also 13. 547) *taedaeque ad funera uersae* of a funeral taking the place of a wedding. *Ferales* also has the secondary meaning of 'fatal'. Lucan seems to recollect Verg. *Aen.* 7. 319–22, especially the phrase *funestae...taedae*.

114. **quod si tibi fata dedissent**: cf. Verg. *Aen.* 11. 112 and Prop. 2. 1. 17.

115. **maiores**: 'longer'. The meaning of the word must be understood from its context, cf. 635 and 674 and see the discussion of the trope *e praecedentibus sequentia* (Introduction, p. lv).

furentem: attempts to emend this word on account of *parentem* in the next line are unnecessary, as the rhyme is no more unusual in Lucan than it would be in Vergil. See Heitland, *Introd.* pp. xcvii–xcviii.

116. **inde...hinc**: Lejay remarks that this use is that of a strong μέν...δέ, cf. 173–6–8–81 and 9. 377 *inde polo Libyes, hinc bruma temperet annus.*

117. **excusso...ferro**: 'striking the sword from their grasp' (Haskins).

118. **Sabinae**: for the reconciliation effected by the Sabine women compare Liu. 1. 13 and Ouid. *Fast.* 3. 226 *dant soceri generis accipiuntque manus. Mediae* = 'coming between them', cf. Ouid. *Fast.* 3. 217 *cum raptae ueniunt inter patresque uirosque.*

120. **aemula uirtus**: cf. Hor. *Epod.* 16. 5.

121. **acta**: see·the Critical Apparatus.

triumphos: these were three in number, cf. 8. 814–15 and Postgate *ad loc.* The first was held in 79 B.C. for the subjugation of the Marian forces under Domitius Ahenobarbus in Sicily and Africa, the second in 71 for the defeat of the troops of Sertorius in Spain and of Spartacus in Lucania, and the third in 61 for the conquest of the pirates and Mithridates.

122. Pompey was afraid that his victory over the pirates would be forgotten in the glory gained by Caesar for his conquest of Gaul.

123. **Magne**: Lucan's favourite appellation of Pompey. According to Plut. *Pomp.* 13 this surname was given to Pompey by Sulla as a result of the campaign against the Marians in Africa.

te: Caesar, not Pompey, as is shown by *series...laborum*, 124 *fortuna* (cf. 226), and 125. Bentley's *hunc* for *te* and Lejay's *illum* for *te iam* are unnecessary. Compare 4. 112–13, where *tu* apostrophizes two different deities.

series ususque laborum: 'continual familiarity with exertion', an instance of hendiadys. Cf. Ouid. *Her.* 9. 5 *seriesque inmensa laborum.*

124. **erigit**: 'arouses', cf. Nepos, *Them.* 1. 2 *quae contumelia non fregit eum sed erexit.*

125. For similar statements see Caes. *B.C.* 1. 4. 4, Vell. Pat. 2. 29. 3, *ibid.* 33. 3, Sen. *Marc.* 14. 3, *Ep.* 94. 65, Florus 2. 13 (4. 2. 14), and Dio Cass. 41. 54. 1.

126. **quis**=*uter*, cf. 5. 602 and Verg. *Aen.* 12. 719 and 727.
Similarly in 127 *quisque*=*uterque*.

induit: see the Critical Apparatus.

127. **scire nefas**: cf. Hor. *Carm.* 1. 11. 1 and Ouid. *Fast.* 3. 325.

magno...tuetur: *i.e.* each had the verdict of a judge whose
decisions were to be valued highly. Caesar's side was supported
by Heaven and Pompey's by Cato. Cf. Cic. *Lig.* 6. 19 *nunc melior
est iudicanda ea* (*causa*) *quam etiam di adiuuerunt.*

128. As Haskins observes, the Stoics did not hesitate to place
their 'wise men' (*sapientes*) such as Cato on the same footing as the
gods; cf. Sen. *Prou.* 6. 6 and *Ep.* 9. 15 *nihil necesse sapienti est.*
Lucan's famous line has often been quoted, *e.g.* by Boethius (*Cons.
Phil.* 4. 6) as an illustration of the superior knowledge of the divine
intellect! The same thought is apparent in Sen. *Ep.* 71. 8 *nihil
interest, utrum Pharsalica acie Cato uincatur an uincat? e.q.s.*
Professor A. Souter suggests to the editor that Lucan's original
may well be found in a quotation from a letter of Brutus [Cic.
Ep. fr. 8 (7). 17] preserved in Quint. *Inst. Orat.* 9. 4. 75 *neque illi
malunt habere tutores aut defensores, quamquam* [*quoniam causam*
Halm] *sciunt placuisse Catoni.*

129. **pares**: 'equally matched' like gladiators. See 7 n. and cf.
Hor. *Epist.* 1. 5. 25–6 *ut coeat par...pari.*

alter: *i.e.* Pompey.

129–30. **uergentibus annis in senium**: cf. 2. 105–6 and Sen.
Clem. 1. 11. 1.

130. **senium**: not merely *senectus*, but *senectus* with its con-
comitant ills and infirmities, cf. Cic. *Tusc. Disp.* 3. 12. 27 (*Tarquinius*) *dicitur...senio et aegritudine esse confectus.* Pompey, however, at the outbreak of the Civil War was only fifty-seven years of
age and Caesar was six years his junior.

togae: 'civil life', see 365 n. and cf. the following statements
regarding Pompey, viz. 8. 813–14 *dic semper ab armis | ciuilem
repetisse togam* and 9. 199 *praetulit arma togae.*

131. **dedidicit**: supply *esse* or *se praestare.* It is also likely that
ducem (cf. 144) is an instance of the concrete for the abstract
and = 'leadership', 'the art of being a general'. See Introduction,
p. lvi and cf. 10. 134 (*iuuentus*) *exsecta uirum*, where *uirum* =
'virility'.

petitor: used in the literal sense of 'a seeker after'.

132. **in uolgus**: stronger than the mere dative and implying
that Pompey showered games and largesses in profusion (*multa*)
upon the people.

popularibus auris: cf. Verg. *Aen.* 6. 816 and Hor. *Carm.*
3. 2. 20.

133. **sui...theatri**: cf. 7. 9 *Pompeiani...sede theatri*. This, the
first stone theatre at Rome, was built between 54 and 52 B.C., and,
according to Postgate *ad loc. cit.*, could hold 40,000 spectators.

134. **reparare nouas uires**: cf. Ouid. *Her.* 4. 90 *haec reparat
uires fessaque membra nouat*, an indication that *nouas* is here
proleptic.

-que: the enclitic has the force of *sed*, coming as it does after *nec*.
See Appendix B and cf. 633.

135. **stat** = *restat*, as in 145, cf. *Octauia* 71 *magni resto nominis
umbra*.

nominis: 'name' in the sense of 'reputation'. Cf. 8. 449–50 *quis
nominis umbram | horreat?*, Verg. *Aen.* 11. 223 *magnum reginae
nomen obumbrat* (to which phrase Lucan is probably indebted here),
and Quint. 12. 10. 15 *umbra magni nominis delitescunt*.

The expression *stat magni nominis umbra* may have been a play
on Vell. Pat. 2. 1. 4 *Pompeium magni nominis uirum*, and was current
in Claudian's day, as may be seen from his epigram (*Carm. Min.* 10)
on a beaver coat which had seen better days (cf. also *Epist. ad
Serenam* 46). For its quotation in the Middle Ages see Professor
Eva Matthews Sanford in *A.J.P.* lv, 1934, pp. 6–7.

136–7. For the simile of an oak cf. Verg. *Georg.* 3. 332–3, and
for the custom of hanging spoils on trees cf. *Aen.* 10. 423 and
11. 5–7. The oak was held sacred to Jupiter.

137. **ueteris**: this epithet, which properly calls attention to the
age of the tree, is transferred by hypallage from *exuuias* to *populi*;
but cf. Stat. *Theb.* 6. 67 *ueterum exuuias...auorum*.

138*. **nec iam ualidis** = *et iam inualidis*.

radicibus haerens: cf. Lucr. 3. 325 and 5. 554 *radicibus haerent*,
as well as Manil. 4. 828 *concutitur tellus ualidis conpagibus haerens*
(an echo of Lucr. 4. 1204).

139. **pondere fixa suo est**: cf. Ouid. *Met.* 9. 41.

nudos: *i.e.* 'stripped of their leaves', not bare, because they
still carry the spoils.

140. The usual punctuation of this line involves the addition
of a comma to *frondibus* or at any rate the assimilation of *non
frondibus* to *trunco*. In this way such a translation as 'making a
shade not with leaves but with its trunk' (Duff) is evolved. Better
sense is obtained by punctuating only after *trunco*, so that this
word is taken with *effundens* and the meaning is seen to be 'does not
make a shade with its leaves (but only with the spoils which are on

the boughs in place of the leaves)'. For this kind of ellipse with a negative cf. 145 and Housman's note there.

141. **Euro**: the S.E. wind, cf. Sen. *N.Q.* 5. 16. 4 *ab oriente hiberno Eurus exit.*

142. **siluae**: 'trees' by synecdoche, cf. 7. 807 *erige congestas Oetaeo robore siluas,* and for *robore* cf. also 390. Note the absence of a connective (asyndeton) between this line and 141.

143. **tamen**: the correlative of 141 *quamuis*.

colitur: Haskins compares Quint. 10. 1. 88 *Ennium sicut sacros uetustate lucos adoremus in quibus grandia et antiqua robora iam non tantam habent speciem quantam religionem.*

tantum: the commentators generally understand this word as an adverb and translate 'But Caesar had more than a mere name' (Duff). It is better, however, to take it as an adjective (cf. 9. 597 *quis tantum meruit populorum sanguine nomen?*) referring to 135 *magni nominis.* Caesar was the younger man (see 130 n.), and he began his military career much later in life than Pompey. The total of the' latter's exploits far outweighed the conquest of Gaul and Britain, for which Caesar had not yet received a triumph.

144. **fama ducis**: supply *tanta* from *tantum* by syllepsis, and translate 'reputation for generalship' (abstract for concrete, cf. 131 n.), or 'reputation of being a general', where the want of the gerundive of *sum* is felt.

144–5. For the juxtaposition of *uirtus* and *pudor* cf. Verg. *Aen.* 5. 455.

nescia uirtus stare loco: cf. Verg. *Georg.* 3. 84 *stare loco nescit.*

145. **non uincere bello**: *i.e.* 'to gain the victory by any method except war'. The scholiasts correctly interpret Lucan's meaning as *sine bello uincere.* Housman furnishes a good selection of parallels for this explanation, which is more suited to Caesar's character than the commonplace sense 'not to conquer (*i.e.* to be defeated) in war', cf. 2. 439–40 *Caesar in arma furens nullas nisi sanguine fuso | gaudet habere uias, e.q.s.*

146. **quo spes quoque ira uocasset**: cf. Ouid. *Met.* 5. 668 *qua uocat ira sequamur* and Sen. *Ag.* 142 *quocumque me ira..., quo spes feret.*

147. **ferre manum**: a Vergilian phrase (*Aen.* 5. 403). Note the use of the simple verb for the compound *conferre.*

temerando: correctly explained by Housman, who follows the scholiast *c* and mentions the almost parallel use of *lacessere ferrum*

(Verg. *Aen.* 10. 10) as 'drawing the sword lightly (*temere*)', *i.e.* 'without good reason', cf. 225. For the similarity of meaning between *lacessere* and *temerare* cf. also 3. 193–4 *inde lacessitum primo mare, cum rudis Argo | miscuit ignotas temerato litore gentes.*

148. **urguere**: 'press', *i.e.* 'make the most of', cf. Cic. *Fam.* 7. 8. 2 *quin tu urgues istam occasionem et facultatem qua melior numquam reperietur?* (Haskins).

instare: 'follow up', cf. Tac. *Hist.* 5. 15 *Ciuilis instare fortunae, Agric.* 18 *non ignarus instandum famae* (Haskins).

149. **inpellens**: 'pushing out of his way' and so 'overthrowing', cf. Sen. *Ben.* 6. 31. 11 *diuina atque humana inpellentem et mutantem quidquid obstiterat.*

150. **uiam fecisse**: an Ovidian phrase (*Her.* 18. 158, *Met.* 5. 423).

151. For the Stoic belief that thunder and lightning are caused by the collision of clouds, Lejay quotes Diels, *Doxographi*, p. 369 οἱ Στωικοὶ βροντὴν μὲν συγκρουσμὸν νεφῶν, ἀστραπὴν δ' ἔξαψιν ἐκ παρατρίψεως and Aristoph. *Nub.* 404 sqq., Lucr. 6. 96 sqq. and 295 sqq., Ouid. *Met.* 1. 56, 6. 695–6, 11. 435–6, Sen. *N.Q.* 1. 1. 6, 1. 14. 5, 2. 23. 1, *Prou.* 1. 3.

151–3. **fulmen...emicuit**: cf. 533–4.

152. **mundi**: hyperbole for *caeli*, cf. *Culex* 352 *ruere in terras caeli fragor* and Liu. 40. 58. 4 *cum ingenti fragore caeli tonitribusque et fulguribus praestringentibus aciem oculorum.* See 154 n. and 664 n.

153. **rupit** = *perrupit*. Lejay compares Manil. 1. 864 *caelum fulmine ruptum.*

diem: 'the daylight sky', cf. 7. 189 and 8. 217, and see Postgate's notes *ad loc.*

154. **obliqua**: 'slanting', cf. 528, Sen. *Marc.* 18. 3 *miraberis... obliqua fulmina et caeli fragorem, Thy.* 358–9 *quem non concutiet cadens | obliqui uia fulminis?*

praestringens: 'dazzling', cf. 7. 157 (*aether*) *oculos ingesto fulgure clausit* and Sen. *Pol.* 12. 3.

lumina flamma: cf. Ouid. *Met.* 11. 368 *rubra suffusus lumina flamma.*

155. **in sua templa furit**: for *suus* in the sense of 'under its own sway', 'where it is master' cf. 407 and 9. 321 (*Auster*) *in sua regna furens.*

templa: the expression *caeli templa* may have been used first by Ennius (Vahl. *Ann.* 49), and the word is explained by Varro, *Ling. Lat.* 7. 6–7. Cortius points out that the word had a technical meaning in augury, and, according to Cic. *Diu.* 2. 42–5 and Plin. *H.N.* 2. 142–4, the Etruscan augurs, whose task it was to observe the flashing of the lightning and its return heavenwards, divided the sky into sixteen parts (cf. Lucr. 6. 86–9).

The theme *emicuit...flamma* corresponds to the variation *cadens*, and in the same way the variation *reuertens* corresponds to the theme *in sua templa furit*, which Haskins correctly translates 'rages against the quarter of the sky whence it came'. Cf. Sen. *N.Q.* 2. 58. 1 *quidam existimant utique fulmen reuerti.*

155–6. **nullaque exire uetante materia**: 'nor can any solid matter forbid its free course' (Duff). For the irresistible might of thunderbolts cf. Lucr. 6. 219–378, especially 227 (*ignem*) *cui nil omnino obsistere possit* and 331 *nec facile est tali naturae obsistere quidquam.*

exire: this verb refers not so much to the moment of its departure from the sky as to its *outward* and downward course, and there-fore = *abire*. Cf. Sen. *Ep.* 49. 10 *dic exeunti* potes non reuerti, *dic redeunti* potes non exire.

157. **dat stragem**: a Lucretian phrase (1. 288) adopted by Vergil (*Georg.* 3. 556 etc.).

sparsosque recolligit ignes: cf. 606–7, Sen. *Ben.* 1. 9. 5 *sparsa...recolligere, Oed.* 506 *Luna...plena recolliget ignes*, but here Lucan may have in mind Lucr. 6. 343–4.

158–9. Both *belli* and *suberant* should be taken with both *causae* and *semina* (see 72–3 n.). For the zeugma, the punctuation of 158, and the fact that *causae suberant* is an Ovidian phrase, see *C.Q.* xxx, 1936, p. 57. For *causae belli* cf. 10. 171 *causas Martis* and Verg. *Aen.* 7. 553, and for *semina belli* cf. 3. 150 and 6. 395 *semina Martis.* Note Cic. *De Off.* 2. 8. 29 *nec uero umquam bellorum ciuilium semen et causa deerit.*

The decadence of Roman standards of conduct was a favourite theme of poets and historians, cf. Sall. *Cat.* 5. 9, Hor. *Carm.* 2. 15, 4. 4. 35–6, Liu. *Praef.* 9, Tac. *Hist.* 2. 38, and Florus 1. 47 (3. 12. 7). For the increase of luxurious living at Rome cf. Sen. *Ep.* 114. 9, 115. 8–9 and Tac. *Ann.* 3. 53.

159. **semina...mersere**: for mixed metaphor in Lucan see Introduction, p. liii.

161. **intulit**: *i.e.* into Rome.

162. **hostiles**: 'taken from the enemy' (Duff).

163. **auro tectisue**: 'the gold with which the ceilings of their dwellings were decorated' by hendiadys, for which see Introduc-

tion, p. lxiv. Cf. Sen. *Ep.* 114. 9 *deinde in ipsas domos inpenditur cura...ut tecta uarientur auro*, id. 115. 9 *cum auro tecta perfudimus*, and Sil. 13. 351-60 (where cf. 356 *nec modus argento* with Lucan's *non auro...modus*).

mensas: 'meals', cf. 4. 307, 375-6, and 6. 116.

164. **cultus**: 'clothes'.

164-5. **gestare decoros uix nuribus** = *uix decoros qui a nuribus gestarentur*. For this epexegetic use of the infinitive cf. 463-4 and 510-11, and see Heitland, *Introd.* p. cv.

165. **nuribus** = *mulieribus* or *feminis* by synecdoche and so employed because of the impossibility of fitting either word into the hexameter, cf. Ouid. *Met.* 2. 366 *nuribus mittit gestanda Latinis*. Haskins compares Suet. *Calig.* 52 for the wearing of silk by men. Compare also Sen. *N.Q.* 7. 31. 2 *colores meretricios matronis quidem non induendos uiri sumimus*.

mares: used contemptuously in contrast with the *uiri* which might have been applied by the poet to the male population of Rome, had they been worthy of this name.

166. **toto...orbe**: cf. Sen. *Helu.* 10. 3 *epulas quas toto orbe conquirunt*, as well as Manil. 5. 55-6 *totusque per usus | diuersos rerum uentis arcessitur orbis*.

167. **quo gens quaeque perit**: 'the special bane of each nation' (Duff).

longos; proleptic as in 170. The passage refers to the growth of *latifundia*, which were a sign of the decadence of Rome. Haskins compares Liu. 34. 4. 9 *ingens cupido agros continuandi* and Plin. *H.N.* 18. 35 *uerumque confitentibus latifundia perdidere Italiam iam uero et prouincias*.

168-9. **duro...uomere**: cf. Verg. *Georg.* 3. 515 *duro sub uomere* and Ouid. *Trist.* 3. 10. 68 *uomere sulcat*. For the whole passage compare Hor. *Carm.* 1. 12. 41-4, with the mention there of Curius and Camillus who were produced by *saeua paupertas*.

169. **Curiorum**: plural for singular, see Introduction p. liv.

170. **sub**: 'under the control of'.

ignotis: this word implies not only that the owners were 'nobodies' who are contrasted with illustrious men (*noti*) like Camillus and Curius (see Professor W. B. Anderson in *C.Q.* x, 1916, p. 100), but also that they were newcomers or interlopers (Housman). In the same way *longa* is opposed to the idea of the tiny farms of the heroic Romans of old. This is better than to assume with M. Bourgery that the *ignoti* were slaves who may be

spoken of as being too numerous to be known to their masters, as
appears from such passages as Sen. *Contr.* 2. 1. 26 *ignoti seruorum
domino greges* and Sen. *Vit. Beat.* 17. 2 *tam neglegens es, ut non
noueris pauculos seruos.*

171. **is**: Lejay observes that this is one of the three examples in
Lucan (the other two being 3. 611 and 4. 546) of the pronoun,
which is very rare in the poets of the Augustan age.

173. For *inde* here and *hinc* in 176, 178, and 181 see 116n. and
translate 'not only...but also...and...and'.

174. **decus**: for this word with the infinitive Lejay compares
Tac. *Ann.* 1. 43 *decus istud et claritudo sit subuenisse Romano nomini,
compressisse Germaniae populos.*

175. **potuisse**: a frequentative perfect, similar to the Greek
gnomic aorist. See 327n. The use of such perfects is often determined by the convenience of their metrical form as substitutes for
presents, cf. 258 *timuisse* and 326 *uicisse.* For *plus patria potuisse
sua* cf. Cic. *Fam.* 7. 3. 5.

175–6. **mensuraque iuris uis erat**: 'might was the standard
of right'.

176. **coactae**: 'passed by violence' (Duff). The participle (with
sunt understood) is nominative plural agreeing with *leges*, not
genitive singular agreeing with *plebis*. The feminine noun is
preferred to the neuter for purposes of agreement, just as in Cic.
Legg. 1. 1. *init.*, which Housman quotes, the masculine noun is
preferred to the feminine.

177. Duff explains: 'Order should be represented by the consuls,
and progress by the tribunes, but both bodies were equally
factious.' In other words government and opposition alike joined
in confounding the laws.

178. **fasces**: 'curule office', an instance of the concrete for the
abstract.

sector: usually 'one who bids' at an auction of the goods of
bankrupts, etc., when these were confiscated by the state, but
here by metonymy the word = *praeco*, 'auctioneer'. Compare Sen.
Ep. 29. 11 *malis artibus popularis fauor quaeritur.*

179. **ambitus**: the term suggests canvassing for office by illegal
methods, especially bribery, as opposed to the more favourable
word *ambitio.*

180. **Campo**: elections were held at Rome in the Campus
Martius.

181. **auidumque in tempora fenus**: of four suggestions put

forward by Haskins to explain this phrase, the best is 'greedily looking to the times of payment', *i.e.* the Kalends, etc., cf. Hor. *Epod.* 2. 69–70 and *Serm.* 1. 3. 87.

183. **cursu superauerat**: cf. Ouid. *Trist.* 1. 11. 5 *cursu superauimus Isthmon.*

184. **motus**: 'rebellion', cf. 265, though there is a verbal echo of Verg. *Georg.* 1. 420–2 *pectora motus…concipiunt*, where *motus* ='impulses'. Note the theme *motus* and the variation *bellum.*

185. **ceperat** = *conceperat.*

Rubiconis: the scholiast *c* observes that this river was so called from its reddish colour. Cf. 214 *puniceus Rubicon* and Sidon. Apoll. *Ep.* 1. 5. 7 (*Rubiconem*) *qui originem nomini de glarearum colore puniceo mutuabatur, quique olim Gallis Cisalpinis Italisque ueteribus terminus erat.*

186. **ingens**: the conjecture of Heinsius *lugens*, as Heitland (*C.R.* xi, 1897, p. 39) remarks, 'thrusts upon Lucan a wretched tautology'. Ghosts and persons seen in dreams were thought to appear not only greater than the earthly shape of those whom they represented. but also in consequence more huge than the person who saw them, cf. Verg. *Aen.* 2. 773 (of the ghost of Creusa) *nota maior imago.* The same belief was extended to gods, cf. Ouid. *Fast.* 2. 503–4 *humano maior…* | *Romulus in media uisus adesse uia.* Furthermore *ingens* has a pathetic sense of 'great in adversity', and is thus used of Pompey at 2. 730, 7. 679, 8. 28, 266; cf. 3. 719 and 9. 885.

ingens, clara, maestissima, and *effundens* are all parallel and unconnected by conjunctions. For the wide separation of *uisa* from 189 *adstare* see 12 n.

With Lucan's account compare Caesar's dream before crossing the Rubicon as recounted by Plutarch (*Caes.* 32), who says that he had a vision of having incestuous intercourse with his mother. Suetonius (*Iul.* 32) speaks of an apparition which encouraged him to cross the Rubicon by itself setting the example.

188. **turrigero**: for a discussion of this and other endowments of *dea Roma* with an attribute of Cybele on account of Verg. *Aen.* 6. 781–7, see *Proc. Camb. Philol. Soc.* 1939 (*Camb. Univ. Report.* 14 March 1939, pp. 711–12).

canos effundens uertice crines: cf. Claud. *Bell. Gild.* 1. 24–5 (also of Roma) *laxata casside prodit* | *canitiem.*

189. **caesarie**: this word is used of women's hair also at Verg. *Georg.* 4. 337.

190. gemitu permixta: 'words broken with sighs' (Haskins).

192. ciues: *i.e.* not as rebels.

huc usque: Lejay observes that this use (=*hac temus*) is found for the first time in Seneca.

193. gressumque coercens: this phrase seems to be a coinage of Lucan on the analogy of Verg. *Aen.* 6. 389 *conprime gressum*.

194. languor: 'faint-heartedness', 'irresolution', cf. 393 and Cic. *Att.* 14. 6. 3 *uides languorem bonorum* (Haskins).

195. magnae...urbis: *i.e.* Rome.

196. Tarpeia: according to Varro, *Ling. Lat.* 5. 41, the Capitol was formerly called the Tarpeian Hill after Tarpeia who betrayed the citadel, of which her father was governor, to the Sabines (Liu. 1. 11. 5–9). The poets found this name more convenient metrically than Capitolinus. The reference here is to the temple of Jupiter on the Capitol, cf. Liu. 1. 55. 1 *Iouis templum in monte Tarpeio*.

Tonans: Lejay observes that in the Cantabrian War, Augustus once miraculously escaped being struck by lightning, and in consequence he vowed to Iuppiter Tonans a temple (Suet. *Aug.* 29), which was erected in 22 B.C. on the south side of the Capitol (Plin. *H.N.* 34. 78, 36. 50). Either Lucan is guilty of an anachronism, or, as is more likely, he is identifying Iuppiter Tonans with Iuppiter Capitolinus. See also Frazer on Ouid. *Fast.* 2. 69 and 6. 33.

Phrygiique penates: according to Tac. *Ann.* 15. 41 these were kept in the temple of Vesta, though Varro, *Ling. Lat.* 5. 144, seems to refer to them as being still at Lavinium in his day. Cf. also Iuu. 4. 60–1.

197. gentis Iuleae: Aeneas had brought the Penates from Troy (cf. Verg. *Aen.* 3. 148–50), and so Caesar, who claimed descent from Ascanius or Iulus the son of Aeneas, could speak of them as belonging to the *gens Iulia*; cf. Verg. *Aen.* 1. 288 *Iulius a magno demissum nomen Iulo*.

Iuleae: Lejay observes that the form of this adjective, which occurs also at 9. 995, is due to Greek adjectives in -εῖος, and is found first in Prop. 4. 6. 17. The etymology which derived *Iulus* from ἴουλος helped not only to make this name trisyllabic in the poets (cf. 3. 213), but also to suggest the Grecised adjective.

rapti secreta Quirini: for the Quirinalia or feast of Quirinus on Feb. 17 see Ouid. *Fast.* 2. 511–12 and Frazer on *id.* 2. 475 and 6. 796. The temple of the god stood on the Quirinal, and according to Dio Cass. 41. 14. 3 it was burned in 49 B.C. It is curious that Lucan fails to mention this disaster. Caesar as a former *pontifex* *maximus* seems to have been interested in the cult of Quirinus, for in 45 B.C. his statue was set up in the temple of that god (Dio Cass. 43. 45. 3).

For *rapti* applied to Romulus cf. Liu. 1. 16. 2 *sublimem raptum procella*. Note the similarity of the idea to that of *Gen.* 5. 24: 'And Enoch walked with God: and he was not; for God took him.' The poetical account was that Romulus was carried to heaven by the steeds of his father Mars, cf. Hor. *Carm.* 3. 3. 15–16 and Ouid. *Fast.* 2. 496.

198. **Latiaris**: this form generally has older and better MSS authority than *Latialis*, and is attested also by the Greek spelling Λατιάριος and by Macrob. *Sat.* 1. 16. 16 (cf. 535). The cult of **Iuppiter Latiaris in his shrine on the Alban Mount (Monte Cavo)** was connected with the *feriae Latinae* (cf. 550), for the origin of which, after the destruction of Alba Longa by Tullus Hostilius, through the command of a heavenly voice on the summit of the mount, see Liu. 1. 31. 1–4. On account of his ancestor Ascanius who founded Alba Longa, Caesar presumably had a special reason for invoking Iuppiter Latiaris.

199. **Vestalesque foci**: the worship of Vesta at Rome was introduced from Alba Longa, see Frazer on Ouid. *Fast.* 4. 41 and 6. 257. According to Iuu. 4. 61 a minor cult of Vesta was retained at Alba. For the connexion of the *gens Iulia* with the goddess see Ouid. *Fast.* 3. 419–28 and 4. 949–50, as well as Frazer *ad loc.*

summi...numinis: Cybele seems to be meant on account of the resemblances between her and Roma, see 188 n. The commentators, however, take *summi numinis* as meaning generally 'the greatest of the gods', as at 8. 860. But Cybele was the *Magna Mater* and a *magna dea* (cf. Catull. 63. 91 *dea magna, dea Cybebe* and Prop. 3. 17. 35 *uertice turrigero iuxta dea magna Cybebe*), and, as the mother of the gods, had the right of taking precedence over them, cf. Ouid. *Fast.* 4. 359–60.

numinis instar: this phrase, according to Lejay, is an Ovidian coinage (*Am.* 3. 11. 47, *Met.* 14. 124).

200. **Roma, faue coeptis**: repeated at 8. 322, this time in a speech uttered by Pompey. Compare Sen. *Epigr.* 5. 1.

furialibus armis: cf. Ouid. *Met.* 6. 591. *Furia* may be used of a public enemy, *e.g.* Cicero (*Sest.* 14. 33) calls Clodius *illa furia ac pestis patriae*.

202. **ubique tuus...miles**: 'now in any place whatever I am your (loyal) soldier as well, if I am but permitted'.

liceat modo: for this parenthesis, which applies to what follows, Lejay compares Ouid. *Met.* 8. 38–9 *impetus est illi, liceat modo, ferre per agmen* | *uirgineos hostile gradus*, which is against Housman's punctuation whereby the parenthesis is extended to *nunc quoque*.

204. **moras soluit**: the usual verb with *moram* and *moras* in Vergil and his successors is *rumpere*, cf. 264, 2. 525, Verg. *Georg.* 3. 43, *Aen.* 4. 569, 9. 13, and Ouid. *Met.* 15. 583; but for *soluere* cf. Sen. *Troad.* 1126–7 *moram...solui.* Note 281 *tolle moras.*

205–12. For the simile cf. Hom. *Il.* 20. 164–74, Verg. *Aen.* 12. 4–8, and Sen. *Oed.* 919–20.

205. **squalentibus**: this word, which etymologically means 'covered with scales', is apt for the description of parched and burnt land (Lejay). Compare 5. 39 *Libyae squalentibus aruis* and Verg. *Georg.* 1. 507 *squalent abductis arua colonis.*

206. **aestiferae**: 'sultry'. This adjective is used already by Lucretius in the passive sense, on account of the unsuitability of *aestuosus* for the hexameter.

Libyes: see the Critical Apparatus.

leō: for this and other shortenings see Heitland, *Introd.* p. ci.

207. **colligit iram**: cf. Lucr. 1. 723 *colligere iras.*

208. **uerbere**: concrete for abstract, cf. Ouid. *Met.* 14. 300 *uerbere uirgae.* For this habit of the lion Haskins compares Plin. *H.N.* 8. 49. Ellis on Catull. 63. 81 quotes Eustathius 1201 φάσι δὲ κέντρον ἐνεῖναι μέλαν τῇ τοῦ λέοντος ἀλκαίᾳ ἤγουν οὐρᾷ ὡς κεράτινον, ᾧ μαστίζει τὰς πλευρὰς ἐν καιρῷ μάχης ἐρεθίζων ἑαυτόν, but is in error when he dismisses this statement as 'a strange theory'.

209*. **murmur** =*fremitum*, a natural cognate accusative after *infremuit.* For *murmur* of a lion's roar cf. Mart. 8. 55. 1–2, and for 211 cf. *ibid.* 11 *grandia quam decuit latum uenabula pectus!*

212. 'He passes along the weapon to its end without thought of so severe a wound'—a bold hypallage, with which the commentators compare Sen. *De Ira* 3. 2. 6 (*barbari) gaudent feriri et instare ferro et tela corpore urguere et per suum uolnus exire.* For the transference of motion from the moving to the stationary body, compare such a phrase as Verg. *Aen.* 5. 503 (*sagitta) uolucres diuerberat auras*, where the epithet is transferred from *sagitta* to *auras.* In the same way it is customary at the present day to speak of stationary objects 'speeding past' a moving vehicle. Here, of course, both the lion and the weapon are in motion in contrary directions. Compare also 7. 623–4 *qui pectore tela* | *transmittant* and Sen. *Ep.* 9. 19 *uir, qui per ferrum...euasit.*

213. **cadit**: according to Lejay this verb is always employed in Lucan with the ablative and without a preposition.

inpellitur undis: cf. Ouid. *Met.* 15. 181 *unda inpellitur unda*.

214. **puniceus Rubicon**: see 185n. and 402n. Page on Verg. *Aen.* 3. 516 and 693 calls attention to the fact that Vergil 'is fond of placing with a Greek proper name a Latin word which suggests its derivation', e.g. *pluuiae Hyades, Plemmyrium undosum, stagnans Helorus, arduus Acragas*. Compare 10. 318 *praecipites cataractae* and Verg. *Aen.* 8. 663 *exsultantes Salios* (see 603n.).

216. **disterminat**: cf. 9. 957. According to Lejay, this is the first instance of the verb with such a complement as *ab Ausoniis... colonis*, for in Cic. *Arat.* 94 it is followed by the accusative only.

217–19. For an explanation of these lines see *C.Q.* xxx, 1936, pp. 57–8, where it is shown that *tertia Cynthia* = 'the moon on the third night after she was new', when her slender crescent shape permits the phenomenon of earth-shine. This, the appearance of the new moon 'wi' the auld moon in her arm' is what Lucan means by *grauido cornu*, and such a phenomenon portends rain (*pluuialis*).

219. **Euri**: see 141n. This is a rain-bearing wind, cf. 2. 459 *nubifero...Euro* and the description in 4. 59–77, as well as Hor. *Epod.* 16. 54 *aquosus Eurus* (Housman).

Alpes: either Lucan is guilty of a geographical mistake here, or he is calling the Apennines *Alpes* by an easy metonymy. For the ready possibility of the interchange of the names of two mountain ranges so well known note Sil. 2. 333 *geminas Alpes Apenninumque*. It is, of course, possible to apply the name *Alpes* to any high mountains; and to this day the lofty Apennine range above Massa and Carrara is called the Apuan Alps (Alpi Apuane) from the name of the Apuani, a Ligurian tribe.

220–2. This was Caesar's usual method of crossing a river, cf. *B.G.* 7. 56. 4. The cavalry took up their position 'slantwise across the stream' (Duff) to break its force (*excepturus aquas*), and the infantry were thus enabled to ford the water easily.

220. **in obliquum...amnem** = *obliquus in amnem* by hypallage. See Housman's note for parallels.

sonipes: as an adjective this word goes back to Accius and Lucilius, and as a substantive is found in Catull. 63. 41 (see *Archiv f. latein. Lexicogr.* VII, p. 326). It may be translated either 'horses' (singular for plural) or 'cavalry' (metonymy). For the interchange of *equus* and *eques* in Latin poetry compare Gell. 18. 5, Macrob. 6. 9. 8–12 and our use of 'horse' for 'horsemen'.

opponitur: Lejay observes that the use of this verb with *in* is unusual, for its usual construction is either with the dative or with *ad* and the accusative. Note also Ouid. *Fast.* 4. 178 *ante oculos opposuitque manum*.

225. **temerataque**: *i.e.* already by Pompey and the senatorial party, cf. 277.

Lucan lost an opportunity of working into Caesar's speech here the famous expression *iacta est alea* (Suet. *Iul.* 32)—a defect which Petronius (*Bell. Ciu.* 174) remedied with *iudice Fortuna cadat alea*. Compare Plut. *Pomp.* 60 ἀνερρίφθω κύβος.

227. **fatis**: Housman ingeniously but unnecessarily conjectured *satis his*, cf. 673. As Lejay observes, the correspondence of the tenses is similar to Hor. *Carm.* 3. 5. 1–3 *caelo tonantem credidimus Iouem | regnare, praesens diuus habebitur | Augustus*. Caesar's meaning is, then, 'my trust has always been in my destiny and still is in it, so away with treaties which are of no use. I must avail myself of the arbitration of warfare, for this is inherent in my destiny'. *Fortuna* and *fata* seem to be synonymous here, as at 393–4, where see note. Similarly at 2. 454–60 *Auster* and *Notus* are synonymous.

Lejay quotes for Caesar's well-known belief in Fortune *B.G.* 6. 30. 2 and *B.C.* 3. 68. 1. Lucan frequently alludes to it, cf. 264–5, 309–10; 5. 292–3, 325, 482, 581–3; 7. 285–7, 297–8, and finally 7. 547 *fortuna Caesaris*. In *Gnomon*, ii, 1926, p. 510 Professor Eduard Fraenkel also rejects Housman's emendation, comparing 7. 254–5. Like Caesar, Pompey too put his trust in his former fortune, cf. 134–5.

iudice bello: cf. Petronius as quoted in 225 n.

228. **noctis tenebris**: cf. 6. 624 *noctis geminatis arte tenebris* and Ouid. *Met.* 11. 521 *caecaque nox premitur tenebris hiemisque suisque*. Lucretius is fond of attaching a genitive to *tenebrae*.

rapit agmina: the phrase is Vergilian, cf. *Aen.* 12. 450 *rapit agmen*. Lucan elsewhere uses it of Caesar, *e.g.* in 3. 299 and 5. 403. Compare 6. 14 (also of Caesar) *Dyrrachii praeceps rapiendas tendit ad arces*. Lejay observes that Caesar's rapidity was one of his qualities to which tribute was paid in antiquity, see Cic. *Att.* 8. 9. 4, Plin. *H.N.* 7. 91, and Suet. *Caes.* 37. At the time of the siege of Gergovia he and his army covered about 46 miles in 24 to 30 hours (*B.G.* 7. 39–41), and alone he could travel 92 miles in the course of a day (Suet. *Caes.* 57).

229. **it**: see the Critical Apparatus.

Balearis...fundae: for the analogy of Balearic slingers cf. Verg. *Georg.* 1. 309 *stuppea torquentem Balearis uerbera fundae* and Ouid. *Met.* 2. 727–9.

uerbere: the thong of the sling, by which the pocket containing the missile was rotated round the head. There were two of these thongs, which are called *habenae* in Vergil (*Aen.* 9. 587 and 11. 579) and *scutalia* in Livy (42. 65. 10). Compare 3. 469–70 *saxum quotiens ingenti uerberis actu | excutitur*, and for *torto* cf. *ibid.* 465 *lancea... tenso ballistae turbine rapta*.

230. Parthi: the Parthians were notorious for feigning flight and harassing their pursuing enemy with arrows, cf. Verg. *Georg.* 3. 31, Hor. *Carm.* 1. 19. 11–12, 2. 13. 17–18, etc.

231. et: 'when'. Housman compares Ouid. *Fast.* 6. 383–4 *fratris uirgo Saturnia iussis | adnuit* (not *paruit*), *et mediae tempora noctis erant*.

231–2. ignes solis: plural for singular, as *ignis* is used of the light of one heavenly body, cf. Hor. *Carm.* 1. 12. 47–8 *inter ignes | luna minores*. The singular for the plural is found in Ouid. *Met.* 10. 448–50 *fugit aurea caelo | luna, tegunt nigrae latitantia sidera nubes, | nox caret igne suo.* For the *ignis* (sing.) of the sun cf. 8. 228 *Phoebi surgentis ab igne*.

232. Lucifero...relicto: the planet Venus when Morning Star rises before the sun, and, being brighter than the other planets and fixed stars, is the last of them to fade at dawn. Compare Ouid. *Met.* 2. 114–15 *diffugiunt stellae, quarum agmina cogit | Lucifer et caeli statione nouissimus exit.*

233. dies=*sol*, cf. 9. 431–2 *ora | sub nimio proiecta die*, and similarly *Phoebum*=*diem* in 10. 227 *ante parem nocti Libra sub iudice Phoebum*.

tumultus: 'this word is perhaps purposely used on account of the special sense which it bears of a war in Italy; cf. Cic. *Phil.* 8. 2–4 especially *itaque maiores nostri tumultum Italicum, quod erat domesticus, tumultum Gallicum, quod erat Italiae finitimus, praeterea nullum nominabant*' (Haskins). Compare 303–5. There is, however, no possibility of this special meaning at 6. 53 and 10. 425. *Belli tumultus* occurs in Ouid. *Her.* 16. 369.

234. seu sponte: Housman, who objects to the asyndeton, emends the first *seu* of this line to *sed* unnecessarily. Though his parallels for the suppression of the first of two *seu*'s cannot be questioned, he admits that *seu* is always doubled elsewhere in Lucan; and his objection to *seu sponte seu Auster inpulerat* as a 'singularis lectio' is itself singular on account of his own citation of Stat. *Theb.* 2. 20 *seu Iouis imperio, seu maior adegit Erinys.* His refusal to discuss 5. 136 *seu sponte deorum* is merely arbitrary. The asyndeton of this line as well as of 229 may surely be justified by the equally violent 244, where *sed* must be understood; compare also 2. 34–5 *nec cunctae summi templo iacuere Tonantis:* | *diuisere deos,* where the sense is '(but) they divided the gods between them'. Translate, then: 'But whether by the will of Heaven' etc.

turbidus Auster: see 498n.

235. **maestam**: a good instance of the pathetic fallacy, as Ruskin, *Modern Painters,* iii, ch. 12 called it. For a discussion of the pathetic fallacy in Latin poetry see Professor A. S. Pease in *Classical Journal,* xxii, 1927, pp. 645–57.

tenuerunt = *retinuerunt,* cf. Ouid. *Am.* 1. 13. 30 *spissa nube retentus equus (Aurorae).*

236. **miles**: singular for plural.

237–8. In these verses by onomatopoeia (for which see Introduction, p. lvii) Lucan conveys the sound of the martial instruments of music used by the Romans. Lejay compares Verg. *Aen.* 8. 526 *Tyrrhenusque tubae mugire per aethera clangor.*

237 The blending of the sounds described by *stridor* and *clangor* is emphasized by *concinuit.* Such a combination of two nouns expressing a single idea is naturally followed by a verb in the singular, cf. Caes. *B.G.* 2. 19. 1 *ratio ordoque agminis aliter se habebat.*

238. **non pia** = *inpia,* which reters as usual to the impiety of the civil war, cf. Verg. *Georg.* 1. 511 *saeuit toto Mars inpius orbe.* For *non* negativing an adjective Francken compares 5. 58 *non fidae* = *infidae,* 7. 830 *non sanum* = *insanum* and 9. 54 *non iusti* = *iniusti.* Observe 138n.

239. **stratis**: this neuter participle, when used as a noun, originally means 'bed-coverings' (Lucr. 4. 849 *lecti mollia strata*), then, as here, 'beds' by synecdoche.

excita: both the long and the short *i* are found, but Lucan always employs *excire* in all its forms with the long vowel. On the other hand, at 5. 597 the rare *concita* is found once, but elsewhere he uses the form with *i* (Lejay).

iuuentus: 'the men of military age', its usual meaning (Haskins).

240. **adfixa penatibus arma**: for the language compare Hor. *Carm.* 3. 5. 18–21. In time of peace arms were hung up on the hearth near the Lares and Penates, cf. Prop. 4. 1. 91 and Ouid. *Trist.* 4. 8. 21–2.

241. **quae pax longa dabat**: 'which a long period of peace had been ruining'. See Introduction, p..lv for the explanation of this meaning of *dabat*, which not merely = 'had been providing', as in 5. 521 *quem dabat alga toro*, but has the additional sense of 'had been providing in a dilapidated condition', as the poet goes on to describe in the next two lines.

nuda: 'stripped of their leather' (through its decay).

crate: the wicker framework of the shields.

iam…fluentes: 'which had long been rotting', 'falling to pieces', cf. 294 *iam*. With *fluentes* cf. 2. 166 *(colla) cum iam tabe fluunt* and Plin. *H.N.* 27. 138 *capillos fluentes*.

242. **inuadunt**: 'rushed upon', and so 'seized' (historic presents should be rendered in English by past tenses), cf. 9. 198 *inuasit ferrum*. For the change from the singular of *iuuentus deripuit* to the plural here cf. 484-6.

curuataque cuspide pila: 'javelins bent at the point', cf. Ouid. *Met.* 2. 199 *uolnera curuata minitantem cuspide uidit*, where, however, the meaning is different.

243. **nigrae**: according to Lejay this epithet for rust, as opposed to the bright colour of iron or steel in condition, is Lucan's own coinage. Vergil (*Georg.* 1. 495) and Ovid (*Fast.* 1. 687) use *scabra*.

245. **celsus**: the usual epithet of a general on horseback, cf. Liu. 30. 32. 11. Note, however, Verg. *Aen.* 7. 285 *sublimes in equis*. For the whole line cf. *id.* 8. 587-8 *ipse agmine Pallas | in medio, chlamyde et pictis conspectus in armis*.

246-7. See the Critical Apparatus.

248. **male**: for the amphibole see Introduction p. lxiv.

uicinis…Gallis: ablative of attendant circumstance.

condita: for the founding of Ariminum see 254 n.

249. **tristi…loco**: ablative (of cause), as is pointed out by Housman, who compares among other passages Ouid. *Met.* 3. 335 *aeterna damnauit lumina nocte*.

omnes: 'all other', see 31 n.

249-50. Supply *sunt* with *pax* and *quies*, see 237 n.

250. **populos**: 'cities'. *Populus* primarily means the people of a city-state, see Cic. *Rep.* 1. 25. 39 and cf. the Span. *pueblo*.

251. **prima**: this word qualifies both *praeda* and *castra*.

dedisses: the full construction would be *melius (fecisses, si) dedisses tueri*.

252-3. The construction is *sedem errantesque domos* and *orbe sub Eoo gelidaque sub Arcto*, though of course Lucan intends the *sedem* to be *orbe sub Eoo* and the *errantes domos* to be *gelida sub Arcto*. In both instances *-que* = 'or'.

252. orbe: this word may mean either a part of the sky, as here (cf. 53), or a part of the world or *orbis terrarum* (cf. 166). For *orbis Eous* in the latter sense cf. 8. 289, Ouid. *Fast.* 3. 466, 5. 557, and *Pont.* 4. 9. 112.

sedem: 'a fixed home', as contrasted with *errantes domos*, cf. 344–5.

253. errantesque domos: *i.e.* such as the caravans of the nomad Scythians, cf. 3. 267 *errantes Scythiae populi*, Hor. *Carm.* 3. 24. 9–10 *campestres...Scythae,* | *quorum plaustra uagas rite trahunt domos*, and Sen. *H.F.* 533 *Scythiae multiuagas domos*.

Latii...claustra: 'the door of Latium', *i.e.* of Italy, cf. Liu. 9. 32. 1 *quae urbs (Sutrium) uelut claustra Etruriae erat*. For *Latii* as a metonymy for *Italiae* see 427 n.

254*. Senonum: the Senones were the tribe from Cisalpine Gaul who defeated the Romans at the. battle of the Allia in 387 B.C. In 285 they again caused trouble by attacking Arretium, but were driven across the Rubicon by Curius Dentatus. As a result of their defeat on this occasion, the *ager Gallicus* in Picenum and Umbria was appropriated by the Romans, and Ariminum was founded afterwards in 268 (cf. Vell. Pat. 1. 14. 7 and Strabo 5. 1. 11). See Introduction, p. xxxix.

motus: see 184 n.

Cimbrum: singular for plural. The Cimbri and Teutones had threatened Rome between 113 and 101 B.C., but had been defeated by Marius, the Teutones at Aquae Sextiae in 103 and the Cimbri at Vercellae in 101. The Teutones never invaded Italy or even Cisalpine Gaul. See Introduction, p. xl.

255. Martem Libyes: 'the Punic war'. The reference is to the occasion during the second Punic war when Hasdrubal took the eastern route into Italy from Cisalpine Gaul before he was defeated at the Metaurus in 207 B.C. Ariminum was in a strategic position, as it commanded the easier of the two passes between Cisalpine Gaul and Italy, see Strabo 5. 2. 9 as well as Polyb. 3. 61. 11. In 225, during the war with the Gauls, it was occupied by a Roman army, as was the case all through the second Punic war (Polyb. 2. 23 and 3. 61, 77; Liu. 21. 51 and 24. 44), when it remained faithful to Rome (Liu. 27. 10. 9). For the part which it played in the Gallic war of 200 see Liu. 31. 10. Lucan lost the opportunity of mentioning that it was plundered by Sulla (Cic. *Act. Sec. in Verr.* 1. 14. 36).

cursum = *incursum*, cf. 183.

255–6. furoris Teutonici = *furentum Teutonum* (abstract for concrete), cf. Ouid. *Rem.* 119 *cum furor in cursu est, currenti cede furori.*

258. timuisse: see 175 n.

258–9. uox nulla dolori credita: 'they did not trust themselves to speak in their grief'. Compare 520.

259. quantum: sc. *est*, so that *cum* embraces not only *coercet* but also *silent* and *tacet*. *Quantum* is correlative to 261 *tanta* and is the neuter adjective, not the adverb, because it is complementary to the *cum* clause. Compare 3. 392 *quantum est quod fata tenentur.* Housman in his note on 260 condemns others for adopting *iacet* in preference to *tacet*, but fails himself to understand the construction of *quantum*. See 293 n.

coercet: 'restrains the voice of'. The phrase comes from Ouid. *Met.* 11. 77–8 *illam (uolucrem) | lenta tenet radix exsultantemque coercet,* but the verb is apt with such an accusative as *uerba* or *uocem*, cf. Tac. *Hist.* 2. 94 *nec coercebat eius modi uoces Vitellius.*

260. rura silent: note the asyndeton, which is similar to that of 665.

-que: 'or', cf. 252–3 n. The silence of the birds and the countryside is independent of the silence of mid-ocean, as Housman observes in comparing Val. Flacc. 2. 585 *ubi iam medii tenuere silentia ponti.*

tacet: see the Critical Apparatus. Lucan was aware, like Valerius Flaccus (*cit. supr.*), that when the sea approaches the shore, it always has a slight motion and is never completely quiet, while silence can reign only in mid-ocean. Compare Stat. *Theb.* 12. 729 and *Ach.* 1. 230–1, as well as Sen. *H.F.* 536.

261. gelidas lux soluerat umbras: cf. Verg. *Aen.* 11. 210 *tertia lux gelidam caelo dimouerat umbram.*

262–4. faces...stimulos...moras: for mixed metaphor in Lucan see Introduction, p. liii.

262. dubiae: for Caesar's hesitation see also 192–4 and 280–1.

in proelia: Housman, who follows the scholiasts, takes these words not with *dubiae* but with *urguentes* and compares for this unusual order 312 (where see note) as well as other passages. Lejay states that *dubiae in proelia* is a coinage of Lucan on the analogy of *auidus in proelia* (cf. 181), and for this view 5. 728–9 *dubium trepidumque ad proelia, Magne, | te quoque fecit amor* should be considered. Certainly *in proelia* should be understood by an ἀπὸ κοινοῦ construction with both *dubiae* and *urguentes*. Compare 276, where *in te* should be taken with *transferre* in the first instance and with *dubios* in the second.

263. **addunt stimulos**...**pudoris**: cf. Quint. 10. 7. 16 *addit ad dicendum etiam pudor stimulos*.

264. **laborat**: according to Lejay, who cites J. Schmidt, *De usu infinitiui apud Lucanum, Valerium Flaccum, Silium Italicum*, Halle, 1881, p. 114, the infinitive alone is found after *non laborare* in Ciceronian prose, and after *laborare* in poetry and in the prose of the Silver Age. Schmidt quotes only two passages from Justin (28. 3. 10 and 36. 1. 7) to parallel this use of the verb with the accusative and infinitive construction.

265. **motus**: see 184n.

266. **ancipiti**: because, as Lejay explains, the city was divided into two factions, namely the supporters of Caesar and those of Pompey and the Senate.

discordes: *i.e.* from the point of view of the senatorial party.

tribunos: Antony and Q. Cassius Longinus. They were also accompanied by Caelius. See Introduction, p. xxxi.

267. **uicto iure**: 'overcoming the legal rights of the tribunes', *i.e.* the *ius* (cf. 276) due to them by virtue of the *tribunicia potestas*.

minax: adjective for adverb (see Introduction, p. lxv) and a good instance of the figure ἑτεροίωσις or alteration of the normal idiom, cf. 329n. *Minax iactatis*...*Gracchis = cum minaciter exitium Gracchorum iactauisset*, or, to employ the Ciceronian phrase (*Quinct.* 14. 47 *minae iactentur*), *cum minas de exitio Gracchorum iactauisset* ('boasted of the doom of the Gracchi' in Duff's translation). After having been tribunes both Tiberius and Gaius Gracchus met their deaths as the result of the hostility of the Senate.

iactatis: Caelius in a letter to Cicero (*Fam.* 8. 6. 5) applies this very word to Curio's boastful utterances.

curia = *senatus* by metonymy, cf. 487.

269. **audax**: compare the description in Vell. Pat. 2. 48. 3 *non alius maiorem flagrantioremque quam C. Curio tribunus plebis subiecit facem: uir nobilis, eloquens, audax*.

uenali: for the bribe which Curio took from Caesar compare 4. 820 *Gallorum captus spoliis et Caesaris auro* and 824 *hic uendidit urbem*. Its size is discussed by Rice Holmes, *The Roman Republic*, ii, p. 321.

270–1. The construction is *uox quondam populi* (*fuit*) *aususque est libertatem tueri et*...*miscere*.

When Curio was a young man he hated the triumvirs and used to attack them (Cic. *Att.* 2. 18. 1, 2. 19. 3; *Q.F.* 2. 3. 2; *Fam.* 8. 4. 2). About the end of 51 or the beginning of 50 B.C. he went over to Caesar's party, as is apparent from Cic. *Fam.* 8. 6.

271. **plebi**: not the *plebs* as opposed to the patricians or rather *optimates*, but Roman citizens as a whole opposed to the triumvirs, *i.e.* the ordinary people, cf. 9. 193–4 *plebe parata* |...*seruire* (*Pompeio*). See 86 n.

miscere: 'to bring down armed chiefs to the level of the people', cf. 3. 138–9 *permiscuit imis* | *longus summa dies*. Curio had proposed to the Senate that Pompey and Caesar should lay down their arms simultaneously (App. 2. 28–31) (Haskins). Compare also Cic. *Fam.* 8. 13. 2 and 8. 14. 2.

272. **uoluentem pectore curas**: cf. Verg. *Aen.* 5. 701–2 *pectore curas* | *mutabat uersans.*

275. **traximus**: the technical verb is, of course, *prŏrŏgāre*, which is impossible for the hexameter. Curio had first vetoed a motion of the Senate on Dec. 1, 50 B.C. to the effect that Caesar should resign his command, and on Jan. 1, 49 B.C. he brought the latter's proposals before that body (App. 2. 32). See 317 n.

rostra tenere: Lucan in commenting on Curio's death at 4. 799–801 refers to the *rostra* in the *forum* as the *arx tribunicia* or stronghold of the tribunes.

276. **dubios in te transferre**: see 262 n.

277. **leges bello siluere coactae**: cf. Cic. *Mil.* 10 *silent enim leges inter arma*, which of course refers particularly to the circumstance alluded to in 323. Observe how *bello* accordingly may be used as a metonymy for *armis*, and for this see Introduction, p. xlix.

278. **uolentes**: this participle refers to present, not to past, time, as is thought by some commentators, who imagine that there is a contradiction with 266. Curio means that the tribunes and he are willing to be exiles, because they know that they will recover their citizenship when Caesar is victorious.

280. **nullo firmatae robore**: cf. 2. 245 *dubium certo tu robore firma* and 527 *ut inmixto firmaret robore partes*. Lejay observes that the Pompeians had only two legions at Luceria, and, as these had come from Caesar, reliance could not be placed on them (Caes. *B.G.* 8. 54 and Cic. *Att.* 7. 13. 2). They were the 6th and the 15th, both veteran legions. It would appear, however, from Caes. *B.C.* 1. 6 that Pompey was counting on levying ten legions.

partes: this word may refer either to one's own side, as in 2. 527 (*cit. supr.*) and 2. 596 *uerba ducis nullo partes clamore sequuntur*, or to that of the enemy, as here and in 10. 78–9 *partesque fugatas | passus...coalescere.*

281. **tolle moras**: an Ovidian expression (*Her.* 4. 147 and *Met.* 13. 556). See 204n.

semper nocuit differre paratis: frequently quoted in the Middle Ages according to Professor Eva Matthews Sanford in *A.J.P.* lv, 1934, pp. 5–6.

differre: this verb without an accusative appears in another proverbial context, namely Ouid. *Fast.* 3. 394 *differ: habent paruae commoda magna morae*, where the maxim with its advice contrary to that tendered by Curio relates, however, to marriage and not to war.

paratis: masculine and dative after *nocuit*. Curio intends that the proverb should refer in this case to Caesar's followers, who unlike Pompey's forces are ready for action.

282. For the interpretation of this line, which Housman brackets through failure to understand its meaning, and for an explanation of the two figures *e sequentibus praecedentia* and hypallage which are involved in it, see Introduction, pp. lv and lvii. Translate: 'The toil and the danger are no greater (than they were before), but the prize aimed at is more considerable.'

283. **geminis...lustris**: 'ten years' (two periods each of five years). The case is ablative of time through which an action happens, and this is a Ciceronian usage, though the accusative is much more frequent. Caesar was given the command of Gaul in 59 B.C., though he did not go to crush the Helvetii and Ariovistus until 58 B.C. Compare 300.

284. **pars quota terrarum**: cf. Sen. *H.O.* 95–6 *sed quota est mundi plaga | oriens subactus!*

facili: 'easily attained'. The expression *facilis euentus* seems to be a coinage on the part of Lucan on the analogy of *facilis exitus* (Cic. *Att.* 9. 3. 1, Caes. *B.C.* 3. 22, Verg. *Aen.* 6. 894, Sen. *Tro.* 601), and is imitated by Frontinus (*Strat.* 3. 1. 2).

285. The force of the future perfects is: 'Once you win a few battles, you will find that it is for you (*tibi*) that Rome in the past has subdued the world.'

286. **pompa triumphi**: an Ovidian phrase (*Pont.* 2. 1. 19–20).

287. **aut**: having been negatived by the *neque* of 286, this conjunction itself = *neque*.

poscunt...**laurus**: a triumphant general was crowned with bay, and the crown was then dedicated in a temple (Plin. *H.N.* 16. 9–10). For the *laurus* at a triumph compare also Ouid. *Met.* 1. 560–1.

288. edax: the Ovidian epithet of *liuor* (*Am.* 1. 15. 1, *Rem.* 389).

288–9. gentesque...feres: 'scarce will you go unpunished for having subdued foreign nations'. For **gentes** see 9n. The commentators aptly compare the jealous attitude of Tiberius towards Germanicus (Tac. *Ann.* 2. 26), and this may have been in Lucan's mind.

289. inpune feres: cf. Catull. 78. 9, 99. 3, Prop. 1. 4. 17. It is a frequent expression in Ovid, cf. *Met.* 2. 474; 8. 279, 494; 11. 207; 12. 265; 14. 383; *Fast.* 4. 595.

290*. decretum...est with the infinitive is, as Lejay points out, a Livian construction.

291. et ipsi: Haskins and Lejay render *ipsi* as 'his general', 'his master', but this interpretation ignores the *et*, which connects awkwardly with *accenditque*. *Et ipse* is simply the phrase, so frequent in Livy, which corresponds with καὶ αὐτός. W. R. Hardie in *C.R.* iv, 1890, p. 13 has well observed that *et ipsi* | *in bellum prono* = the Homeric μεμαῶτι καὶ αὐτῷ (cf. *Il.* 13. 46 etc.). See also 293 n.

292. in bellum prono: as Lejay observes, this is a construction which has already been used by Horace (*Epist.* 1. 18. 10 *alter in obsequium plus aequo pronus*) and Livy.

tamen: this word correlates with a *quamuis* suppressed, the full expression being *duci* (from 293 *ducem*) *quamuis et ipsi in bellum prono*, while on the contrary in the ensuing simile the *quamuis* is expressed in 294 and the *tamen* omitted but understood with *clamore iuuatur Eleus sonipes*. For *quamuis* suppressed compare 333 and Housman's note *ad loc.* as well as 378, and for *tamen* suppressed compare 354. Both *quamuis* and *tamen* are sometimes omitted, cf. 577n.

293. ducem: only when this word is reached does it become clear that with *et ipsi* in 291 the reader must understand *duci* by an *e sequentibus praecedentia* construction. See Introduction, p. lv.

quantum: as Housman points out, this word correlates with the adverb *tantum*, which must be supplied with *accendit* from the substantival *tantum* in 292.

iuuatur: 'is encouraged' (Duff), cf. Ouid. *Pont.* 1. 6. 18 *adloquioque iuua pectora nostra tuo*.

294. Eleus sonipes...carcere: cf. Tibull. 1. 4. 32 *qui prior Eleo est carcere missus equus* and Ouid. *Her.* 18. 166. For *Eleus* = 'at

Olympia' see 106 n. Elis may be used for Olympia by synecdoche (whole for part).

iam: 'has been for some time...', see 241 n.

carcere: when this word denotes the barriers or starting-places (of which there were twelve, cf. Sidon. Apoll. *Carm.* 23. 319) in the race-course, it is normally plural, but the singular is common in poetry. Compare Enn. (Vahl. *Ann.* 85) *omnes auidi spectant ad carceris oras.*

Ennius (Vahl. *Ann.* 374–5, cited by Cic. *Sen.* 14) uses the simile of the aged horse which had been formerly victor at Olympia. Compare also Ouid. *Trist.* 5. 9. 29–30.

295. **pronusque**: to replace this adjective Hosius conjectured *pedibusque* on account of Ouid. *Met.* 2. 155 *pedibusque repagula pulsant*, and he was followed by Lejay. It may be argued on the one hand that, if Lucan is indebted to Ouid. *Trist.* 5. 9. 29–30 as well, *pedibusque* is required to correspond with Ovid's *pede* just as *inmineat foribus* corresponds with *pressa fronte*; and on the other that *inmineat foribus* is the theme and *pronusque repagula laxet* merely the variation. In the latter case *pronus* according to Housman = Ovid's *pressa* (v. l. *ipsa*) *fronte*, and the best translation of it is 'throwing his weight forward', 'pushing hard'. This is suggested by Professor W. B. Anderson (*C.Q.* x, 1916, pp. 100–1), who compares Stat. *Theb.* 10. 509–11. *Pronus* then may be retained, as the repetition from 292 is no real objection to it (see 25 n.).

298. **dextraque silentia iussit**: Haskins compares Pers. 4. 7–8 *fert animus calidae fecisse silentia turbae | maiestate manus.*

299. **bellorum o socii**: a metrical equivalent of Caesar's favourite *commilitones* (Suet. *Caes.* 67. 2).

mille: 'innumerable'. *Mille* is commoner in poetry than *sescenti* with this general meaning.

300. **decimo...anno**: see 283 n. The meaning is 'now in the tenth year you are (find yourselves) victorious', which is a more precise way of saying 'you have been victorious for ten years' (cf. 347). Compare for *iam* with ordinals Verg. *Aen.* 1. 755–6 *te iam septima portat...aestas* and *id.* 5. 626.

301. **hoc** is developed by what follows according to an *e sequentibus praecedentia* construction (see Introduction, p. lv). Caesar means that after their victories in Gaul his soldiers really deserve a triumph and then retirement (341–5), but instead they find that they have to deal with a new war and with the edict that has gone forth against their general.

cruor...diffusus: cf. 615 and Verg. *Aen.* 10. 908 *undantique animam diffundit in arma cruore.*

Arctois: *i.e.* in the northern lands of Gaul and Britain, cf. 371.

302. **mortes**: *i.e.* of their lost companions.

sub: 'immediately behind', *i.e.* in Transalpine Gaul. Lejay compares Verg. *Aen.* 5. 323–4 *Euryalumque Helymus sequitur, quo deinde sub ipso | ecce uolat calcemque terit iam calce Diores* and Hor. *Carm.* 4. 4. 17–18 *uidere Raetis bella sub Alpibus | Drusum gerentem Vindelici.*

303–4. **non secus...quam**, as the commentators on Cic. *Mur.* 4. 10 following Zumpt point out, = *non minus quam*, while *non secus ac* = *non aliter ac*. Of these constructions Vergil uses only *non secus ac* and Ovid both.

303. **tumultu**: see 233n.

304. **transcenderet**: see the Critical Apparatus.

305*. **ualidae**: proleptic and, according to Professor W. B. Anderson (*C.Q.* x, 1916, p. 101), ironical. He compares for Lucan's irony 5. 277 *en inproba uota* and 9. 1108 *o bona libertas.*

tirone: singular for plural, cf. Verg. *Aen.* 2. 20 *armato milite conplent.*

306. **in classem**: 'to make ships'. *In* having the meaning 'with a view to', 'so as to produce' is, as Mr S. G. Owen observes on Ouid. *Trist.* 2. 409, a use of the preposition of which Ovid is fond. Compare 5. 525 *scintillam...pauit in ignes.*

307. **agi**: 'to be chased', *i.e.* like an animal. The commentators compare Verg. *Aen.* 7. 481 *ut ceruum ardentes agerent.*

quid: sc. *facerent, i.e.* 'what would the Pompeians do?'

iacerent: 'lay prostrate'.

308. **Marte...aduerso**: a Vergilian expression (*Aen.* 12. 1).

feroces: Haskins compares Tac. *Agric.* 11 *plus tamen ferociae Britanni praeferunt, ut quos nondum longa pax emollierit: nam Gallos quoque in bellis floruisse accepimus.*

309. **populi**: 'tribes' of a barbarian country, compare 250n.

309–10. **secundis...rebus**: ablative of attendant circumstance.

310. **agat**: an example of syllepsis (see Introduction, p. lxiii), for the verb must be taken with both *Fortuna* and *superi*, but it agrees in number with the preceding rather than the following subject. Cortius compares Sen. *Ep.* 104. 29 *Catonem...cum quo et infestius Fortuna egit et pertinacius.*

superique ad summa: note the play upon words, for which cf. 312 *in bella togatae.*

311. temptamur: 'I am challenged', *i.e.* by the Pompeians.
longa...pace solutus: cf. 241.
dux: Pompey.

312. **milite**: see 305 n.

cum: Lejay observes that this is the only example in Lucan of the use of *cum* whereby the assistance of soldiery is denoted, rather than by the simple ablative of instrument.

subito: for the haste with which Pompey's soldiers were raised see Plut. *Pomp*. 60. 3 and App. 2. 34.

in bella togatae: note the strong antithesis. For *togatae* see 130 and the note *ad loc*. *In bella* should, of course, be taken with both *togatae* and *ueniant*, see 262 n.

313. See Appendix C.

314. **extremi**: 'vile', *i.e.* = *infimi*, as is shown by Housman, who follows one of two suggestions by Farnaby.

clientes: the *uolgus* of 132, whom he had bought (*empti*) and made his 'clients' by his extravagant bounty (Housman).

315. **continuo per tot...tempora regno**: 'with a renewal of his despotic power during so many periods of time', *i.e.* during so long a time. For the plural *tempora* cf. 671. This line refers to the command conferred by the *Lex Gabinia* of 67 B.C. against the pirates and then prolonged by the *Lex Manilia* of the following year for the purpose of combating Mithridates. Afterwards Pompey was consul with Crassus in 55, had proconsular *imperium* over Spain in 54 without leaving the vicinity of Rome, and in 52 was sole consul.

316. **currus**: for this word with reference to a triumph cf. 3. 77; 8. 810, 814; 9. 79, 598–600.

Pompey had defeated Iarbas in Numidia and claimed a triumph, which Sulla ultimately granted him in 80 or 79 B.C. while he was still a mere *eques* (cf. 8. 810 *currus quos egit eques*) and only twenty-five or twenty-six years of age. A magistrate who might legally be granted a triumph would normally be older.

317. **dimittet**: cf. 9. 200 *iuuit sumpta ducem, iuuit dimissa potestas*.

honores: especially those which he had been enjoying since his sole consulship in 52 B.C. He would not resign his *imperium*, though on Jan. 1 of 49 Curio announced on Caesar's behalf to the Senate that the latter would give up his command if Pompey would do the same (App. 2. 32).

318. **rura**: in the first instance this word = 'country estates', and so, as here, their produce, *i.e.* 'crops'. Compare Verg. *Aen.*

1. 430–1 *apes...per florea rura* | *exercet sub sole labor* and Hor. *Carm.* 4. 5. 18 *nutrit rura Ceres almaque Faustitas.*

318–19. On Sept. 7, 57 B.C., Cicero proposed in the Senate that Pompey should have control of the corn-supply of the world for five years with proconsular *imperium* and fifteen legates. The hired ruffians of Clodius attacked Pompey for having kept back the corn-supply when he was commissioner, cf. Cic. *Q.F.* 2. 3. 2.

319. **iussam seruire famem**: 'famine forced to be his servant'. **castra** = *milites* by metonymy.

319–23. In April of 52 B.C. when Milo was accused of *uis* and defended by Cicero, Pompey's forces occupied the Forum to preserve order and intimidate the court.

320. **gladii...triste micantes**: Cortius compares Stat. *Theb.* 4. 153–4 *enses* | *triste micant.*

321. **insolita...corona**: cf. Cic. *Mil.* 1. 2 *non enim* corona *consessus uester* cinctus est, ut solebat, *non usitata frequentia stipati sumus.* The ring (*corona*) made by Pompey's soldiers round the court created a great impression both at the time and afterwards.

322. **medias**: emphatic with *perrumpere*. Compare 5. 583 *medias perrumpe procellas.*

perrumpere...leges: cf. 4. 27 *ruptis legibus.*

milite: see 305 n.

323. **clauserunt** = *incluserunt.*

324. **lassum**: 'weary' after a life of fighting, cf. Sall. *Iug.* 53. 5 *Romani...proelio fessi lassique erant* and Iustin. 28. 4. 5 *lassos (milites) reficiebant.* Haskins compares Hor. *Carm.* 2. 6. 7–8 *sit modus lasso maris et uiarum* | *militiaeque.*

priuata: 'spent in private life', cf. 7. 266 *priuatae...uitae.*

325. **suetus ciuilibus armis**: the theme which is explained by the variation of 326. After Pompey had raised three legions and defeated the Marians, he joined Sulla, who gave him the title of Magnus. See 123 n.

326. **docilis**: 'quick to learn'. Apart from a possible instance in Hor. *Epist.* 1. 2. 64–5, this and Sen. *Phaedr.* 814 are probably the first examples of the use of *docilis* with the infinitive on the analogy of *doctus.*

scelerum: this genitive depends on *magistrum*. Even Cicero was afraid that Pompey would follow in Sulla's footsteps, cf. *Att.* 8. 11. 2 and 9. 10. 6.

uicisse: see 175 n.

327. tigres: 'tiger-cubs', as is shown by *matrum*. See Introduction, p. lvi.

posuere: a frequentative perfect. See 175 n., 390 n., and 432 n. The verb also = *deposuere*. Compare Ouid. *Rem.* 497 *positos... furores*.

327–9. With this simile Haskins compares the picture of the lion's whelp in Aesch. *Ag.* 717 sqq.

328. Hyrcano: Hyrcania was a barbarous region to the S.E. of the Caspian, and 'Hyrcan' or Caspian tigers are famous in literature from Verg. *Aen.* 4. 367 to Shakespeare. Compare Stat. *Theb.* 10. 288–92.

sequuntur: 'make for', cf. Verg. *Aen.* 4. 361 *Italiam non sponte sequor*.

329. altus: adjective for the adverb *alte* to ensure the balance in the line of adj. A, adj. B, verb, noun A, noun B. Just as *minax iactatis* in 267 = *minaciter iactatis* (see note *ad loc.*), so here *altus caesorum* = *alte caesorum* ('with deeply inflicted wounds'), cf. 32 and 8. 690–1 *putrisque effluxit ab alto | umor*. Haskins's parallel 3. 572–3 *cruor altus in unda | spumat* has a different meaning—that of blood flowing deep below the surface of the sea, and 2. 214–15 *iam sanguinis alti | uis sibi fecit iter* refers to a river of blood. Compare Ouid. *Met.* 4. 121 *cruor emicat alte*.

armentorum: for spondaic lines in Lucan see Heitland, *Introd.* p. xcvii.

330. Sullanum...ferrum: cf. Petron. *Bell. Ciu.* 98 *ex quo Sullanus bibit ensis*.

lambere ferrum: a phrase apparently coined by Lucan. For *lambere* in this context with *sitis*, compare 3. 346 *(parati sumus) effossam sitientes lambere terram*.

331. durat: this word here unites the meaning of 'hardens' with that of 'lasts'.

331–2. nullus...sanguis: 'never does blood' etc. *Nullus* in the sense of the adverb *numquam* is used with verbs of motion in Cicero's letters. Compare the common example *nullus uenit* = 'he never came' and *Att.* 15. 22 *ego autem scripsi Sextum aduentare, non quo iam adesset, sed quia certe id ageret ab armisque nullus discederet*. Lejay compares Catull. 8. 14 *at tu dolebis, cum rogaberis nulla* and Prop. 1. 17. 12. For this use in Lucan see Heitland, *Introd.* p. cviii (ς).

For the sentiment, which was inspired perhaps by Ouid. *Met.* 1. 226–35, compare 4. 239–41.

332. **pollutas...fauces**: cf. Ouid. *Met.* 15. 98 *nec polluit ora cruore*.

333. **tamen**: *quamuis* must be supplied with *tam longa*. Housman supplies a number of parallels including 378 but not 292, where see note.

potentia: unofficial power, as opposed to the *potestas* of the magistrates.

334. **quis scelerum modus est**? cf. Sen. *Thy.* 1052 *sceleri modus debetur ubi facias scelus*.

inprobe: 'unsatisfied', 'incapable of satisfaction' like the wild beasts of the simile, cf. Verg. *Aen.* 10. 727–8 *lauit inproba taeter | ora (leonis) cruor*.

335. **descendere**: Sulla resigned his dictatorship in 79 B.C., a year before his death. Compare Sen. *Clem.* 1. 12. 2 *descenderit licet (Sulla) e dictatura sua*.

336. **post Cilicas uagos** = *post proelia contra Cilicas uagos gesta*. The *Cilicas uagos* are the pirates who were finally routed by Pompey off the Cilician coast.

uagos: the adjective may be applied also to peaceful travellers, cf. Hor. *A.P.* 117 *mercator uagus*.

lassi...regis: Mithridates (see 315 n.), who had had to face Sulla in the first Mithridatic war. Then in the third war of the same name first Cotta and afterwards Lucullus opposed him for seven years from 74 B.C. onwards. Finally Glabrio was sent out, but did little after his arrival. Caesar in depreciation of Pompey suggests that when the latter arrived on the scene in 66 B.C., he found Mithridates already worn out after so many campaigns.

337. **barbarico...ueneno**: 'poison taken in a foreign land', see 106 n. After his final defeat Mithridates fled to the Cimmerian Bosporus (the Crimea) to rouse the wild Sarmatae and Getae against Rome, but committed suicide after a few years by taking poison (63 B.C.). The commentators, however, suggest that *barbarico* refers to the fact that Pontus was famous for poisonous herbs, and compare Verg. *Ecl.* 8. 95–6.

uix: Housman is right in preferring the explanation of the scholiast *a* 'quia diu pugnatum est quippe a tot ducibus' to that of *c*, which suggests that Mithridates found that poisoning himself was a difficult task, as he had been in the habit of taking antidotes. *Vix* implies that the difficulty was on Pompey's side, and is in harmony with the sneer contained in *lassi*. Caesar implies that Pompey did not bring the king in triumph to Rome as he ought, but merely drove him into such a position that he was compelled to take poison. Pompey, however, states his own point of view at 2. 580–2.

consummata: Ovid is the first poet to use this essentially prose word.

338. **prouincia**: very sarcastic. 'Is Pompey, who has had so many *prouinciae*, going to have in Caesar his last (and greatest) sphere of operations?'

340. **merces**: *i.e.* what the *cruor diffusus* (301) really *meruit*. The word is here a synonym for *pretium*, cf. 4. 220 *pretium mercesque*.

341. **his**: explained by *miles* in the next line. See Introduction, p. lvi.

saltem: like *tamen* (see 292 n. and 333 n.) this word virtually calls for an understood *quamuis* before *non cum duce*.

non cum = *sine*, cf. 7. 96 *ne non cum sanguine uincant*.

342. **miles…iste**: 'these soldiers of mine', repeating the *his* of the previous line. For *iste* = 'this' see Heitland, *Introd.* p. cviii (η), Postgate on 8. 122 and 670 n.

343. **exsanguis…senectus**: 'they in their feeble old age' (abstract for concrete), cf. Stat. *Theb.* 11. 323 *exsangues crudescunt luctibus anni*.

344. **rura**: 'assignations of land', cf. 170.

345. **moenia**: *i.e.* of military colonies. Compare Verg. *Aen.* 3. 85 *da moenia fessis*.

346. After Pompey had defeated the pirates off the coast of Cilicia, he settled some of them in Calabria, cf. Vell. Pat. 2. 32. 4. Servius quotes this line in his comment on Verg. *Georg.* 4. 125–8 *namque sub Oebaliae memini me turribus arcis, | qua niger umectat flauentia culta Galaesus, | Corycium uidisse senem, cui pauca relicti | iugera ruris erant* (Corycus was a town of Cilicia).

347. **iam pridem**: to be taken with *uictricia*, *i.e.* 'long-victorious', cf. 300.

348. **uiribus…quas fecimus**: the commentators compare Quint. 10. 3. 3 *uires faciamus ante omnia, quae sufficiant labori certaminum et usu non exhauriantur* for the expression *uires facere* used of the training of athletes. Gaul had been their school for the big issues that were now to face them. The phrase *uires facere* is Ovidian (*Met.* 4. 528, 8. 143, *Trist.* 3. 6. 21).

348–9. **arma…negat**: 'He who refuses his due to him who is armed gives him everything', *i.e.* by justifying him in taking more.

349–50. See the Critical Apparatus.

351. **dominos**: plural for singular, probably, with reference to Pompey, because *dominum* is inconvenient metrically for this line.

352-3. **non claro murmure...incerta fremit**: cf. 9. 1008 (and Ouid. *Fast.* 3. 273) *incerto...murmure*.

uolgus...fremit: cf. 10. 11 *fremitu uolgi* and Ouid. *Met.* 15. 606-7 *frementis...uolgi. Volgus* = 'the soldiers' as opposed to their general, cf. 7. 45-6 *mixto murmure turba | castrorum fremuit* and 9. 217 *fremit...discordia uolgi*.

353. **pietas patriique penates**: 'love of their country and their ancestral homes', cf. 7. 346 *patriam carosque penates* and 9. 230-1 *patrios permitte penates | desertamque domum...reuisere*.

354. **quamquam**: to be taken with *feras* and *tumentes*, while *tamen* should be supplied with *frangunt*, see 292 n.

feras: 'made savage', *i.e.* = *efferas*, for the use of which with the ablative cf. Verg. *Aen.* 4. 642 *coeptis inmanibus effera Dido*. Or Lucan may have transferred an epithet which is natural with *caedes*, cf. Ouid. *Trist.* 4. 2. 38.

feras mentes animosque tumentes: cf. Verg. *Aen.* 6. 49 *rabie fera corda tument*.

355. **diro ferri**: an unconscious reminiscence of Verg. *Aen.* 1. 293-4 *dirae ferro... | claudentur Belli portae*. For the sentiment Haskins compares Hom. *Od.* 16. 294 αὐτὸς γὰρ ἐφέλκεται ἄνδρα σίδηρος. Lucan seems still to be thinking of the *ferae tigres* which have once tasted blood, see 327-32.

356. **summi...pili**: Haskins says: 'he was a *centurio primi pili* otherwise termed *primipilaris* or *primipilus*: this title originally belonged to the first centurion of the first maniple of *triarii* who ranked next to the *tribuni militum*. After the distinctions between *hastati, principes*, and *triarii* were abolished by Marius when he raised the levy against Jugurtha B.C. 107-6, the *primipilus* was probably the first centurion of the first maniple of the first cohort, who acted as *aquilifer*. In later times the *primipilares* seem to have been a small corps acting as the general's bodyguard.' Lejay observes that these centurions served as intermediaries between Caesar and his soldiers, and cites *B.G.* 1. 41. 3 and 7. 17. 8.

munera: *i.e.* the insignia that had been presented to him. Note the variation on this theme in the following line.

357. **Laelius**: the speech which follows takes the place of the enthusiastic reception of Caesar's words by his soldiers, as mentioned in *B.C.* 1. 7-8. It is possible that there may have been such

a person as Laelius and that he was mentioned by Livy, but this
must be merely conjecture.

emeriti: not in the meaning which occurs in 344, but in that
of *meriti*, *i.e.* 'which he had earned'. Haskins compares Sil. 7. 19
surge age et emerito sacrum caput insere caelo and Mart. 1. 31. 3
grata Pudens meriti tulerit cum praemia pili.

358. **referentem**: 'recalling', 'bringing back the memory of',
cf. Verg. *Aen.* 5. 563–4 *paruus*... | *nomen aui referens Priamus*.

praemia: to be taken with *seruati*...*ciuis*, cf. Tac. *Ann.* 12. 31
(of the civic crown) *seruati ciuis decus meruit*.

quercum: cf. Verg. *Aen.* 6. 772 *umbrata gerunt ciuili tempora
quercu*. The reference is to the *corona ciuica* or *querna corona* (Ouid.
Fast. 1. 614, where see Frazer), the oaken crown awarded to a
soldier for saving the life of a fellow Roman.

359–60. **Romani**...**nominis**: 'of all that is called Roman', a
common phrase in Livy.

360. **ueras expromere uoces**: cf. Verg. *Aen.* 2. 280 *maestas
expromere uoces*.

361. **quod**: 'that'. Note the construction which gradually
replaced the accusative and infinitive in Latin and was continued
in the Romance languages (*e.g.* Fr. *que*).

362. **conquerimur**: 'we all complain' (*con-*).

363. Lejay observes that the idea of a man's life being contained
in his blood is found in Homer and Empedocles, *e.g.* in Hom.
Hymn. Apoll. 361–2 λεῖπε δὲ θυμὸν | φοινὸν ἀποπνείουσα (with which
cf. Verg. *Aen.* 9. 349 *purpuream uomit ille animam*). *Anima* in the
Latin poets may mean 'life-blood', cf. the Vergilian line just
quoted *id.* 10. 908 *undantique animam diffundit in arma cruore*;
so may *uita*, cf. Val. Flacc..6. 188 *mixtaeque uirum cum puluere
uitae* and ibid. 705–6 *subitos ex ore cruores* | *saucia tigris agit uitamque
effundit erilem*, and even Cic. *Phil.* 14. 11. 30 *grata eorum uirtutem
memoria prosequi, qui pro patria uitam profuderunt*. For *sanguis
=uita* cf. 2. 76–7 *hosti concessa potestas* | *sanguinis inuisi*. Blood is
identified with the vital power in 3. 679 and 4. 287. See *Genesis* 9. 4.

365. **degenerem**...**togam**: 'private life (cf. 130n.) that is
unworthy of you', not, as the scholiasts say, 'civilians (*togam
=togatos*) who have lost their courage'. Housman supports the
former interpretation by citing four passages, of which 3. 367
dimissis degener armis and 10. 441 *degeneres passus latebras* apply to
Caesar himself. To them may be added 2. 522–3 *Romamne petes
pacisque recessus* | *degener?* (of Domitius), and especially 5. 381–2
Romam | *iam doctam seruire togae* (*i.e. Caesari togato*).

366. Compare Verg. *Aen*. 12. 646 *usque adeone mori miserum est?*

367–72. In establishing the punctuation of these lines Housman shows that 367–8 form the protasis and 372 the apodosis. 369–71 are thrown in to strengthen the pride of the utterance and give an additional reason for 372. Laelius says in effect: 'We have crossed the Channel and bridged the Rhine; we can also march through Scythia, the Syrtes, or Libya, if necessary.'

367. **inhospita Syrtis**: cf. Verg. *Aen*. 4. 41.

Syrtis: genitive to correspond with *Scythiae* and *Libyes*, according to Housman, rather than accusative. Though at 9. 710 *Syrtidos* occurs, elsewhere the MSS of Lucan and the authority of Priscian vouch for the accusative *Syrtim*, and the genitive *Syrtis* appears in Sen. *Thy*. 292, Sil. 1. 408, etc. Francken understands the case to be the accusative, and Housman then compares 3. 295 *usque Paraetonias Eoa ad litora Syrtis* and Verg. *Georg*. 4. 168 *ignauom fucos pecus* for an apposition which is already exemplified in 313 *nomina uana Catones*.

368. **Libyes**: see the Critical Apparatus.

369. **haec manus**: 'these hands of ours'.

uictum...orbem: Britain. *Orbis* by synecdoche may mean *a part* of the world (see 252 n.). The commentators compare Verg. *Ecl*. 1. 66 *penitus toto diuisos orbe Britannos* and Vell. Pat. 2. 46. 1 (of Caesar crossing the Channel to Britain) *alterum paene imperio nostro ac suo quaerens orbem*.

370. **conpescuit undas**: cf. Hor. *Carm*. 2. 14. 9 *conpescit undā* and *Epist*. 1. 12. 16 *quae mare conpescant causae*.

371. **fregit**: i.e. by the piles of Caesar's bridges. The two crossings of the Rhine were effected in 55 B.C. (Caes. *B.G*. 4. 17) and in 53 B.C. (*B.G*. 6. 9).

Arctoo spumantem uertice Rhenum: practically a hypallage for *Arctoum spumanti uertice Rhenum*. Lucan regarded Gaul as a northern country, cf. 301, 458, and 482.

372. **sequi** = *exsequi*. 'I must be able and willing to execute your commands.'

374. **signa decem felicia castris**: 'by the victorious standards of ten camps' (i.e. legions). This, as well as the usual explanation 'prosperous in ten campaigns' (cf. 283 n.), is given by the scholiast *c*. For the use of the dative instead of the genitive (antiptosis) see Introduction, p. lxiv and 25 n. *Castra* (frequently with an ordinal numeral) is used of the camp pitched at the end of a day's march, and consequently of a day's march itself, cf. 5. 374 *Brundisium decimis iubet hanc attingere castris* and see *Thes. Ling. Lat*. iii, p. 563

for other examples, but the commentators do not cite any good example of *castra* with the meaning of 'a year's campaign'. Lejay, who observes that the present season is winter, quotes Caes. *B.G.* 5. 53. 3 *ipse* (*Caesar*) *cum tribus legionibus...trinis hibernis hiemare constituit*, from which it appears that each legion had its winter camp. Therefore *castra* may be used as a metonymy for *legiones*. Caesar had according to Plut. *Pomp.* 58 ten legions, according to Cicero writing in December B.C. 50 (*Att.* 7. 7. 6) eleven, the extra legion having been raised probably in 52 (*B.G.* 7. 65).

felicia: for *felix* with the dative cf. 10. 51 *non felix Parthia Crassis*.

376. Compare Ouid. *Met.* 13. 458-9 *aut tu iugulo uel pectore telum | conde meo.*

377. **condere**: for this verb with the ablative lacking a preposition cf. 541. In employing *condere* Vergil uses a preposition with nouns denoting parts of the body, *e.g. Aen.* 9. 347-8 *pectore in aduerso...ensem | condidit* and 12. 950 *ferrum aduerso sub pectore condit.* According to Lejay, this is the only instance in Lucan where it is found also with *in* and the accusative, just as on one occasion (9. 86) it is followed by *in* and the ablative.

uiscera: cf. 5. 79 *premeret cum uiscera* (*matris*) *partus* and Ouid. *Met.* 15. 88 *heu quantum scelus est in uiscera uiscera condi!*

378. **inuita peragam...dextra**: cf. Ouid. *Pont.* 3. 2. 66 *inuita peragens tristia sacra manu.*

peragam: future indicative, as may be seen from the parallel *miscebit* of 380. Note the contrast of moods between the *iubeas* of the protasis and the *peragam* of the apodosis. Caesar's wishes are merely a possibility, but Laelius's execution of them will follow without hesitation.

tamen: *quamuis* must be supplied with *inuita...dextra*, see 292 n. and 333 n.

379. **deos**: *i.e. templa deorum*, as is clear from *templis* in the variation of the theme *spoliare deos*. Translate: 'If you bid me despoil the temples of the gods by setting fire to them', etc., and compare 5. 305 *spoliandaque templa*. For the accusative of a noun which = the accusative of another noun (to be supplied by the context) together with the genitive of the first noun, see 566 n. and 2. 246 *alii Magnum uel Caesaris arma sequantur*, where *Magnum = Magni arma.*

380. **castrensis...monetae**: 'the mint controlled by the soldiers'. The temple of Iuno Moneta (for Cicero's derivation of

the word see *Diu.* 1. 45. 101) stood on the Capitol on the site of the modern church of Santa Maria in Araceli. In this temple money was coined, whence *moneta* with the meaning of 'mint'. Compare 6. 404–5 *aurumque moneta | fregit*, which Housman quotes in addition to Bentley's parallels from Sen. *Contr.* 4. 4 and Stat. *Silu.* 3. 3. 105. Laelius means that, if it is Caesar's will, he himself will set up a mint in the camp and melt down the images of the gods. Is Lucan thinking of Nero's action as described by Suetonius (*Ner.* 32 *fin.*) *templis conpluribus dona detraxit simulacraque ex auro uel argento fabricata conflauit* (cf. Sen. *Const. Sap.* 4. 2)?

381*. **Thybridis**: Lejay observes that Lucan uses only this, the Hellenized, name of the Tiber. Compare, however, the adjective *Tiberinus* in 475 and 2. 216.

382. **Hesperios**: 'Italian', see 29 n. For the meaning 'Spanish' compare 555 and 4. 14 *Hesperios inter Sicoris non ultimus amnes.*

metator: 'camp-surveyor', cf. Cic. *Phil.* 14. 10 *peritus metator et callidus decempeda* (Haskins). Lejay observes that *metari castra* may be used as a synonym of *ponere castra* (cf. Caes. *B.C.* 3. 13 and Sall. *Iug.* 106. 5), because measuring was an essential task in pitching a camp.

383. **effundere**: not only 'knock down', but also 'spread the stones (cf. 384 *disperget saxa*) over the level ground'. Compare Sen. *Phoen.* 343 *disicite passim moenia, in planum date* and Stat. *Theb.* 3. 250 *effundam turres.*

385. **urbem**: note the attraction of the antecedent into the case of the relative pronoun, as in Verg. *Aen.* 1. 573 *urbem quam statuo uestra est.* See Löfstedt, *Synt.* ii, pp. 114–15.

386. **his**: sc. *dictis.*

387–8. **elatasque...promisere manus**: 'and they promised the help of their hands as they raised them'. The phrase *promisere manus* is imitated by Statius (*Theb.* 4. 353 and 6. 663).

388. **it...clamor**: cf. Verg. *Aen.* 12. 409 *it tristis ad aethera clamor.*

389*. **Thracius**: a conventional epithet for 'northern', and taken over from Greek. To the Greeks Thrace was of course a northern country. Compare Hor. *Carm.* 1. 25. 11–12 *Thracio... uento, Epod.* 13. 2–3 *siluae | Threicio Aquilone sonant,* and Ouid. *A.A.* 2. 431 *Threicio Borea.* In Sil. 1. 587 even the Provençal mistral is called *Thracius Boreas.*

390. **rupibus**: cf. 6. 333–4 *Thessaliam...rupes Ossaea coercet* and *Ciris* 33 *Ossaeis...saxis.*

incubuit: a frequentative perfect, see 175 n.

curuato robore: ablative of attendant circumstance. Compare 9. 364 (*serpens*) *robora conplexus rutilo curuata metallo.*

391. **rursus redeuntis**: for the pleonasm cf. 7. 719 *rursus in arma potes rursusque in fata redire* and Verg. *Aen.* 4. 531–2 *rursusque resurgens | saeuit amor.*

392. **acceptum tam prono milite**: when *acceptus=gratus* it is constructed with the dative or else with *in* and the accusative, cf. Ouid. *Met.* 13. 467 *acceptior illi.* Here the use of the ablative for the metrically impossible dative (antiptosis, see Introduction, p. lxiv) has not been understood by commentators like Haskins. With *prono* cf. 292.

393. **ferre**: the use of this verb seems to imply a metaphor taken from navigation, where it is applied to favouring winds. The commentators compare Cic. *Act. Sec. in Verr.* 5. 40. 105 *ita sui periculi rationes ferre ac postulare* and Verg. *Aen.* 4. 430 *exspectet facilemque fugam uentosque ferentes.*

languore: see 194n.

394. **Fortunam**: a synonym here of *fata* in the preceding line. See 227n. and cf. 8. 701–2 *Fortuna…Magni tam prospera fata | pertulit.*

395. **euocat**: catalogues, such as that which now follows, belong to the apparatus of the Epic from Homer onwards. Pompey's forces also are listed in 3. 169–297.

396. **deseruere**: the subject of this verb is either *cohortes* to be supplied from 394, or *illi* to be understood from 399 *hi* which otherwise has no pronoun to correspond to it. The latter construction, which is a good example of *e sequentibus praecedentia* (see Introduction, p. lv), is more likely.

cauo: *i.e.* set deeply amid the surrounding hills. The epithet is truer of the eastern than of the western end of the lake. Compare 2. 422 *Rutubamque cauum,* 4. 157–8 *attollunt campo geminae iuga saxea rupes | ualle caua media,* 4. 723 *caua…in ualle,* and Verg. *Georg.* 1. 326 (4. 427) *caua flumina.*

tentoria: Lejay observes that this word is not exact, because in winter camps the tents of skin were replaced by huts (*casae,* cf. Caes. *B.G.* 5. 43. 1), but goes on to point out from *id.* 8. 5. 2 that the names *tentoria* and *casae* may be interchanged on occasion.

fixa: 'erected', cf. Ouid. *Her.* 7. 119–20 *fixi moenia.*

397. **Vogesi**: see the Critical Apparatus, and Introduction, p. xli.

curuam…ripam: for *curuus* applied to the course of a river cf. Ouid. *Fast.* 3. 520 *Tiberis curuis…aquis.*

398. **pugnaces pictis...armis**: Housman compares Liu. 22. 37. 8 *Mauros pugnacesque alias missili telo gentes*. Pichon sees in *pictis* an allusion to the shields ornamented with enamel and made at Bibracte (Autun), while Professor Wight Duff (*op. cit.* p. 320n.) refers to the exactness of this description for the Aeduan antiquities at that town. Compare Diod. Sic. 5. 30. 2 ὅπλοις δὲ χρῶνται... πεποικιλμένοις ἰδιοτρόπως.

cohibebant: cf. Tac. *Ann.* 12. 31 *cunctaque castris...cohibere parat*.

Lingonas: the Lingones occupied the modern departments of Haute-Marne and Vosges, and their chief town was Andematunnum (Langres). See the Critical Apparatus, and Introduction, p. xli.

armis: 'shields' by synecdoche, see 423n. and Introduction, p. liii. Compare 3. 475–6 *armisque innexa priores | arma ferunt* and Seru. ad Verg. *Aen.* 4. 495, where *arma* is defined as follows: *gladium dicit abusiue, proprie enim arma sunt quae armos tegunt, hoc est scutum.* Servius Danielis *ad loc.* goes on to cite *Aen.* 10. 841 *at Lausum socii exanimem super arma ferebant.* Compare also Liu. 1. 20. 4, where *caelestia arma* = the *ancilia* or sacred shields which fell down from heaven.

399. **uada**: a word applicable to the slow motion of a river, cf. 222 and Sen. *N.Q.* 6. 7. 3 *illic quoque aliae (aquae) uasto cursu deferuntur et in praeceps uolutae cadunt, aliae languidiores in uadis refunduntur et leniter ac quiete fluunt.*

Isarae: the Isère. In *C.Q.* xxx, 1936, pp. 59–60 there are set forth reasons why it should be believed that Lucan was thinking of the Arar (Saône), even though this river is mentioned specifically at 434. The language of 399–401 suggests a river which flows gently, and the Arar but not the Isara suits this description. Compare especially Plin. *H.N.* 3. 33.

gurgite...suo: 'by its own course', 'in its own channel'; cf. 5. 466 *neuter longo se gurgite lassat* referring to two rivers, where Mr Duff translates 'neither river is wearied by the length of its course'. *Gurgite* may also be used of a swift river, cf. 433, where the *Cinga rapax* (4. 21) is described by this word.

ductus = *deductus*, i.e. 'descending'. For the 'older and freer timeless use' of the perfect participle passive see Conway on Verg. *Aen.* 1. 246 (Cambridge, 1935). Such an expression as Plaut. *Aul.* 708 *ego me deorsum duco de arbore* shows how the simple *ducere* may replace the compound *deducere*, and for the use of *mittere* instead of *demittere* see Verg. *Aen.* 4. 253–4 *hinc toto* *praeceps se corpore ad undas | misit* and Prop. 2. 26. 19 *iamque ego conabar summo me mittere saxo.* For *ductus* compare, in addition to the parallels cited in *C.Q. loc. cit.*, Sidon. Apoll. *Carm.* 5. 373–5 *conscenderat Alpes | Raetorumque iugo per longa silentia ductus | Romano exierat populato trux Alamannus.*

400. per tam multa: sc. *uada* from the preceding line. These words, which furnish an extreme instance of an ἀπὸ κοινοῦ construction, have been needlessly suspected. Housman compares Tibull. 1. 7. 14 (*Cydne, qui*) *placidis per uada serpis aquis.* Regarding *tam multa* it may be observed that the Saône is the longest tributary of the Rhone.

amnem: the Rhone.

401. lapsus: this perfect participle has, like *ductus*, a present meaning. Note the asyndeton between *ductus* and *lapsus*, and cf. 229 crit. n.

ad aequoreas...undas: cf. 4. 22–3 *nam gurgite mixto | qui praestat terris aufert tibi* (*i.e. Cingae*) *nomen Hiberus,* 6. 375 *in alterius nomen cum* (*Titaresos*) *uenerit undae,* Ouid. *Fast.* 4. 338 (*Almo*) *nomen magno perdit in amne minor* (*i.e.* in the Tiber), and especially Amm. Marc. 15. 11. 17 (*Rhodanus*) *Ararim quem Sauconnam appellant...suum in nomen adsciscit.*

pertulit: cf. 10. 253–4 *omnia flumina Nilus | ...non uno gurgite perfert.*

402. soluuntur: 'are relieved from' (Haskins).

flaui: M. Bourgery suggests that this may be an etymological epithet, cf. 214n.

Ruteni: a people of Gallia Aquitania, whose chief town was Segodunum (Rodez). They occupied the modern departments of Tarn, Aveyron, and Lozère so close to the borders of the Roman *prouincia* (Plin. *H.N.* 4. 109 *Narbonensi prouinciae contermini Ruteni*) that Lucan may well have imagined them to be within it, and accordingly used the epithet *longa* (*i.e.* 'long before Caesar').

403. Atax: the Aude.

Latias: 'Roman' by metonymy, cf. 253n.

non ferre: for the navigability of the Atax, Haskins compares Strab. 4. 1. 14 ἐκ δὲ Νάρβωνος ἀναπλεῖται μὲν ἐπὶ μικρὸν τῷ Ἀτακι. Note also Mel. 2. 81 *Atax...exiguus uadusque est, et...nisi ubi Narbonem adtingit nusquam nauigabilis.*

404. promoto limite: here no anachronism such as the scholiast *c* suggests is to be understood, for Lucan is describing the Var as it was in his day. By the *Lex Roscia* which was passed later in

49 B.C. (see Dio Cass. 41. 36 and *Camb. Anc. Hist.* ix, pp. 643–4) under Caesar's direction in order to enfranchise the Cisalpine Gauls, this river became the boundary between Italy and the *prouincia*, cf. Strab. 4. 1. 9, 5. 1. 1 and Plin. *H.N.* 3. 31.

405*. quaque: 'and the place where', cf. 409, 432–4 etc. (Housman).

portus: the harbour was called the *portus Herculis Monoeci* (Plin. *H.N.* 3. 47, Sil. 1. 585–6, Tac. *Hist.* 3. 42, and Amm. Marc. 15. 10. 9 *Monoeci...arcem et portum ad perennem sui memoriam consecrauit*), and was sacred to Hercules the solitary dweller (Μόνοικος), whence the modern name of Monaco. Compare the allusion to this place with reference to the army collected by Caesar from Gaul in Verg. *Aen.* 6. 830–1.

406. urguet: 'encroaches upon' (Haskins).

rupe caua: ablative of description, so that the meaning is 'lying in the hollow of a rock'—an allusion to the lofty promontory of Monaco, between which and the mainland lies the harbour. What really encroaches on the sea is not the harbour but the promontory, so that here there is a double hypallage or interchange of cases and epithets (see Introduction, p. lvi), and the sense is *rupes portu cauo* (cf. 396 n.) *praedita pelagus urguet*. Compare the description of a sunset in Val. Flacc. 2. 34–5 *iamque Hyperionius metas maris urguet Hiberi | currus*.

Corus: the N.W. wind which prevails on the Gallic shore of the English Channel according to Caes. *B.G.* 5. 7. 3, while *Zephyrus* is the W. wind. Compare Sen. *N.Q.* 5. 16. 5 *aequinoctialis occidens Fauonium mittit quem Zephyrum esse dicent tibi etiam qui Graece nesciunt loqui*; *a solstitiali occidente Corus uenit qui apud quosdam Argestes dicitur* and Plin. *H.N.* 2. 119 *ab occasu solstitiali Corus.*

407. ius habet: cf. 9. 887 and Sen. *Oed.* 447 *ius habet in fluctus... puer.*

sua: 'where it is master', see 155 n.

408. Circius: probably the mistral (see also 389 n.) which is familiar to readers of Alphonse Daudet as a feature of Provence, and is of exceptional strength. Compare Plin. *H.N.* 2. 121 *in Narbonensi prouincia clarissimus uentorum est Circius, nec ullo uiolentia inferior*, as well as Diod. Sic. 5. 26. 1 and Strab. 4. 1. 7. The mistral blows down the valley of the Rhone, and for its chilling violence Sil. 1. 587–94 should be consulted, where it is described under the general name *Boreas*. Strabo (*loc. cit.*) says of it μελαμ-βόρειον, πνεῦμα βίαιον καὶ φρικῶδες. See also Sen. *N.Q.* 5. 17. 5.

prohibet: sc. *naues*, as Oudendorp shows. For the omission of the object see Heitland, *Introd.* p. cvii.

statione: 'anchorage-ground'. Haskins compares Vell. Pat. 2. 72. 5 *exitialem tempestatem fugientibus statio pro portu foret*. See also Strab. 4. 6. 3 ὁ δὲ τοῦ Μονοίκου λιμὴν ὅρμος ἐστὶν οὐ μεγάλαις οὐδὲ πολλαῖς ναυσίν.

409. litus dubium: some commentators understand this of the Vada Sabatia near Genoa, others with more reason of the Belgian coast on account of 411 *Oceanus*. It is not unlikely that Lucan here and at 2. 571 (of Caesar) *Oceanumque uocans incerti stagna profundi* is thinking of Caesar's description of the coast of the Veneti who lived in Southern Brittany (*B.G.* 3. 12. 1 *erant eius modi fere situs oppidorum, ut posita in extremis lingulis promunturiisque neque pedibus aditum haberent cum ex alto se aestus incitauisset, quod bis accidit semper horarum xii* (dub.) *spatio, neque nauibus, quod rursus minuente aestu naues in uadis adflictarentur*). Lucan's language resembles also that used by Mela (3. 1–3) in discussing tides. In Strab. 4. 4. 1 the other Veneti (or Heneti) who inhabited modern Venetia to the north of the Po (cf. *id.* 5. 1. 4) are mentioned in company with them, and indeed it is curious to find an account of tides similar to those of the Ocean occurring in an inland sea like the Adriatic (cf. 4. 427–9). Note the interest in the tides of the Atlantic on the part of Lucan as of other Greek and Roman writers, accustomed as they were to the comparatively tideless Mediterranean (cf. Caes. *B.G.* 4. 29. 1). According to Strab. 1. 1. 9 Poseidonius (see 449 n.) was an authority on the causes of the motions of the Ocean.

dubium: *i.e.* there is uncertainty whether the shore should be regarded as sea or land. See 686 n.

410. alternis uicibus: cf. Ouid. *Met.* 15. 409 *alternare uices* and *Pont.* 4. 2. 6 *per alternas...uices*.

funditur = *infunditur*, cf. Rut. Nam. 1. 641–2 *qualiter Oceanus mediis infunditur agris,* | *destituenda* (cf. 413 *infr.*) *uago cum premit arua salo*.

411. refugis...fluctibus: cf. Ouid. *Met.* 10. 41–2 *nec Tantalus ndam* | *captauit refugam*.

412. With uentus...uolutet destituatque sc. *utrum*. This and the following questions depend on 417 *quaerite*.

ab extremo...axe: 'from the most remote part of the sky', cf. 4. 62–3 (*Eurus*) *suo nubes quascumque inuenit in axe* | *torsit in occiduum...orbem*.

sic: 'as I have just described'.

uolutet: 'keeps rolling on', the frequentative of *uoluat*.

413. destituat: the regular word to denote an ebbing tide (see 410n. and Verg. *Ecl.* 1. 60 *et freta destituent nudos in litore pisces*) is transferred here to the wind which is supposed to carry the tide back.

ferens: 'in the act of carrying it forward'.

sidere...secundo: the moon, see Appendix A. The moon is recognized as the cause of the tides in 10. 204 *luna suis uicibus Tethyn terrenaque miscet* and Sen. *Prou.* 1. 4. Compare Manil. 2. 90–1.

414. Tethyos: the sea, cf. 10. 204.

uagae: 'restless', 'moving forwards and backwards', cf. Ouid. *Her.* 10. 136 *scopulo quem uaga pulsat aqua*, and for the passage generally Sil. 3. 58–60.

lunaribus...horis: 'by the phases of the moon'.

aestuet: 'forms tides' (*aestus*).

415. flammiger: see 48n.

alentes: the belief that vapours arising from water feed the sun and other heavenly bodies is not confined to Stoicism. See 7. 5 (*cit. infr.*) and Postgate *ad loc.*, as well as Cic. *Tusc. Disp.* 1. 19. 43 and *N.D.* 2. 46. 118.

416*. ad sidera: either 'to his own orb' (see 15n. and Appendix A), cf. 7. 5. *attraxit nubes non pabula flammis* (of the sun), where Postgate translates *attraxit* as 'drew *to himself*', and 9. 313 (for which see the Critical Apparatus); or 'to himself and the other heavenly bodies', cf. 10. 258–9 *nec non Oceano pasci Phoebumque polosque | credimus*, Rut. Nam. 1. 643–4 *siue* (*Oceanus*) *alio* (*i.e.* the moon) *refluus nostro colliditur orbe, | siue corusca suis sidera pascit aquis*, and Sen. *N.Q.* 2. 5. 2, 6. 16. 2.

417. quaerite: for discussions concerning the cause of the tides see Strab. 1. 3. 11 and Plin. *H.N.* 2. 212–21, and consult Pease on Cic. *Diu.* 2. 34 (*ed.* p. 409). This may be a hit at the Peripatetics, if value is to be placed in the opinion of John of Salisbury, who quotes these words of Lucan with approval (*Metalog.* 943 b, ed. Webb, p. 213). For the expression *quaerite, quos agitat mundi labor* compare the similar language of Lucr. 5. 1211–14 and note Prop. 2. 34. 51 *harum nulla solet rationem quaerere mundi*

419. late: cf. 3. 458 *causa...latenti*, 10. 190, and Verg. *Aen.* 5. 5 *causa latet*. The phrase is common in Ovid.

Nemetis: singular for plural. In the time of Pliny and Tacitus (*H.N.* 4. 106, *Germ.* 28, *Ann.* 12. 27) the Nemetes dwelt on the left bank of the Rhine near Speyer, but in the time of Caesar, who mentions them (*B.G.* 1. 51) as part of the army of Ariouistus, they were probably not in this locality (see Rice Holmes, *Caesar's Conquest of Gaul*, 2nd ed. pp. 455–6).

420*. Aturi: the Adour, which flows through Aquae Tarbellicae (Dax) in the modern department of Landes.

421. claudit=*includit*, cf. Ouid. *Fast.* 2. 222 *riparum clausas margine finit aquas*.

Tarbellicus = *Tarbelli*, adjective for noun and at the same time singular for plural. Housman mentions other instances, including Verg. *Aen.* 10. 350 where *Threicios* = *Thraces*. The Tarbelli lived in the modern departments of Landes and Basses Pyrénées, and are spoken of by Strabo (4. 2. 1) as dwelling by a lagoon, which, like the Galatic lagoon, is within the coastline of Gallia Narbonitis (τὸν ἐν τῇ Ναρβωνίτιδι παραλίᾳ Γαλατικόν). These *étangs*, such as the Bassin d'Arcachon in Gironde, are characteristic of the coast there to this day.

422. gaudet: cf. 403. This verb has to carry the weight of the nouns of 422–35 by an extreme example of syllepsis, for which see Introduction, p. lxiii.

Santonus: singular for plural, cf. *Biturix, Leucus, Remus*, etc. The Santoni (Santones acc. to Caes. *B.G.* 1. 10. 1 etc.) occupied the modern departments of Charente and Charente-Inférieure and gave their name to the town of Saintes (Mediolanum). They are mentioned in company with the Tarbelli in Tibull. 1. 7. 9–10.

423. Biturix: the Bituriges consisted of two tribes, the Bituriges Cubi, who occupied the modern departments of Cher and Indre as well as the N.W. part of Allier, and gave the name of Bourges to their capital (Auaricum); and the Bituriges Viuisci in Gironde, whose chief town was Burdigala (Bordeaux).

Suessones: a metrical adaptation of the name Suessiones (cf. the shortening of *u* in *Aturi* as noted in 420 crit. n.). They were a people of Gallia Belgica who lived in the modern departments of Aisne and Oise, and gave their name to Soissons (Nouiodunum or Augusta Suessionum).

in: 'in', *i.e.* 'equipped with', not, as Duff translates, 'in spite of'. This is a Caesarian as well as a poetical usage, cf. *B.G.* 7. 11. 6 *duas legiones in armis excubare iubet*.

armis: synecdoche for *gladiis*, as Farnaby observes. See 398 n. and Introduction, p. liii. Lejay remarks that this description (cf. 424 n.) might well be attributed to the Gauls in general, for they were lightly armed in contrast to the Romans, who were at a disadvantage, as Caesar says (*B.G.* 5. 16. 1), *propter grauitatem armorum*. For the long weapons of the Gauls and other northern barbarians cf. 6. 259 *Cantaber exiguis aut longis Teutonus armis* (mistranslated by Duff), Diod. Sic. 5. 30. 3 σπάθας ἔχουσι μακράς and Strab. 4. 4. 3 μάχαιρα μακρά.

424. excusso...lacerto: a general characteristic of the Gauls (cf. *leues* in the preceding line), who were handy with the *ammentum* or leather thong attached to the javelin. The commentators compare Ouid. *Her.* 4. 43 *tremulum excusso iaculum uibrare lacerto* and *Pont.* 2. 9. 57. The javelin was probably the μάδαρις or *matara* mentioned by Strabo (4. 4. 3) as a παλτοῦ τι εἶδος.

Leucus: the Leuci were a people of Gallia Belgica to the N. of the Lingones, and they inhabited the modern departments of Vosges, Meuse, and Meurthe et Moselle.

Remus: the Remi lay to the N.W. of the Leuci in the department of Marne, and they gave their name to Rheims (Durocortorum). Lejay observes that the submission of the Suessiones to the Remi (Hirt. *B.G.* 8. 6. 2) had its effect later when the bishop of Soissons became subordinate to the archbishop of Rheims.

425. gens...Sequana: the Sequani lived in the modern departments of Jura and Doubs, and their chief town was Vesontio (Besançon). Though the ancient name of the Seine was Sequana, the Sequani did not dwell near its source.

flexis in gyrum...frenis: 'in wheeling their bitted steeds' (Duff). The *gyrus* was the ring used for breaking-in horses, cf. Verg. *Georg.* 3. 115–17, Pseud. Tibull. 4. 1. 91–4, Ouid. *A.A.* 3. 384 *in gyros ire coactus equus*, and Xen. *De Re Equestri* 7. 13–19, where στροφαί are described.

426. monstrati: 'invented by others' (Duff), as Sulpitius correctly explains and *docilis* suggests. Housman compares Verg. *Georg.* 1. 19 *uncique puer (Triptolemus) monstrator aratri*.

couinni: the Britons were the inventors of this type of chariot, as appears from Mel. 3. 52 and Sil. 17. 416–17. For a description of this manner of fighting as employed by the Britons in chariots with the general name of *essedae* see Caes. *B.G.* 4. 33, and for the Belgians cf. Verg. *Georg.* 3. 204 *Belgica uel molli melius feret esseda collo*. According to Mart. 12. 24. 1–2 the *couinnus* was used later in Rome as a carriage.

427. Aruerni: this people inhabited Auvergne, *i.e.* the departments of Haute-Loire, Puy-de-Dôme, and Cantal, and their chief town was Augustonemetum (Clermont-Ferrand). For the confusion with the Aedui, who were in fact rivals of the Aruerni (Caes. *B.G.* 1. 31. 3), see Introduction, p. xlii.

Latio: metonymy for *Latinis* or rather *Romanis*, see 253 n. and compare 8. 234 *iustas Latii...iras*.

428. Iliaco: for the hypallage see Introduction, p. xlviii. Compare Verg. *Aen.* 1. 19–21 *progeniem...Troiano a sanguine...hinc populum* and 6. 875 *Iliaca...de gente Latinos*.

428–9. nimiumque rebellis Neruius: the Neruii inhabited the territory which is now East Flanders and Hainault. Caesar defeated them completely in 57 B.C. (Caes. *B.G.* 2. 16–28), but in 54 Q. Cicero was sent into winter quarters in their country (*id.* 5. 24. 2). At the same time a legion under Q. Titurius Sabinus and L. Aurunculeius Cotta encamped in the territory of the Eburones at Atuatuca (? Tongres). Ambiorix, the chief of that tribe, persuaded them against Cotta's will to leave their camp and go to that of Cicero or Labienus, but treacherously cut them to pieces in open country, where Cotta was slain (*id.* 5. 37). The Neruii then joined the Eburones (*ibid.* 38) and attacked Cicero's camp (*ibid.* 39) without success, but next year were reduced by Caesar (*id.* 6. 3). They sent, however, 5000 men to help in relieving the siege of Alesia in 52 (*id.* 7. 75).

429. foedere: see the Critical Apparatus.

430. Sarmata: cf. Val. Flacc. 5. 424 *Sarmaticis permutant carbasa bracis*.

bracis: cf. Ouid. *Trist.* 5. 7. 49 *pellibus et laxis arcent mala frigora bracis*. This trousered dress, which was common to the Gallic nations, is mentioned by Strabo (4. 4. 3) as well as by Polybius (2. 28. 7) in his description of the battle of Telamon (225 B.C.). The Greek name of this garment was ἀναξυρίδες, which Herodotus uses also of the similar Eastern and Scythian dress (3. 87, 7. 64 etc.). Diodorus Siculus (5. 30. 1), however, employs the Latin word in speaking of the clothes of the Gauls: χρῶνται... χιτῶσι...καὶ ἀναξυρίσιν, ἃς ἐκεῖνοι βράκας προσαγορεύουσι. Transalpine Gaul, especially Narbonensis, was known once as *Gallia Bracata* (Mel. 2. 74, Plin. *H.N.* 3. 31).

431. Vangiones: mentioned by Caesar (*B.G.* 1. 51. 2) among the Germans. They probably lived on both sides of the Rhine, *i.e.* in the Palatinate and Hesse around the modern town of Worms.

Batăui: see the Critical Apparatus. The *insula Batauorum* is mentioned in Caes. *B.G.* 4. 10. 1, and it was enclosed apparently by the Waal, the Meuse, and the main stream of the Rhine (Rice

Holmes, *Caesar's Conquest of Gaul*, 2nd ed. p. 694). The Bataui lived, then, in modern Zeeland and South Holland.

truces: cf. Tac. *Germ.* 29 *uirtute praecipui Bataui...tantum in usum proeliorum sepositi...bellis reseruantur.*

aere recuruo: an Ovidian phrase (*Rem.* 210, *Fast.* 6. 240). Lejay, who cites Eustathius on Hom. *Il.* 18. 219 and Diod. Sic. 5. 30. 3, observes that the Gaulish trumpet was curved first slightly upwards, then downwards, and ended in the fantastic head of an animal. Eustathius on Hom. *Il.* 18. 219 mentions that its Greek name was κάρνυξ.

432. stridentes acuere tubae: cf. 237 and Verg. *Aen.* 12. 590 *magnisque acuunt stridoribus iras.*

acuere: a frequentative perfect, see 175 n.

Cinga: see Introduction, p. xli and 399 n.

pererrat: see Introduction, p. xli n.

433-4. Compare 399-401 and consult the notes *ad loc.*, as well as Introduction, p. xli. For the sluggishness of the Arar see Caes. *B.G.* 1. 12. Haskins mentions the comparison drawn by the elder Pitt between the coalition of Newcastle and Henry Fox and the meeting of the Rhone and the Saône.

435*. pendentes either = *inpendentes*, or else this participial adjective is transferred by hypallage from the people to the mountains (see 464 n.). Compare Verg. *Ecl.* 1. 76 (*capellas*) *pendere procul de rupe uidebo* (a context which was probably in Lucan's mind here) imitated by Ovid (*Pont.* 1. 8. 51 *pendentes...rupe capellas*).

cana...rupe: ablative of description if *pendentes* = 'overhanging'. For the snow of the Cevennes cf. Caes. *B.G.* 7. 8. 2 *mons Ceuenna, qui Aruernos ab Heluiis discludit, durissimo tempore anni, altissima niue iter impediebat.*

436-40. See the Critical Apparatus.

441. laetatus: Housman, who cites several examples of the ellipse of the second person of *sum* in Lucan and other poets, observes that *es* must be supplied.

conuerti: *i.e. ex Gallia in Italiam* (Weise).

Treuir: the Treuiri inhabited S.E. Belgium, the Grand Duchy of Luxembourg and the Saar valley. They gave their name to Trier (Trèves).

442-3. Ligur...Comatae: the Ligures occupied not merely S.W. Cisalpine Gaul but also Transalpine Gaul between the Alpes Maritimes and the valley of the Rhone. Being contained in the *prouincia* they had of course given up the barbarous practice of letting their hair grow long. This practice caused Transalpine Gaul

to be called *Gallia Comata* in distinction from Cisalpine Gaul or
Gallia Togata (see Cic. *Phil.* 8. 9. 27 *Galliam Togatam remitto,
Comatam postulo*). Compare Plin. *H.N.* 4. 105 *Gallia omnis Comata
uno nomine appellata* and Suet. *Iul.* 22 *Galliam Cisalpinam...
accepit* (*Caesar*), *mox per senatum Comatam quoque.*

442. **decore**: the adverb is rare in poetry, though Cicero used
it in his *Aratea* (444) and *De Cons. Suo* 55 (ap. *Diu.* 1. 20).

443. **crinibus effusis**: ablative of cause, see 249n.

444–6. For a full discussion of the matter of these lines, including the Celtic triad of deities, the cult of Diana at Nemi, and
the punctuation and reading of 446 see Appendix D.

444. **diro**: 'accursed', *i.e.* because it was human blood, cf.
3. 404–5 *structae diris altaribus arae, | omnisque humanis lustrata
cruoribus arbor* (Haskins).

447. **animas**: 'souls' in sense of 'human beings', 'men', cf.
5. 322 (*seditio*) *detegit inbelles animas* and Hor. *Serm.* 1. 5. 40–2
*Plotius et Varius Sinuessae Vergiliusque | occurrunt, animae, quales
neque candidiores | terra tulit*, etc.

448. **uates**: see 449n.

dimittitis: 'hand down'. Oudendorp compares Stat. *Theb.*
1. 185 *augurium seros dimisit ad usque nepotes*, and Lejay Sen. *Ep.*
31. 10 *in populos nominis dimissa notitia*.

449. **fudistis carmina**: cf. Tac. *Ann.* 14. 30 *Druidaeque circum
preces diras sublatis ad caelum manibus fundentes.*

Bardi: a similar statement is found in Amm. Marc. 15. 9. 8 *et Bardi
quidem fortia uirorum illustrium facta heroicis composita uersibus cum
dulcibus lyrae modulis cantitarunt.* Strabo (4. 4. 4) mentions three
classes, namely Bards, Vates, and Druids, viz. βάρδοι μὲν ὑμνηταὶ καὶ
ποιηταί, Οὐάτεις δὲ ἱεροποιοὶ καὶ φυσιολόγοι, Δρυΐδαι δὲ πρὸς τῇ φυσιολογίᾳ
καὶ τὴν ἠθικὴν φιλοσοφίαν ἀσκοῦσι. His account is taken from Poseidonius (for whom see Athenaeus 6, p. 246 c), who travelled in Gaul
in the early part of the first century B.C. The three classes appear in
Diod. Sic. 5. 31 as Βάρδοι, Μάντεις, and Δρυΐδαι (or Δρουίδαι).

450. **barbaricos ritus**: these are alluded to in Caes. *B.G.* 6. 16,
Tac. *Ann.* 14. 30, Strab. 4. 4. 5, and Diod. Sic. 5. 31. 3.

451. **Dryadae**: for the derivation from δρῦς, 'oak', see Plin.
H.N. 16. 249, and for a good discussion of the Druids consult Rice
Holmes, *Caesar's Conquest of Gaul*, 2nd ed. pp. 523–9. Caesar
seems to use the spelling *Druides* (see *Thes. Ling. Lat.* v, 2070), but
the MSS of Lucan with few exceptions (see Lejay's critical apparatus) favour *dry-* or *dri-*.

positis repetistis ab armis: 'laid aside their arms and went back to their barbarous rites' (to drop the apostrophe in the translation). *Ab* the ablative of origin is dictated as much by the necessities of metre as is *ab* instrumental, which is mentioned in Heitland's *Introd.* p. civ. Haskins compares Ouid. *Her.* 3. 95 *ille ferox positis secessit ab armis.* Lucan seems to imply that the Druids, who usually refrained from warfare (Caes. *B.G.* 6. 14. 1), had been in arms lately against the Romans; and this supports the contention of Jullian and Rice Holmes (*op. cit.* p. 527) that they took part in the rebellion of 52 B.C.

452. solis: not 'alone among mankind' as most commentators say, but 'alone among the Gauls', cf. Caes. *B.G.* 6. 14 and Mel. 3. 19 (*Druidae*) *quid dei uelint scire profitentur.*

nosse deos: cf. 639–40 and 3. 417. Caesar (*B.G.* 6. 13. 4) observes *illi rebus diuinis intersunt, sacrificia publica ac priuata procurant, religiones interpretantur.*

453*. aut solis nescire datum est: like *solis* in the preceding line, this phrase is often wrongly explained by commentators. *Nescire* = 'not to know' who the gods were whom they worshipped, cf. 3. 415–17 (a passage which describes a sacred grove near Marseilles) *non uolgatis sacrata figuris | numina sic metuunt: tantum terroribus addit, | quos timeant, non nosse deos.*

453–4. nemora...lucis: for the juxtaposition of these two nouns of similar meaning cf. 227 n. Haskins compares Prop. 4. 9. 24 *lucus ubi umbroso fecerat orbe nemus,* and Burman Ouid. *Met.* 3. 175–6 *per nemus...errans | peruenit in lucum* together with other passages from the same poet.

remotis...lucis: cf. Mel. 3. 19 (*Druidae*) *docent multa...clam et diu...aut in specu aut in abditis saltibus.*

454. uobis auctoribus: 'according to your teaching' (Haskins). Compare 485 and Hor. *Carm.* 1. 28. 14–15 *iudice te non sordidus auctor | naturae uerique.*

455. profundi: see the Critical Apparatus.

455–6. tacitas Erebi sedes...petunt: cf. Ouid. *Met.* 15. 772 *sedesque intrare silentum.*

Ditisque...regna: Housman compares *Aetna* 78 *Ditis pallentia regna,* to which add Pseud. Tibull. 3. 1. 28 *pallida Ditis aqua.* The passage is reminiscent of Verg. *Aen.* 4. 25–6 *ad umbras | pallentis umbras Erebi noctemque profundam.*

456. regit idem spiritus artus: cf. Verg. *Aen.* 4. 336 *dum spiritus hos regit artus.*

457. **orbe alio**: Lejay with others understands 'in some other region', which is the meaning of the expression in 6. 579 and 8. 315 (see 252 n.), and thinks of lands beyond the Ocean, such as are mentioned in accounts in Celtic literature of voyages like that of St. Brendan. Haskins's rendering 'in a new cycle' has, however, as much probability, cf. Verg. *Aen.* 6. 745 *perfecto temporis orbe* and the following lines in which Plato's cycle of a thousand years is recalled. Lucan's knowledge, as usual, may be inexpert here and contaminated with a recollection of the Vergilian passage.

For the Druid doctrine of the transmigration of souls see Caes. *B.G.* 6. 14 *in primis hoc uolunt persuadere, non interire animas, sed ab aliis post mortem transire ad alios, atque hoc maxime ad uirtutem excitari putant, metu mortis neglecto* (cf. 460 *infr.*), as well as Mel. 3. 19, Val. Max. 2. 6. 10, Amm. Marc. 15. 9. 8, Strab. 4. 4. 4, Diod. Sic. 5. 28. 5–6, and Diog. Laert. *Prohoem.* 6.

longae: 'continuous' (Duff).

cognita = *certa*, see Reid on Cic. *Acad.* 2. 6. 16.

458. **media**: Lejay compares 6. 99 *nec medii dirimunt morbi uitamque necemque*, to which add 6. 610 *medios...abrumpimus annos* ('we break his life off in the middle').

quos despicit Arctos: Lucan, who probably is drawing from Poseidonius, means that the northern tribes are especially warlike, cf. Strab. 4. 4. 2 ἀεὶ δὲ οἱ προσβορρότεροι καὶ παρωκεανῖται μαχιμώτεροι.

459. **ille**: almost the definite article, which this demonstrative became in vulgar Latin and in the Romance languages (Fr. *-le*, Ital. *il-*, etc.), see Postgate, 'Flaws in Classical Research' (*Proc. Brit. Acad.* iii), p. 20, n. 2.

459–60. **timorum...metus**: for the juxtaposition cf. 453–4 n. Disdain of death, of which Lucan as a Stoic approved, appears excellently in Pompey's dying thoughts (8. 622–35, especially 630 *sum tamen, o superi, felix*), and in Lentulus's words (8. 395–6) *mors ultima poena est | nec metuenda uiris*. Compare also the discussion in Sen. *N.Q.* 6. 32.

460. **leti metus**: for this and what follows cf. Ouid. *Met.* 7. 604–5 *mortisque timorem | morte fugant*.

ruendi: to be taken with *mens* rather than with *prona* according to Housman, who compares 6. 1 *pugnae...mente* and 9. 226 *mente fugae*. If *promus* is used with the genitive here, it is a neologism.

460–1. **ruendi in ferrum**: cf. Verg. *Georg.* 2. 503–4 *ruuntque | in ferrum*.

461–2. **capaces mortis**: 'great enough for death' (Haskins), cf. Sil. 11. 171–2 (*animae Romanorum*) *capiunt...Pauli memorabile letum*, where *capiunt = recipiunt* in prose (see Gronov. *Obs*. 1. 17). The construction of *capax* with the genitive is in the first instance Ovidian, cf. *A.A.* 1. 136 *capax populi...circus*, and occurs elsewhere in Lucan at 512 and 10. 183 *mundique capacior hospes*. Haskins compares Shakespeare's use of 'capable', *e.g. King John* 3. 1. 12 'For I am sick and capable of fears'.

462. **ignauum rediturae parcere uitae**: 'the thought that it is cowardly to be careful of a life that will return'. For this omission, not unnatural after *mens*, of a verb of 'thinking', compare such instances of the accusative and infinitive of exclamation as the well-known example in Verg. *Aen*. 1. 37–8 (cf. 510 *infr*.).

463. **crinigeros**: a neologism, which Silius (14. 585) and Claudian later adopted. Once again Lucan is assigning an epithet which is true generally of the barbarians of Gaul and Germany to a particular tribe, see Introduction, p. liv and 402, 423, 424, 430, as well as 442–3 n.

bellis: 'by force of arms', see 277 n. and Introduction, p. xlix. Bentley's emendation *Belgis* implies that the Chauci were prone to wage war on the Belgians, but Tac. *Germ*. 35 (*Chauci*) *quieti secretique nulla prouocant bella* can hardly be said to support a view which is also Housman's. M. Bourgery well remarks: 'il s'agissait moins de protéger les Belges, à peine subjugués, que de tenir les Germains en respect', and this observation is supported by 8. 423–4 (*cit. infr*. 465 n.). See *C.Q*. xxx, 1936, p. 59, n. 4.

arcere: for the epexegetic use of the infinitive see Heitland, *Introd*. p. cv. With this construction of *opponi* contrast 220–1.

Caycos: a variant spelling of *Chaucos*. For the geographical position of the Chauci and the possibility that the name may be used here by synecdoche for *Germanos* see Introduction, p. xliii.

464–5. **petitis...deseritis**: the figure hysteron proteron (so called), see Introduction, p. lxv.

464. **feroces**: the epithet is transferred (see 435 n.) from the inhabitants of the banks (cf. 308), *i.e.* the Chauci, to the banks themselves. Compare Hor. *Carm*. 1. 35. 10 *Latium ferox*. Housman cites Ouid. *Pont*. 4. 9. 76 *ripa ferox Histri sub duce tuta fuit*.

465. **apertum**: proleptic.

gentibus: 'barbarian nations', see 9 n. and 288–9 n.

orbem: the Roman world, cf. 110 and 285. Cortius compares 8. 423–5 *ne qua uacarent | arma, uel Arctoum Dacis Rhenique cateruis | imperii nudare latus*.

466. Caesar, ut...: cf. 392.

inmensae conlecto robore uires: the action of Caesar's march on Rome is not resumed until 2. 439, when the march through Etruria and Umbria to Auximum, Asculum, Nuceria, and Corfinium is described. Unless Lucan is speaking very generally of the events of the next few weeks, these words can refer only to the 13th legion (see Introduction, p. xxxiii).

conlecto robore: cf. Verg. *Georg.* 3. 235–6 *post, ubi conlectum robur uiresque refectae, | signa mouet.*

467. audendi maiora: a Vergilian phrase (*Aen.* 10. 811, 12. 814).

fidem fecere: 'gave him confidence', *i.e. fidem = fiduciam*, which is metrically inconvenient. Compare Liu. 33. 14. 5 *fiduciam Androstheni fecerunt acie decernendi*. This meaning of *fidem facere* is not properly distinguished in *Thes. Ling. Lat.* vi, 687. Normally the phrase = 'to cause belief', 'convince', *e.g.* 5. 141–2 *fecitque...metus ipse fidem*, Cic. *Brut.* 187 *fidem facit oratio*, and Ouid. *Met.* 6. 566 *lacrimae fecere fidem*. For the fluctuations in Lucan of the meaning of *fides* see Heitland, *Introd.* p. cii.

468. spargitur: *Caesar* is of course used by synecdoche for *Caesaris milites.*

470. inrupitque animos: cf. Sen. *Ben.* 3. 3. 2 *inrumpit animum aliorum admiratio.*

populi = *populi Romani*, cf. 2, 171, 179, etc.

471. nuntia: for the application of this epithet to *fama* cf. Verg. *Aen.* 4. 188 (*Fama*) *nuntia ueri*, and with Lucan's *innumeras linguas* cf. Vergil's *multiplici...sermone* (*ibid.* 189).

472. soluit...linguas: cf. Ouid. *Met.* 3. 261 *linguam ad iurgia soluens.*

praeconia: cf. Ouid. *Her.* 17. 207 *uolucris praeconia famae.*

473. tauriferis: a neologism. Oudendorp compares Sil. 6. 647 *sedet ingentem pascens Meuania taurum.*

Meuania: the modern Bevagna in Umbria near the birthplace of Propertius (4. 1. 123 *qua nebulosa cauo rorat Meuania campo*).

474. turmas: the *turma* was a cavalry division. During the Empire the *ala* (cf. 476) was composed of 24 *turmae* of 40 men each, or 16 of 30 men each, according to whether it was *milliaria* or *quingenaria.*

475. adferat: upon this verb depends the reported speech of 473–84, as the punctuation for the first time in any text shows.

Nar: the modern Nera.

476. barbaricas...alas: Lucan may be thinking expressly of such foreign cavalry as was sent to Caesar by the king of Noricum, cf. Caes. *B.C.* 1. 18 *equitesque ab rege Norico circiter ccc.* According to Plut. *Caes.* 32. 1, when Caesar left Ravenna, he had not more than 300 horse, and these were probably Gallic levies.

478–84. For a full discussion of these lines see *C.Q.* xxx, 1936, p. 60.

478. **densis...castris**: 'with camps pitched close together', cf. Caes. *B.G.* 7. 46. 3 *superiorem partem collis...densissimis castris conpleuerant.*

479. **maior**: just as figures seen in dreams appeared larger than life-size (see 186 n.), so the Romans conjured up before their fearful minds a picture of Caesar greater than he really was, because of his conquests.

ferus: positive with the force of a comparative, as is shown by the complementary *maior* and *inmanior*. The comparative and superlative of *ferus* are wanting, and are usually replaced by the corresponding degrees of *ferox.*

480. **uictoque inmanior hoste**: 'more terrible than ever (cf. 554 n.) from the conquest of the foe'. For the ablative of cause with *inmanior* compare Verg. *Aen.* 1. 347 *Pygmalion scelere ante alios inmanior omnes* and Val. Flacc. 2. 614–15 *Asiamque prementem | effugit abruptis Europa inmanior oris.* Similar examples of this ablative may be seen in 443 and 4. 642 *maiorque accepto robore surgit.*

481*. **tunc** = *mox, deinde*, cf. 508 and 608.

Alpemque: see Introduction, p. xliii.

482. **reuolsos**: cf. 8. 309 *effundam populos alia tellure reuolsos* and Ouid. *Met.* 11. 554–5 *Athon Pindumue reuolsos | sede sua.*

483. **pone sequi**: cf. Vergil's *pone sequens* (*Georg.* 4. 487, *Aen.* 10. 226).

484. **Romano**: *i.e.* Caesar (by antonomasia, for which see Introduction, p. lvii). Similarly in 10. 268 he is addressed *Romane* by Acoreus. Compare 637 *Tuscus* (*i.e.* Arruns).

484–9. These lines were quoted aptly with reference to events in France by Sheridan in the House of Commons on March 4, 1793.

484–5. **quisque...famae**: a new presentation of Vergil's (*Fama*) *uires adquirit eundo* (*Aen.* 4. 175).

485. **nulloque auctore malorum**: 'with none to confirm the ill tidings' (Haskins). See 454 n.

486. **timent**: for the change from the singular of the preceding *quisque...dat* to the plural, cf. 242 n.

487. curia: see 267 n.

et ipsi: see 291 n.

489. In fact the consuls as well as the senators fled from Rome on Jan. 18, the day after Pompey's departure for Capua. If, as is likely, *decreta* alludes to the *senatus consultum ultimum* of Jan. 7 (Caes. *B.C.* 1. 5) whereby the consuls, proconsuls, praetors, and tribunes were authorized to act in defence of the Republic and a state of war was declared against Caesar, Lucan's account is again not accurate.

490. tum: see the Critical Apparatus.

491–2*. urguent praecipitem populum: 'they hurry the people into headlong flight' (Haskins).

492. haerentia = *cohaerentia*, cf. Curt. 7. 3. 21 *iuga uelut serie cohaerentia*.

longa: ablative, cf. Verg. *Aen.* 1. 641 *series longissima rerum*.

493. nefandas: because aimed against Rome, cf. 2 n. There may be an unconscious reminiscence here of the phraseology of Ouid. *Her.* 11. 102–3 *fuge turbato tecta nefanda pede.* | *ferte faces in me.*

494. ruina: of the tendency to fall by an earthquake shock, cf. Verg. *Aen.* 3. 414 *loca ui…et uasta conuolsa ruina.*

495. pendere: cf. 24.

496. uelut: 'thinking that', cf. the similar use of *tamquam* in Latin of the Silver Age.

497. excedere: the transitive use of this verb is not earlier than Livy in prose and Ovid in poetry, and is common in Seneca. Ovid indeed constructs *excedere* with the accusative of abstract nouns only (*Met.* 6. 197 *metum* and 7. 166 *fidem*).

498. turbidus Auster: cf. 234 and Hor. *Carm.* 3. 3. 4–5 *Auster* | *dux inquieti turbidus Hadriae.* With the simile which follows M. Bourgery compares Plut. *Caes.* 33 (of Rome before Caesar's arrival) ἐν πολλῷ κλύδωνι καὶ σάλῳ μικρὸν ἀπολιπεῖν αὐτὴν ὑφ' αὑτῆς ἀνατετράφθαι.

499. reppulit: cf. Ouid. *Met.* 15. 292 (*pontus*) *media tellurem reppulit unda.* When the storm raged, the sea was driven by the S. wind away from the quicksands, cf. 9. 322–3 (*Auster*) *longe a Syrtibus undas* | *egit.*

This line and 503 are discussed in *C.Q.* xxx, 1936, p. 61, where *inmensum* is defended against Bentley's less significant (in spite of Hor. *Epod.* 10. 5) *inuersum. Inmensum* aptly describes the sea round the Syrtes, where the land is far away, cf. 9. 341 *procul omnibus aruis* and 344 *litora nulla uident.* Just as the sailors here too do not see the shore when they leap into the vast sea, so the senators and people have no idea where they are going (490–1 *quae tuta petant. . .incerti*).

500. Translate: 'and the heavy mast which carries the sails breaks with a crack'.

502. **nauitaque**: singular for plural.

503. **naufragium sibi quisque facit**: 'each man makes shipwreck (*i.e.* wrecks the ship) to save himself'; in other words the sailors break off or snatch at any loose piece of timber and thus help to wreck the ship in order to support themselves in the water. Similarly at the siege of Massilia the combatants broke up their ships in order to obtain missiles, cf. 3. 674 *in pugnam fregere rates*. To the passages cited in *C.Q. loc. cit. supr.* 499n. may be added Ouid. *Trist.* 1. 6. 8 *naufragii tabulas qui petiere mei*, Curt. 9. 9. 20 *auolsarum tabularum remorumque fragmentis*, *Octauia* 324–5 *alii lacerae puppis tabulis | haerent nudi fluctusque secant*, and especially Sil. 14. 543–7 *hic robore fracto | pugnat inops chalybis* seseque *in proelia rursus* | armat naufragio; *remis male feruidus ille | festinat spoliare ratem, discrimine nullo | nautarum interdum conuolsa sedilia torquens*. With the active and passive meanings of *naufragium facere* compare *silentium facere*, for which see Conington on Pers. 4. 7.

504. **in bellum fugitur**: 'flight is the preparation for war' (Duff). For *in* see 262, 292, 306n., and 312; and for Lucan's love of antithesis consult Heitland, *Introd.* pp. lxxix–lxxx.

nullum: *natum* must be understood with *parens* to balance *coniunx* and *maritum*. See Introduction, p. lxiii and compare Verg. *Aen.* 11. 160–1 *contra ego uiuendo uici mea fata, superstes | restarem ut genitor* (sc. *nato*). The omission of one of four such terms is not very common, *e.g.* Lucan has all four expressed in 4. 563 *fratribus incurrunt fratres natusque parenti*. *Nullum* must be taken also with 507 *tenuere*, but in the sense of *neminem*, cf. 2. 254 *nullum furor egit in arma*.

505. **euatuit**: compound for simple verb. Note that the able-bodied men ran away, leaving their wives and aged parents behind them. Lejay observes that a criticism of this cowardice as depicted by Lucan is implied in Petron. *Bell. Ciu.* 229–31 *sunt qui coniugibus maerentia pectora iungant, | grandaeuosque patres onerisque ignara iuuentus | id pro quo metuit, tantum trahit*.

reuocare: cf. 509 *inreuocabile*.

506. **dubiae**: 'uncertain', cf. Ouid. *Her.* 9. 41–2 *aucupor infelix incertae murmura famae, | speque timor dubia, spesque timore cadit* and *Met.* 15. 438 (*Aeneae*) *flenti dubioque salutis*.

507. conciperent: Housman compares Ter. *Andr.* 626–7 and Liu. 4. 35. 9 for the plural verb in the subordinate clause when the singular *quisquam* or *nemo* occurs in the principal sentence. See 242 n. and 486 n.

limine: cf. Verg. *Aen.* 2. 673–4 *in limine coniunx | haerebat.* Here again Petronius seems to imply a criticism of Lucan in *Bell. Ciu.* 226–8 *ille manu pauida natos tenet, ille penates | occultat gremio deploratumque relinquit | limen.*

508. extremo: compare the description of Pompey's departure from Italy in 3. 4–6. Haskins mentions Liu. 1. 29. 3 *nunc in liminibus starent, nunc errabundi domos suas ultimum illud uisuri peruagarentur.*

forsitan: this adverb qualifies the adjective *extremo*.

510. faciles: cf. Sen. *Ep.* 101. 13 *quid huic optes nisi deos faciles?* and *Oed.* 198–9 *solum hoc (i.e. mori) faciles | tribuere dei.*

dare … tueri: for the epexegetic infinitive in Lucan see 164–5 n. and cf. 2. 656 *Roma capi facilis.* This usage with *facilis* is not earlier in poetry than Propertius (1. 11. 12, 2. 21. 15, 4. 8. 40) and Ovid (*A.A.* 1. 358), and in prose than Seneca (*De Ira* 2. 36. 5).

511. populis: the Italian cities which had received Roman citizenship, cf. Mart. 12. 6. 5 *populi gentesque tuae, pia Roma* (Housman).

513. Caesare: ablative for dative by antiptosis, for which see Introduction, p. lxiv.

514. manus: 'hands', cf. 9. 26 *ignauis manibus proiectos reddidit enses.*

517. rapti: 'seized hastily', cf. Verg. *Aen.* 8. 220 *rapit arma manu.*

agger: cf. 5. 316–17 *aggere fulti | caespitis.* The *agger* was the embankment of earth and turf upon which were set palisades (*ualli*), the whole then forming the *uallum* (516).

518. somnos: 'nights of sleep', see 520 *nox una* and cf. 4. 603–4 *ad somnos non terga ferae praebere cubile | adsuerunt.*

519. tantum: the adverb qualifies *audito*.

520. muris: Haskins observes that at this time Rome of course had extended so far beyond the Servian walls that it was practically an unwalled city.

522. Pompeio fugiente timent: cf. Petron. *Bell. Ciu.* 238–44 *quid tam parua queror? gemino cum consule Magnus, | ille tremor Ponti…, | pro pudor, imperii deserto nomine fugit, | ut Fortuna leuis Magni quoque terga uideret.* Cicero seems to contradict the impression received from Lucan that Pompey's flight struck terror into the hearts of the Romans, for he speaks of it as strengthening their resolve to resist Caesar in *Att.* 7. 11. 4 . . . *uidetur hoc consilium (Pompei) exitum habiturum:.,. fugiens denique Pompeius mirabiliter homines mouet. quid quaeris? alia causa facta est: nihil iam concedendum putant Caesari.*

522–83. This passage should be compared in detail with those describing the portents at the time of Caesar's death, *i.e.* Verg. *Georg.* 1. 463–92 and Ouid. *Met.* 15. 779–802, as well as with Tibull. 2. 5. 71–8.

523. **saltem**: to be taken with *futuri, i.e.* 'they were desperate of the present, and the prodigies prevented their having any hope of the future either' (Haskins). Compare Petron. *Bell. Ciu.* 246 *consensitque fugae caeli timor.*

524. **manifesta fides**: a Vergilian expression (*Aen.* 2. 309, 3. 375).

526. **ignota. . .sidera**: *i.e.* the meteors and the comet which are described in the following lines.

527–8. The theme is **ardentemque polum flammis**, and the variation **caeloque uolantes. . .faces**. It is better to take the construction in this way and assume that *polum* = 'sky' generally (see 47n.), than to understand *polum* of the North Pole and *flammis* of the Aurora Borealis. For the infrequency of this phenomenon in Greece and Italy and for the rarity of references to it in classical literature see Pease on Cic. *Diu.* 1. 18 (*Ed.* pp. 105–6).

With the whole context compare Lucr. 5. 1191 *noctiuagaeque faces caeli flammaeque uolantes*, Sen. *N.Q.* 1. 1. 3–4 and 6. 3. 3 *actde in transuersum faces et caeli magna pars ardens et crinita sidera et plures solis orbes et stellae per diem uisae* (cf. 535–7 *infr.*) *subitique transcursus ignium multam post se lucem trahentium.*

528. **per inane**: a Lucretian expression (1. 1018, etc.).

faces: 'meteors'. For these as omens of war cf. Cic. *Cons. Suo* 20 (ap. *Diu.* 1. 18) *Phoebi fax, tristis nuntia belli.*

crinem: used of the tail of a comet, cf. Verg. *Aen.* 5. 528 *crinemque uolantia sidera ducunt* and Ouid. *Met.* 15. 849–50 *flammiferumque trahens. . .crinem | stella micat.* For mythological explanations of the 'hair' of comets see Frazer on Ouid. *Fast.* 4. 175, and for a description of them in general and of the *lampas* (532 *infr.*) in particular consult Sen. *N.Q.* 1. 15. 4, 6. 3. 3, 7. 4. 3, 7. 20. 1.

529. The theme is **sideris** and the variation **cometen** (cf. 530–1 *fulgura. . .ignis*), so that *et* = 'even'. Compare the Tacitean expression (*Ann.* 14. 22, 15. 47) *sidus cometes* = 'comet'.

mutantem regna: comets were supposed to foretell war, revolution, and the death of monarchs and emperors such as Julius Caesar, Claudius, and Nero. See Sen. *N.Q.* 7. 17. 2 (this book is devoted to comets), Plin. *H.N.* 2. 92, Tac. *Ann.* 14. 22, and Suet. *Ner.* 36, as well as Val. Flacc. 6. 607–8 *iratoque uocati* | *ab Ioue fatales ad regna iniusta cometae*, Stat. *Theb.* 1. 708 *quae mutent sceptra cometae*, and Sil. 1. 461, 8. 637. Haskins compares Shakespeare, *King Rich. II* 2. 4. 15 'These signs forerun the death or fall of kings'. See Pease on Cic. *Diu.* 1. 18 (*Ed.* p. 106) for a fuller discussion of the ominous character of comets.

530. **fulgura**: for lightning as a portent see Sen. *N.Q.* 2. 32 sqq.
fallaci...sereno: cf. Verg. *Aen.* 5. 851 *deceptus fraude sereni* (with *fallacibus auris* in the preceding line), but in *Aen.* 9. 630–1 *audiit et caeli Genitor de parte serena* | *intonuit laeuum* the omen was good because the thunder was on the left. Thunder in a clear sky converted Horace to his allegiance to the gods, cf. *Carm.* 1. 34. 5–8. *Sereno* is explained by 533, and for its use as a substantive cf. 4. 55 *tellus hiberno dura sereno* and 9. 423 *nostris reficit sua rura serenis*.

531. **denso**: see the Critical Apparatus. Housman compares Sen. *N.Q.* 7. 21. 1 *cometas, sicut faces, sicut tubas trabesque et alia ostenta caeli, denso aere creari*.

532. Lucan means that the *ignis* (sc. *fulguris*) took various forms: at one time its light was long and thin like a javelin, and at another it spread out like a torch.
iaculum: cf. Mart. Cap. 2. 151 *plerumque enim quaerentes admonent uel sideris cursu uel fulminis iaculo*.
lampas: cf. 10. 502–3 *solet aetherio lampas decurrere sulco* | *materiaque carens atque ardens aere solo*, Manil. 1. 846 (*ignis*) *lampadas et fissas ramosos fundit in ignes*, Sen. *N.Q.* 1. 15. 4, and Plin. *H.N.* 2. 96 *duo genera earum: lampadas uocant plane faces*.

533. **tacitum**: thunder and lightning were thought to be produced by the clouds as they clashed together (see 151 n.), so that any lightning at all (and especially lightning without thunder) in a cloudless sky was indeed an omen. Compare Lucr. 6. 99–101 and Ouid. *Met.* 8. 339. In the same way thunderbolts did not normally fall when the sky was cloudless, cf. Lucr. 6. 400–1 and Sen. *N.Q.* 2. 26. 7. See Pease on Cic. *Diu.* 1. 18 (*Ed.* p. 109).
sine nubibus: cf. Ouid. *A.A.* 3. 173 *sine nubibus aer*.

534*. **Arctois**: Caesar's advent from the north was, of course, portended by the bolt from that quarter. In the same way before the battle of Cannae lightning flashed from the direction of Africa, see Sil. 8. 650–1 *axe super medio, Libyes a parte, coruscae | in Latium uenere faces.*

535. **Latiare**: see 198 n.

caput: this word may be applied to the summit of hills or mountains, cf. Verg. *Aen.* 4. 249 (*Atlantis*) *piniferum caput.*

stellaeque minores: the heavenly bodies lesser than the sun and moon, *i.e.* the planets and possibly the fixed stars. Lejay compares Hor. *Carm.* 1. 12. 46–8 *micat inter omnes | Iulium sidus uelut inter ignes | luna minores.*

536. **uacuum**: sc. *sole* by the trope *e sequentibus praecedentia*, and translate 'when the sun is absent'.

decurrere: 'to run their courses', cf. Manil. 1. 505 (*Orion contentus*) *toto semper decurrere mundo.*

537. **cornuque coacto**: 'with horns brought together' (Haskins), *i.e.* with her disc completed at full moon: so *toto...ore* in the next line. Compare Ouid. *Met.* 7. 179–80 *tres aberant noctes, ut cornua tota coirent | efficerentque orbem* and *id.* 530–1 *quater iunctis expleuit cornibus orbem | luna, quater plenum tenuata retexuit orbem.* It will be remembered that when Caesar crossed the Rubicon the moon was more than two days old (see 218), so that, if Lucan is accurate, the full moon and eclipse would have taken place some twelve days later. See *C.Q.* xxx, 1936, p. 58.

538*. **redderet**: 'reflected', cf. Ouid. *Met.* 2. 109–10 *gemmae (i.e. currus Solis) | clara repercusso reddebant lumina Phoebo.*

539. **terrarum** = *orbis terrarum.* For eclipses of the moon see 6. 500–4, Lucr. 5. 762 sqq., and Claud. *Bell. Goth.* 235–6 *nec credunt uetito fraudatam Sole sororem | telluris subeunte globo.* The true explanation of eclipses seems to go back to Anaxagoras (Heath, *Greek Astronomy*, p. xxxiii). For an account of that before the battle of Gaugamela see Cic. *Diu.* 1. 121.

subita: for the suddenness of the pallor during the brief period of totality cf. Cic. *Cons. Suo* 19 (ap. *Diu.* 1. 18) *subito stellanti nocte (luna) perempta est.*

percussa: cf. Lucr. 5. 705 *luna potest solis radiis percussa nitere.*

expalluit: an excellent verb to describe the copper colour of the moon in total eclipse. Petronius's version is (*Bell. Ciu.* 130–1) *parte alia plenos exstinxit Cynthia uoltus, | et lucem sceleri subduxit.*

umbra: cf. Cic. *Diu.* 2. 17 (*luna*) *incurrat in umbram terrae.*

540. **caput...Titan**: cf. Ouid. *Met.* 15. 30 *candidus Oceano nitidum caput abdiderat Sol.*

medio...Olympo: 'in the Zodiac', see 58 n. and cf. 9. 543 *et*

fuga signorum medio rapit omnia caelo and Verg. *Aen.* 10. 216
Phoebe medium pulsabat Olympum.

ferret = *efferret*, cf. Ouid. *Met.* 15. 31 *et caput extulerat densissima sidereum Nox.*

541. Compare Verg. *Aen.* 11. 187 *conditur in tenebras altum caligine caelum.*

542. **orbem**: 'his own orb'.

543. **fugiente** = *refugiente*, as in Prop. 4. 6. 15 *fugiens Athamana ad litora portus.* The verb *fugere* may be used also of the setting of a heavenly body, cf. 9. 941 (*Phoebe*) *surgens fugiensque* and Ouid. *Am.* 1. 5. 5 *sublucent fugiente crepuscula Phoebo.*

per = *in*, see Introduction, p. lxv and cf. 683.

544. **Thyesteae**: Thyestes, the son of Pelops and Hippodamia, brother of Atreus king of Mycenae, and father of Aegisthus, seduced Aerope the wife of Atreus and robbed him of the golden-fleeced lamb which Hermes had given him as a symbol of his right to rule. In revenge Atreus killed the three sons of Thyestes and served up their flesh to their father at a banquet, whereupon the Sun-god turned back in horror and set in the east. This was a favourite theme of tragedy (see Owen on Ouid. *Trist.* 2. 391) long before Seneca's well-known play, and furnished a commonplace of Roman literature. See 7. 451–2, Ouid. *Her.* 16. 205–6, *Am.* 3. 12. 39, and *Pont.* 4. 6. 47–8 *utque Thyesteae redeant si tempora mensae,* | *solis ad Eoas currus agetur aquas.*

duxere = *sibi induxere.* Housman compares among other passages 6. 828 *caelo lucis ducente colorem,* and for *inducere noctem* Francken cites Ouid. *Fast.* 5. 163 *inducent obscura crepuscula noctem.*

545. **laxauit**: 'opened', cf. 6. 566–7 *conpressaque dentibus ora* | *laxauit* and Verg. *Aen.* 11. 151 *uia...uocis laxata...est* (of a human mouth).

Mulciber: the author of the *Aetna* alludes to the accounts of the poets that Aetna is the home of Vulcan thus (29–32): *principio ne quem capiat fallacia uatum,* | *sedes esse dei tumidisque e faucibus ignem* | *Vulcani ruere et clausis resonare cauernis* | *festinantis opus.*

546. **uertice prono**: 'eddying downwards' (Haskins), cf. 573.

547. **Hesperium...latus**: 'the coast of Italy', cf. Verg. *Aen.* 3. 418 (*pontus*) *Hesperium Siculo latus abscidit.*

atra: this epithet, which is applied often to *sanguis*, is used of Scylla in Ouid. *Met.* 13. 732 *illa feris atram canibus succingitur aluum.*

548. **sanguineum**: proleptic.

549. **canes**: the dogs are those of Scylla. She is described in Verg. *Aen.* 3. 428 as having dolphins' tails joined to a womb full of wolves. Housman compares Prop. 4. 4. 40 *candidaque in saeuos inguina uersa canes* and Ouid. *Met.* 7. 64–5 *cinctaque saeuis | Scylla rapax canibus Siculo latrare profundo* (cf. also *id.* 13. 732 *cit. supr.* 547 n.). Bentley emended *saeui* to *Scyllae*, but the ownership of the *canes* is inferred naturally from the mention of Charybdis. See Introduction, p. lxiii.

raptus: sc. *est*, as in 245 and 615.

550. **confectas**: 'completed'.

Latinas: see 198 n. for the *feriae Latinae* and 199 n. for the cult of Vesta. The *flamma* was that of the nocturnal sacrifices which marked the end of the *feriae*, cf. 5. 402 (*Iuppiter Latiaris*) *uidit flammifera confectas nocte Latinas*. Lejay observes that, as this festival of the Latin league was in celebration of peace and union, to begin a war simultaneously with its celebration was distressing. See Macrob. *Sat.* 1. 16. 16–17 *nec Latinarum tempore...inchoari bellum decebat.*

551. **partes**: supply *duas* from *gemino cacumine*. This is an example similar to that in 504 of the shortening of a fourfold to a threefold expression, see Introduction, p. lxiii. Compare Ouid. *Trist.* 5. 5. 36 *scinditur in partes atra fauilla duas.*

552. **Thebanos imitata rogos**: 'when Eteocles and Polynices were being burned on the same pyre the flame shot up in two separate tongues, showing that they could not be reconciled even in death' (Haskins). Compare Sen. *Oed.* 321–3 *sed ecce pugnax ignis in partes duas | discedit, et se scindit unius sacri | discors fauilla,* Stat. *Theb.* 1. 35–6 (and the description of the event in *id.* 12. 429–32) as well as Paus. 9. 18. 3.

552–5. This passage is discussed in *C.Q.* xxx, 1936, pp. 61–2.

552. **cardine**: 'from the pole', *i.e.* the earth was supposed to be 'hinged' at the poles to the axis common to itself and to the celestial sphere. Here the north pole is probably intended by the poet.

553. **subsedit**: 'sank down', cf. (in a different connexion) Ouid. *Fast.* 5. 13 *pondere terra suo subsedit* as well as *id.* 3. 330 *terraque subsedit pondere pressa Iouis.* Professor W. H. Semple in *C.Q.* xxxi, 1937, p. 21 compares for the general sense Macrob. *Somn. Scip.* 1. 22. 7.

553–4. **ueterem...niuem**: 'the snow of ages' (Duff).

554. **discussere**: Lejay cites Sen. *Oed.* 175–6 *bis Cadmeum | niue discussa tremuisse nemus.* The ancients seemed to believe that

earthquakes were not uncommon in the Alps (Plin. *H.N.* 2. 194), though they may have been thinking of avalanches. Lucan seems to be trying to give greater precision to the words of Vergil in *Georg.* 1. 475 *insolitis tremuerunt motibus Alpes.* Compare Sil. 8. 648 *non Alpes sedere loco* of a portent before Cannae. For the portentous nature of earthquakes see Pease on Cic. *Diu.* 1. 18 (*Ed.* p. 109).

Tethys: 'the sea'.

maioribus: 'greater than usual', cf. 480 n.

555. **Hesperiam Calpen**: Housman observes that 'Spanish Calpe' (Gibraltar) is hollowed on its western side by the sea according to Mela 2. 95 and Sil. 5. 395–400.

summum = *extremum*, *i.e.* 'remotest', so Housman, who compares Sil. 7. 434 *Atlantem et Calpen extrema habitabimus antra.* This interpretation is confirmed by Verg. *Aen.* 4. 480–2.

inpleuit Atlanta: it is usually objected that Mt. Atlas is not near the sea, and in *C.Q. loc. cit. supr.* it is shown that Lucan must be thinking of Ampelusia or Cotes, the modern Cape Spartel near Tangier, where, as Housman shows from Mel. 1. 26, there was a cave open to the sea and sacred to Hercules. Lucan seems to have been confused between Calpe, Abyla (the two 'pillars' of Hercules), Ampelusia, and Atlas, on account of the connexion of the hero with all these places.

556. **indigetes**: these have been explained as the native gods of Rome, in contrast with the *di nouensides* or incomers from abroad, by Wissowa, whose view is criticized by Mr F. Altheim in his *History of Roman Religion* (tr. H. Mattingly, London, 1938, pp. 106–14). Lists of these gods are supplied by Tertullian and Augustine (Roscher, ii, pp. 143–6).

fleuisse: cf. Tibull. 2. 5. 77 *et simulacra deum lacrimas fudisse tepentes.*

laborem: 'distress' (Haskins).

557. **testatos sudore Lares**: cf. Stat. *Theb.* 4. 374 *Tyrios sudare Lares.* For the sweating and weeping of statues as an omen see Pease on Cic. *Diu.* 1. 98 (*Ed.* p. 271).

557–8. **templis...suis**: *i.e.* from where they had been hung in the temples, a compendious expression. For the falling of statues as an omen see Pease on Cic. *Diu.* 1. 19 (*Ed.* p. 113).

558. **diras**: 'ill-omened'.

diem foedasse: Cortius compares 9. 461–2 *licet...fumo.. uiolare diem*, and Claud. *Rapt. Pros.* 1. 164 *foedat nube diem.* The omen is similar to that described in Tac. *Hist.* 3. 56 *contionanti (Vitellio)—prodigiosum dictu—tantum foedarum uolucrum superuolitauit, ut nube atra diem obtenderent.*

uolucres: the birds may have been owls, cf. Iulius Obsequens in his *Prodigiorum Liber* 40 *auis incendiaria et bubo in urbe uisae* (also *ibid.* 46) and Sil. 8. 634 *obseditque frequens castrorum limina bubo.*

559–60. Compare for this omen Sil. 8. 638 (a portent before Cannae) *castra quoque et uallum rabidae sub nocte silenti | inrupere ferae* and Claud. *Eutrop.* 1. 2–3 *moenibus et mediis auditum nocte luporum | murmur, et attonito pecudes pastore locutas.* Haskins cites Shakespeare, *Julius Caesar* 2. 2. 17 'A lioness hath whelped in the streets'.

561. Lucan is thinking probably of the portent of oxen giving voice (*bos locutus est*), which is well known to readers of Livy (3. 10. 6 *et saepe*).

562–3. Compare Claud. *Eutrop.* 1. 1 *semiferos partus metuendaque pignora matri* and Dracont. *Laud. Dei* 1. 45–7 *infantem discors natura biformem | protulit inparibus membris numeroque modoque | et pauet infelix enixa puerpera natum.* Haskins cites Shakespeare, *King Richard III* 1. 2. 21–4 'If ever he have child, abortive be it, Prodigious, and untimely brought to light, Whose ugly and unnatural aspect May fright the hopeful mother at the view'. See Pease on Cic. *Diu.* 1. 93 (*Ed.* pp. 262–3) and on 1. 121 (*Ed.* pp. 313–14), as well as 590–1 *infr.* n.

564. **Cumanae**...**uatis**: the Sibyl of Cumae. The Sibylline books, which were said to have been brought to Rome in the time of either Tarquinius Priscus or Tarquinius Superbus by the Sibyl herself, had perished in the fire of 83 B.C., and a new edition was compiled later 'from the numerous collections of oracular trash which were treasured in many cities and by many private individuals' (Frazer on Ouid. *Fast.* 4. 257). Such were the *carmina*, or oracles couched in verse, which Lucan mentions here. Few, however, of the upper clases in Caesar's time believed in them (Cic. *Diu.* 2. 54–5).

565. **Bellona**: originally an Italian goddess of war, she was identified by the Romans with Ἐνυώ (Hom. *Il.* 5. 333, 592; cf. *infr.* 687). Her cult, like that of Cybele, took a fanatical turn; and it was identified also with that of the Cappadocian goddess Mâ, whose worship began at Rome about the time of the first Mithridatic war and was similarly orgiastic. Compare Hor. *Serm.* 2. 3. 223 *gaudens Bellona cruentis* and Mart. 12. 57. 11 *turba...entheata*

Bellonae. Her priests, according to Acro on the former of these two passages, were called *Bellonarii.* Oudendorp compares Tibull. 1. 6. 45–50, where note especially 47 *ipsa (sacerdos) bipenne suos caedit uiolenta lacertos*; and Haskins refers to Lamprid. *Vit. Com.* 9. 5, saying 'Commodus ordered that they should really gash their arms (*Bellonae seruientes uere exsecare bracchium praecepit studio crudelitatis*), from which it appears that they were usually mere jugglers who pretended to do so'. See 567 n. *infr.*

566*. **deos**: *i.e. deorum mentem,* cf. 639. Housman compares Prop. 4. 1. 104 *sibi commissos fibra locuta deos.* For a similar instance of brachylogy see 379 n.

566–7. **crinemque...sanguineum**: see the Critical Apparatus.

567. **ulularunt**: this verb, so often used of the cries of women (*e.g.* in Verg. *Aen.* 4. 168), is employed here aptly of the emasculated Galli. For the howling of such priests (and for the self-mutilation of the Bellonarii, cf. 565 n. *supr.*) see Sen. *Vit. Beat.* 26. 8.

Galli: for these eunuch priests of Cybele and her cult see Ouid. *Fast.* 4. 221–372 and Frazer *ad loc.*, as well as Catull. 63 throughout.

568. **conpositis**: 'laid to rest'. The commentators quote Verg. *Aen.* 1. 249 *placida conpostus pace quiescit,* Hor. *Serm.* 1. 9. 28 *omnes conposui,* and Prop. 2. 24. 35–6 *tu mea conpones et dices 'ossa, Properti, | haec tua sunt'.*

gemuerunt: Petronius substitutes for this unusual omen a more commonplace mention of ghosts, see *Bell. Ciu.* 137–8 *ecce inter tumulos atque ossa carentia bustis | umbrarum facies diro stridore minantur.*

569*. For the punctuation of this line see *C.Q.* xxx, 1936, p. 62. The *fragor armorum* was heard not *per auia,* but in the sky, cf. Verg. *Georg.* 1. 474–5, Tibull. 2. 5. 73–4, Iul. Obseq. 41 *'fremitus caelestis auditus et pila caelo cadere uisa,* and see Pease on Cic. *Diu.* 1. 97 (*Ed.* pp. 269–70).

569–70. **auia...nemorum**: 'the pathless (regions of the) woods', cf. Verg. *Aen.* 2. 736–7 *namque auia cursu | dum sequor et nota excedo regione uiarum.*

570. **uenientes comminus**: 'meeting in the shock of battle' (Haskins).

572. **urbem cingebat**: 'made the circuit of the city' (Haskins), cf. 594.

Erinys: 'Fury'. Lejay observes that, except for the almost abstract expression *belli furias* (5. 246), Lucan employs the Greek name, though he makes use of the adjective *furialis* (200).

573. excutiens: Cortius compares Sen. *H.F.* 982 *flammifera Erinys uerbere excusso sonat* and *Med.* 961–2 *ingens anguis excusso sonat | tortus flagello*, as well as Ouid. *Met.* 4. 492 (*Erinys*) *caesariem excussit: motae sonuere colubrae.*

pronam: 'turned downwards' (Haskins), cf. 546.

flagranti uertice: either 'with its tip blazing', cf. Verg. *Aen.* 10. 270–1 *cristique a uertice flamma | funditur*; or 'with eddies of flame', cf. 546.

574. stridentes: *i.e.* with serpents, see 573n. and cf. Tibull. 1. 3. 71–2 *serpentum Cerberus ore | stridet.*

Agauen: Agaue, the mother of Pentheus king of Thebes, was inspired with Bacchic frenzy and tore her son to pieces. This is the theme of the *Bacchae* of Euripides, cf. also Ouid. *Met.* 3. 710–33.

575. contorsit: 'helped to throw'.

Lycurgi: Lycurgus was the king of the Edoni in Thrace, and, like Pentheus (their names are frequently coupled), had resisted the introduction of the worship of Dionysus into his kingdom. He attacked the nurses of Bacchus (Hom. *Il.* 6. 130–40) and was blinded by the gods. Then he killed his son Dryas, thinking that he was tearing down the vine (Apollodorus 3. 5. 1).

576. Eumenis: the euphemistic name of a Fury ('the kindly one'), cf. Verg. *Georg.* 1. 278, etc. It was Lyssa (Madness) who gave the decisive impulse (*inpulit*) to the Bacchantes (Eur. *Bacch.* 977), and, at the bidding of Hera, inspired Herakles (*id. H.F.* 858–73) to slay his wife Megara and his children.

Iunonis iniquae: cf. Verg. *Aen.* 8. 292.

577. uiso iam Dite: sc. *quamuis*, see 292n. and cf. 579. Hercules already had visited the underworld to bring Cerberus back with him.

Megaeram: according to Sen. *H.F.* 102 it was this Fury who enraged Hercules. Lejay observes that in Eur. *H.F.* 882 Lyssa was armed with the κέντρον, and indeed Madness is represented as being caused by the Furies in Verg. *Aen.* 7. 346–8 and Ouid. *Met.* 4. 491 sqq.

578. insonuere: see the Critical Apparatus.

579*. silentibus auris: sc. *quamuis*, see 577n.

580. Campo: 'Sulla was buried in the Campus Martius, cf. 2. 222 *his meruit tumulum medio sibi tollere Campo?*' (Haskins).

582. Anienis: on Sulla's orders the corpse of Marius was disinterred and thrown into the Anio (Cic. *Legg.* 2. 22. 56, Val. Max. 9. 2. 1).

583*. fracto...sepulchro: cf. Sen. *Thy.* 671–2 *errat antiquis* *uetus | emissa bustis turba* and Sil. 8. 642 (a portent before Cannae) *Gallorum uisi bustis erumpere manes.*

584. **haec propter**: Lejay observes that *propter* governing a demonstrative pronoun without a relative to follow is found also in Varro, *Re Rust.* 3. 16. 14. Note the anastrophe (i.e. the preposition preceded by the noun or pronoun which it governs).

Tuscos: the Etruscans were famed for having invented the art of the *haruspex* who exercised the power of divination from entrails. See Pease on Cic. *Diu.* 1. 16 (*Ed.* pp. 94–8) for extispicine. Haskins compares not only Liu. 1. 56 (see 586 n.) for an occasion when *haruspices* were called in to explain portents, but also Tac. *Ann.* 11. 15.

de more uetusto: a Vergilian phrase (*Aen.* 11. 142), like *maximus aeuo* (*ibid.* 237).

586. **Arruns**: Lejay observes that the name is Etruscan and that it was given especially to the younger of two brothers, cf. Liu. 1. 34. 2, 1. 56. 7, 2. 6. 6.

desertae: *i.e.* by its inhabitants on Caesar's approach.

Lucae: the modern Lucca, near Pisa.

587. **edoctus**: 'thoroughly schooled in', a 'Greek middle' participle governing an accusative case, for which see Page's Appendix to his Edition of Vergil's *Aeneid I–VI*. Compare Ouid. *Met.* 15. 558–9 *Tages, qui primus Etruscam | edocuit gentem casus aperire futuros.* See Conway on Verg. *Aen.* 1. 246 (cf. 399 n.).

motus: see the Critical Apparatus.

calentes: 'yet warm'. The entrails were taken from the body of the animal as soon as it was killed, cf. 617 n. and 6. 557 *exta...trepidantia*; and see Pease on Cic. *Diu.* 1. 16 (*Ed.* p. 97), where he quotes a number of passages indicating haste on the part of the priest.

588. **fibrarum**: 'entrails' by synecdoche. This is a frequent use in poetry. Compare Sen. *Thy.* 758 *adhuc calentes uiscerum uenas notat*, but see 623 and 627 n.

errantis: see the Critical Apparatus.

in aere = *per aera*, as Lejay observes. See Introduction, p. lxv.

pinnae: Haskins compares Verg. *Aen.* 3. 361 *praepetis omina pinnae*. Arruns, then, was an augur as well as an haruspex.

589–90. **discors...natura**: 'nature at variance with herself' (Duff).

590. **rapi**: for the passive followed by the active *urere* in the next line see Housman's note on 8–10 regarding 9 *praebere* and 12 *geri*.

590-1. **nefandos...infaustis**: note the verbal similarity to Sen. *Oed.* 637-9 *utero...infausto...inpios...fetus* (of Oedipus and his relationship with Iocasta).

The scholia *a* understand the words *nefandos...fetus* to apply to the offspring of mules, regarding which Lejay quotes Plin. *H.N.* 8. 173 *obseruatum...mulas non parere*; *est in annalibus nostris peperisse saepe, uerum prodigii loco habitum.* Compare also Cic. *Diu.* 1. 36 and see Pease *ad loc.* (*Ed.* p. 154). It is more likely, however, that they refer to the unnatural births mentioned in 562-3 *supr.*, and this view is supported by Bentley's citation of Manil. 4. 101-3 *permiscet saepe ferarum | corpora cum membris hominum: non seminis ille | partus erit; quid enim nobis commune ferisque?*

591. **infaustis**: Broukhusius, whom Oudendorp cites, understands this epithet to apply to certain unlucky woods, cf. Macrob. *Sat.* 3. 20. 3 (a quotation from the *Ostentarium Arborarium* of Tarquitius Priscus) *arbores quae inferum deorum auertentiumque in tutela sint, eas infelices nominant...quibus portenta prodigiaque mala comburi iubere oportet.* Haskins compares Catull. 36. 8 *infelicibus ustulanda lignis,* Cic. *Mil.* 13. 33 *infelicissimis lignis semustilatum* (of Clodius's corpse), and Plin. *H.N.* 13. 116.

593. **ambiri**: the *amburbium* was a solemn procession round the city preparatory to a sacrifice, see Apul. *Met.* 3. 2 and Seru. ad Verg. *Ecl.* 3. 77.

festo: *i.e.* it was held on a day set apart for the purpose.

lustro: in the time of the Republic a *lustrum* was a ceremony of purification held by the censors on behalf of the people once every five years after the completion of the census, cf. Liu. 1. 44. 1 *ibi instructum exercitum omnem suouetaurilibus lustrauit, idque conditum lustrum appellatum, quia is censendo finis factus est.* For this sacrifice of a boar, ram, and bull (*suouetaurilia*) see Frazer's *Fasti of Ovid,* vol. v, pl. 14, where its representation on the balustrade of the Rostra in the Forum is displayed.

594. **pomeria**: plural for singular. The origin of the *pomerium,* or sacred boundary round the city, is discussed fully by Frazer on Ouid. *Fast.* 4. 819. Compare Liu. 1. 44. 4 *pomerium, uerbi uim solam intuentes, postmoerium interpretantur esse: est autem magis circamoerium*—an explanation which is justified by Postgate, 'Flaws in Classical Research' (*Proc. Brit. Acad.* iii), 1908, pp. 14-16. See also Pease on Cic. *Diu.* 1. 33 (*Ed.* p. 149). It follows, then, that *per extremos fines* = 'along the outer limit', for the *pomerium* had

been extended recently by Sulla (Sen. *Breu. Vit.* 13. 8, Tac. *Ann.* 12. 23).

595. pontifices: as this was a ceremony of state, the college of pontiffs took the lead. Haskins observes that the description is taken probably from the lustration of the city in the time of Nero (Tac. *Ann.* 13. 24).

596. turba minor: 'the throng of the inferior religious colleges'. Apart from the *pontifices*, the other three *amplissima collegia* or superior colleges were those of (*a*) the *augures* (601), (*b*) the *xv uiri sacris faciundis*, who were entrusted with Greek cults and especially with the care of the Sibylline books (599, see Liu. 5. 13. 6 and Seru. ad Verg. *Aen.* 6. 73) and (*c*) the *uii uiri epulonum*, who had charge of the festival of Jupiter (602, see Cic. *De Orat.* 3. 19. 73). The *turba minor* probably included the Vestals, the Titian guild, the Salii, etc., but see below.

ritu...Gabino: the *cinctus Gabinus* consisted in girding up the toga by throwing a corner of it over the left shoulder and bringing this corner under the right arm to the breast, cf. Verg. *Aen.* 7. 612 and Seru. *ad loc.* Francken objects that there is no word elsewhere of priests wearing the Gabine cincture, and that therefore the *turba minor* is probably composed of attendants.

597. uittata sacerdos: 'priestesses wore a band (*infula*) round their temples, from which a fillet (*uitta*) hung down on either side. The band was sometimes broad and apparently plain; sometimes it was made of white and scarlet stuff twisted together' (Frazer on Ouid. *Fast.* 6. 457). From Verg. *Aen.* 2. 168 and 296 it appears that both the Palladium and the statue of Vesta displayed the fillets of maidenhood, whence this same symbol of chastity was worn by the Vestal virgins.

598. Troianam...Mineruam: the Palladium or statue of Minerva with lance and shield (Roscher, i, p. 690) was believed by the Romans to have been brought from Troy by Aeneas, and to have been housed finally in the temple of Vesta at Rome. See 9. 993–4 *nullique aspecta uirorum | Pallas, in abstruso pignus memorabile templo*, and also Verg. *Aen.* 2. 163–8 for its theft from Troy by Diomedes and Ulysses. There is a full account of its history in Frazer's note on Ouid. *Fast.* 6. 421.

soli: Servius on Verg. *Aen.* 2. 166 states that one priestess only was allowed to see the Palladium.

599. qui: see 596 n.

600. lotam: for the annual washing of the image of Cybele in the Almo, a tributary of the Tiber just outside and to the S. of

Rome, see Ouid. *Fast.* 4. 337 sqq. and Frazer *ad loc.* In Ovid's day this festival was held apparently on April 4, the anniversary of the arrival of the goddess in Rome.

paruo: the Almo is a tiny stream, whence its modern name Acquataccia (a contemptuous diminutive of *acqua*). Compare Ouid. *loc. cit.* 338 *nomen magno perdit in amne minor.*

reuocant: 'restore' rather than 'recall'. Cybele is not 'recalled' *from* the river, but 'restored' to her original purity through being cleansed *by* its waters. Burman suggests *renouant*, and indeed the variants *reuocare* and *renouare* occasionally vex the textual critic (see Drakenborch on Sil. 14. 112), but Heitland in *C.R.* xi, 1897, p. 41 compares Verg. *Georg.* 4. 282, *Aen.* 1. 214 *reuocant uires* and *ibid.* 235 *reuocato a sanguine Teucri.*

Almone: instrumental ablative.

Cybeben: see the Critical Apparatus.

601. **augur**: see 596 n.

seruare: 'observe', a technical term in augury, see Seru. Dan. ad Verg. *Aen.* 6. 198 *seruare . . . et de caelo et de auibus uerbo augurum dicitur.* Lejay compares 5. 395 *nec caelum seruare licet, tonat augure surdo* and 6. 428–9 *quis fulgura caeli | seruet et Assyria scrutetur sidera cura.*

sinistras: Roman augurs observed the direction in which birds were travelling, and those who followed the Etruscan custom (Pease on Cic. *Diu.* 1. 32, *Ed.* pp. 144–5) faced southwards while they regarded the heavens. Only some birds, including crows and woodpeckers, which were seen on the left were lucky according to Pease on *id.* 1. 12 (*Ed.* pp. 76–7).

602. **septemuir**: singular for plural, like *augur*, *Salius*, and *flamen.* See 596 n.

epulis festus = *epulo*, as Housman observes. See the Critical Apparatus. The *Thes. Ling. Lat.* vi, 630, cites for *festus* used of persons Sen. *Ag.* 311–12 *f. turba*, 643 *f. matres*, 645 *f. patres*, and 780 *f. coniunx.*

Titiique sodales: one of the three ancient Roman tribes was that of the Titienses, who were supposed to represent the Sabine stock added in the days of Romulus and were so called, according to most authorities, after the name of the Sabine king Titus Tatius. Probably this guild performed some of the primitive rites of the Sabines. See Tac. *Ann.* 1. 54.

603. **Salius**: for the Salii (from *salire*) or dancing priests of Mars who guarded the *ancilia* (cf. 398 n.) see Frazer on Ouid. *Fast.* 3. 259.

laeto: Burman compares Val. Flacc. 1. 109 *umeris gaudentibus*. The hypallage is the same as that of *generoso = generosus* in the next line and of *electa = electum* in 609. Cf. also Prop. 3. 14. 9 *gaudentia bracchia* and Ouid. *Trist.* 4. 2. 45 *colla...animosa*.

ancilia: when the original *ancile* fell from heaven, Numa ordered eleven other shields of the same size and shape to be made lest it should be stolen (Plut. *Num.* 13, see Frazer, *op. cit. supr.*). For Lucan's rationalizing account of the legend of the fallen *ancile* see 9. 471–80.

604. **apicem**: the pointed cap which the flamens wore (see Frazer on Ouid. *Fast.* 2. 475). Haskins compares Verg. *Aen.* 8. 664 *lanigeros apices et lapsa ancilia caelo* and Liu. 6. 41. 9 *apicem dialem* (the cap of the *flamen dialis* or flamen of Jupiter). The peak of the cap was an olive branch wreathed with a fillet of wool (*filum*, whence the etymology of Varro and Festus *filamen, flamen*).

generoso: Haskins observes that this is an allusion to the three *maiores flamines* (*Dialis, Martialis*, and *Quirinalis*), who, according to Liu. 1. 20. 2, were founded by Numa and chosen, of course, from Romans of patrician stock. Compare 8. 680 *generosa fronte* (of Pompey) and Ouid. *Met.* 12. 234 *generosa pectora*.

605. **effusam**: perhaps there is here a hypallage for *effusi*, but cf. Sen. *Contr.* 1. 6. 4 *effusa moenia (Romae)*.

606–8. For the gathering and burial of traces of fallen thunderbolts (*fulmina condere*) as practised by the Etruscans compare 6. 520 (*Thessala*) *nocturna fulmina captat* and 8. 864 *inclusum Tusco uenerantur caespite fulmen* (*i.e.* the place of burial was surrounded by a wall so as to resemble the head of a well, and was called *puteal* or *bidental*). See Frazer on Ouid. *Fast.* 6. 731 and Pease on Cic. *Diu.* 1. 33 (*Ed.* pp. 147–8).

607. **terrae**: for the dative instead of *in* and the accusative, which is the more usual construction after *condere*, Haskins compares 2. 89 *uacuis mapalibus actus*, 6. 115 *utero demittere*, and Liu. 5. 51. 9 *sacra...terrae celauimus*. See also Heitland, *Introd.* p. civ.

maesto: cf. *Octauia* 923 *gutture maestum fundere murmur*.

murmure: of the recital of a formula which was more or less intelligible. Lejay compares schol. Iuu. 6. 587 *quadam tacita ignorataque prece* and Ouid. *Met.* 7. 251 *precibusque et murmure longo*.

608. **numen**: see the Critical Apparatus. By the burial of the pieces of the thunderbolt Arruns made the place sacred.

609. **electa**: see 603 n. Lejay compares Stat. *Theb.* 1. 506–7

nigri tibi, diua, litabunt | electa ceruice greges. It was important, of course, that the animal should have a fine neck for the sacrifice, cf. *id.* 4. 446–7 *quaecumque gregum pulcherrima ceruix | ducitur.*

marem: sc. *uictimam* from 611 *uictima.* It was a bull (see 633 *infr.*), not a sheep (*bidens*), which, according to schol. Pers. 2. 26, was usually sacrificed on such an occasion and suggested the ancient etymology of *bidental.* See Pease on Cic. *Diu.* 1. 16 (*Ed.* pp. 94–5). For a full description of an ill-omened sacrifice see Sen. *Thy.* 682 sqq.

fundere = *infundere.*

610. **obliquo**...**cultro**: 'slanting the knife', cf. 4. 774 *obliquis et rectis*...*hastis.*

molas: plural for singular. This is the *mola salsa* or salted meal with which, as well as with wine (*Bacchum*, cf. also Verg. *Aen.* 4. 60–1), the head of the victim was sprinkled. Compare Cic. *Diu.* 2. 37 *simul ac molam et uinum insperseris*, where Pease cites among other passages Sen. *Thy.* 687–8 and Val. Max. 2. 5. 5 (add Sen. *Oed.* 335). See Frazer on Ouid. *Fast.* 1. 337.

inducere: 'draw over', 'spread over', cf. 2. 386–7 *membra super*...*induxisse togam* and Ouid. *Met.* 2. 307 *nubes latis inducere terris.*

cultro: for the sacrificial knife, which was short and wide near the handle, see figs. 2117 and 2118 in S. Reinach's account (Dar.-Sagl. p. 1585).

611. **non grati** = *ingrati* (for metrical reasons, cf. 634 *non fanda*), *i.e.* 'unacceptable' to the gods. They were angry, according to Haskins, who compares Tac. *Hist.* 3. 56 where a similar case of reluctance on the part of a bull is thus recorded. Compare also the actions of the bull in Sen. *Oed.* 337 sqq.

uictima: generally *uictimae* comprised larger animals like bulls and cows, while *hostiae* included smaller victims such as sheep and goats (Frazer on Ouid. *Fast.* 1. 335).

612. **succincti**: cf. 596 and see the note on *ministri.*

torus: Heinsius unnecessarily conjectured *torta*, but *toruus* is a suitable epithet for bulls and cows, cf. Verg. *Georg.* 3. 51–2 *optima toruae | forma bouis*, Ouid. *Met.* 6. 115 *toruo*...*iuuenco* and 8. 132 *toruum*...*taurum.*

ministri: the *popae* or assistants who felled the victim with a hammer. Haskins compares Prop. 4. 3. 62 *succinctique calent ad noua lucra popae*, where Butler and Barber observe that, though 'they wore a long apron extending from the waist to the feet' (Seru.

ad Verg. *Aen.* 12. 120), they may have girded up this dress to give themselves greater freedom when they set to work.

613. deposito...poplite: *i.e.* the victim sank on its knees, cf. Eur. *Hec.* 561 καθεῖσα πρὸς γαῖαν γόνυ (Haskins).

614. emicuit: *i.e.* as it should from a narrow thrust, cf. Sen. *Oed.* 345–6 *utrum citatus uolnere angusto micat,* | *an lentus altas inrigat plagas cruor?*

laxo: see the Critical Apparatus.

615. diffusum: sc. *est*, see 441 n.

nigrum: see the Critical Apparatus. The sight of black blood or gall in a victim was a bad omen, cf. Sen. *Oed.* 358 *felle nigro tabidum spumat iecur* and 377 *infecit atras liuidus fibras cruor*. See 620 n.

616. feralibus: 'portending death', cf. 112.

617. raptis: see 587 n. and cf. Ouid. *Met.* 15. 136 *ereptas uiuenti pectore fibras*, Sen. *Oed.* 391 *fibra uiuis rapta pectoribus* and *Thy.* 755 *erepta uiuis exta pectoribus.*

extis: Lejay observes that for prophetic purposes these were six in number: spleen, stomach, kidneys, heart, lungs, and liver.

618. color: the theme, of which *pallida* and *liuor* comprise the variation.

taetris: the characteristic of gore, cf. Verg. *Aen.* 10. 727–8 *taeter...cruor.*

619. gelido...cruore: 'with congealed gore' (Duff). Haskins observes that the usual distinction between *cruor* and *sanguis* (cf. Lucr. 2. 194–5) does not appear to be maintained in this passage.

infecta: cf. Verg. *Georg.* 3. 481 *infecit pabula tabo.*

620. liuor: *i.e.* colour which was *niger*, cf. 615 and Ouid. *Am.* 3. 5. 26 *sed niger in uaccae pectore liuor erat.*

621. tabe...madidum: 'reeking with corruption', cf. Ouid. *Pont.* 3. 1. 26 *tinctaque mortifera tabe sagitta madet.*

622. hostili: the two main lobes of the liver were called the *pars hostilis* (or *inimica*) and the *pars familiaris*, cf. Cic. *Diu.* 2. 28 and see Pease *ad loc.* (*Ed.* p. 394). When these were swollen, a conflict was portended, cf. Sen. *Oed.* 359 and Val. Max. 1. 6. 9. For the swelling of the *pars hostilis* and the appearance of *uenae* upon it cf. Sen. *Oed.* 363–4 *hostile ualido robore insurgit latus* | *septemque uenas tendit*. The *uenae* are probably the *fissa* or streaks on the surface of the liver, see Cic. *Diu.* 1. 16 and Pease *ad loc.* (*Ed.* p. 95). To them the term *fibrae* could also be applied, cf. Seru. ad Verg. *Georg.* 1. 120 *fibrae per iecur, id est uenae quaedam et nerui.*

In this case, the *pars hostilis* was that of Caesar, and the *pars familiaris* that of Pompey.

anheli: an *epitheton ornans*, for the omen consisted in the stifling of the lungs, cf. Sen. *Oed.* 367–8 *non animae capax...pulmo...iacet.* For a similar epithet which, unless regarded as conventional, implies a meaning contrary to the rest of the passage see Verg. *Aen.* 4. 486 *spargens umida mella* soporiferumque *papauer*, where the business of the *Hesperidum templi custos* was to keep the dragon awake.

623*. fibra: cf. 6. 630 *pulmonis rigidi stantes sine uolnere fibras.*

limes: it is uncertain whether the diaphragm or some membrane is meant. Compare Sen. *Oed.* 364–5 *has omnes (uenas hostilis lateris) retro | prohibens reuerti limes obliquus secat,* and especially *ibid.* 361–2 *tenuis...membrana.*

624. latet: *i.e.* the heart is not merely hidden but absent. Van Jever compares Suet. *Iul.* 77 *haruspice tristia et sine corde exta quondam nuntiante* and Iul. Obseq. 67 *Caesari dictatori exta sine corde inuenta.*

saniem: 'corrupted blood' (Duff), and not merely 'gore', cf. Sen. *Oed.* 140–1 *nec cruor, ferrum maculauit atra | turpis e plaga sanies profusa.*

625. produnt: *i.e.* the caul was open and exposed the intestines which it normally hid (*latebras*), cf. Sen. *Oed.* 369–70 *non molli ambitu | omenta pingues uisceri obtendunt sinus.*

latebras: the usual meaning is 'hiding-place', 'place where something lies hidden', but for the meaning 'that which something hides' cf. Stat. *Theb.* 8. 585 *latebras...inguinis.*

626. inpune: 'without ill consequence' (Haskins).

627. capiti: the *pars familiaris* or familiar lobe itself (λοβός, see 622n. and cf. 628–9 *pars...pars*), and not the projections (as Lejay thinks) known as the *processus papillaris* ánd the *processus caudatus* or *pyramidalis*, for which see Pease on Cic. *Diu.* 1. 16 (*Ed.* p. 95).

fibrarum: 'of the liver' by synecdoche, so in 636.

increscere: 'growing upon', cf. Sen. *H.O.* 1070 *increuit Tityi iecur.* The construction is found already in Ouid. *Met.* 4. 577 (*serpens*) *cuti squamas increscere sentit.*

628. alterius capitis: 'the other lobe', *i.e.* the *pars hostilis*, the increase in the size of which was a bad omen, cf. Sen. *Oed.* 363 (quoted in 622n.).

pars: sc. *familiaris.*

aegra et marcida: cf. Sen. *Oed.* 356 *cor marcet aegrum.*

pendet: 'drooped in a flaccid manner', cf. Ouid. *Met.* 15. 231 *fluidos pendere lacertos* (of an aged athlete).

629. **pars**: sc. *hostilis.*

micat: 'throbbed'.

inproba: 'incessantly'.

pulsu: 'with a pulsating movement'.

630. **his**: sc. *ominibus.*

magnorum fata malorum: 'the destiny that brings or imposes great calamities' (Heitland in *C.R.* xi, 1897, p. 41). Bentley unnecessarily conjectured *feta*, for Housman compares Plin. *H.N.* 28. 14 *magnarum rerum fata et ostenta.*

631. **monetis**: see the Critical Apparatus.

632–3. **litaui...sacrum**: a Vergilian phrase (*Aen.* 4. 50).

633. **-que**=*sed*, see 134n.

pectora: see the Critical Apparatus.

634. **uenere**: the gods, if they were willing, entered into *exta*, see Blecher, *De Extispicio*, 1905, pp. 229 sqq. (quoted by Pease on Cic. *Diu.* 1. 16, *Ed.* p. 97).

non fanda=*infanda* or *nefanda*, see 611n.

635. **maiora**: 'worse', see 115n. and cf. 674.

metu: 'than what we fear'. For the brachylogy cf. Sen. *Phaedr.* 1032–3 *malum | maius timore.*

secundent: 'render favourable', cf. Verg. *Aen.* 3. 36 *rite secundarent uisus omenque leuarent.*

636. **fides**: 'reason for believing', *i.e.* 'truth'.

conditor: 'founder', cf. Dracont. *Rom.* 8. 479 *Troius ille puer Ganymedes, conditor artis* (*i.e. augurii*).

637. **Tages**: the scholia *c* on this passage derive his name thus: *Tages est appellatus ἀπὸ τῆς γῆς, et lingua Etrusca significat 'uox terra emissa'*. For the history of Tages, the founder of haruspicine in Etruria, see Cic. *Diu.* 2. 50–1 and the full account by Pease *ad loc.*

637–8. With **flexa**, as with **multa, ambage** must be understood by an ἀπὸ κοινοῦ construction (see Introduction, p. lxiii). Housman compares Lucr. 5. 375 *patet* inmani *et* uasto *respectat* hiatu and Sil. 5. 5–6, and for *flexa...ambage* Lejay and he cite Sen. *Oed.* 214 and Stat. *Theb.* 4. 645.

639–72. This passage is discussed by John of Salisbury (*Policrat.* 441 a-d, see the *ed.* of Webb, tom. i), who quotes 648–68 and merits consultation.

639. Figulus: P. Nigidius Figulus was a Neo-Pythagorean savant and a friend of Cicero, who wrote among other works treatises on private augury, extispicine, dreams, thunder, and astrology, and indeed was a champion of divination. See Pease's edition of Cicero's *De Diuinatione*, Introd. pp. 12, 28, 29 and note on 1. 72 (pp. 217–18). The commentators on Lucan allude to the story in Suet. *Aug.* 94 that he foretold from the circumstances of Octavian's birth the greatness of the future Emperor. According to Gell. 3. 10. 2 he called the planets *errones*.

deos: see 566n. and cf. 379.

640. Aegyptia Memphis: merely 'Egypt', 'Egyptian astrologers', an instance of synecdoche ('part for the whole'). There was an Egyptian as well as a Babylonian school of astrology, see Pease on Cic. *Diu.* 1. 2 (*Ed.* pp. 42–3) and cf. Sen. *N.Q.* 7. 3. 2.

641. aequaret: 'potential' subjunctive.

numerisque sequentibus astra: 'and calculations that keep pace with the stars' (Duff), for *sequentibus = persequentibus*. See the Critical Apparatus.

642–3. errat...mundus: cf. Manil. 2. 71–2 *erraretque uagus mundus standoue rigeret, | nec sua dispositos seruarent sidera cursus*.

642*. nulla cum lege: Haskins observes that this is the Epicurean view and compares Hor. *Epist.* 1. 12. 17 *stellae sponte sua iussaene uagentur et errent*, while the alternative 644 *si fata mouent* is that of the Stoics. For the latter phrase he brings forward as a parallel Manil. 4. 49 *hoc nisi fata darent numquam fortuna tulisset*.

per aeuum: a Lucretian phrase (1. 549 etc.).

643. incerto...motu: cf. Manil. 3. 82 *nec tamen incerto confunderet omnia motu*.

discurrunt: 'speed here and there' as contrasted with 536 *decurrere*.

644*. paratur: sc. *fatis*. Henry on Verg. *Aen.* 2. 121 *cui fata parent* observes that *parare* is repeatedly joined with *fata* (e.g. Luc. 2. 68 and 6. 783), with *Fortuna* (e.g. Val. Flacc. 1. 326 *sin aliud Fortuna parat*), or with *superi* (e.g. infr. 649 and Sil. 1. 136 *magna parant superi*).

645. matura: cf. Sen. *Tro.* 600–1 *me fata maturo exitu | facilique soluant*.

lues: 'destruction' (from *luere*), cf. Sen. *H.F.* 358 *nostri generis exitium ac lues*.

terraene dehiscent: a Vergilian phrase (*Georg.* 1. 479, etc.).

646. subsidentque urbes: a Lucretian phrase (6. 590, where also an earthquake is described).

tollet: Figulus wants to know if heat will prove to be the destruction of *temperies*, the mean between heat and cold to which men owe their lives, and for which Housman compares 9. 435 *temperies uitalis abest*.

feruidus aer: for the attribution of heat to the air, which the Stoics usually regarded as cold, see Cic. *N.D.* 2. 26–7 and Mayor *ad loc.*, as well as Sen. *N.Q.* 2. ·10.

648. infusis...uenenis: cf. 8. 691 *infuso facies solidata ueneno est*.

649–50. Housman observes that these lines recall the uneven arrangement of Verg. *Georg.* 4. 505 *quo fletu Manes, quae numina uoce mouere?* (where, however, there is a variant *qua* for *quae*). Still more uneven is, for example, Val. Flacc. 1. 847–8 *tum porta quanta sinistra | poena docet maneat Pelian, quo limine monstrat*.

650–1. Haskins translates 'many men's days of doom have met at one point of time', *i.e.* 'many are doomed to die at one and the same time in this war'. Compare Ouid. *Her.* 1. 114 *extremum fati...diem*.

651. summo...caelo: 'in the tenth temple of the dodecatropos'. For a solution of the astrological difficulties of this passage see *Proc. Camb. Philol. Soc.* 1939 (*Camb. Univ. Report.* 14 March 1939, p. 711) and *C.Q.* xxxv, 1941, pp. 17–22.

frigida: an epithet of astrology, because Saturn was the outermost planet, cf. Vitruu. 9. 1. 16 *Saturni autem (stella), quod est proxima extremo mundo ac tangit congelatas caeli regiones, uehementer est frigida*. Haskins compares Verg. *Georg.* 1. 336 *frigida Saturni sese quo stella receptet*.

652. stella: here, as frequently, 'planet'. See Housman on Manil. 2. 961.

nocens: also a commonplace of astrology, to which the scholiast on Pers. 5. 50 alludes thus: *Saturnus stella nocens secundum astrologos*. See in addition Cic. *Diu.* 1. 85 and Pease *ad loc*. This commentator (*Ed.* p. 508) compares also Ambr. *Hexaem.* 4. 17 *noxia eum stella conspexit: Saturni ei sidus occurrit*. Both Saturn and Mars were baneful planets, the one, as has been seen in 651 n., being cold and the other hot, whence its name *Pyrois*. For the heat of Mars compare 658–60 and Vitruu. 9. 1. 16 *Martis stella feruens ab ardore solis efficitur*. The other superior planet, Jupiter, was, like Venus, benignant, cf. 660–1, Cic. *N.D.* 2. 119 *ut cum summa Saturni refrigeret, media Martis incendat, his interiecta Iouis illustret et* *temperet*, and Vitruu. 6. 1. 11 *Iouis stella inter Martis feruentissimam et Saturni frigidissimam media currens temperatur.*

nigros: Housman explains this epithet too as due to the stock opinions of astrologers about the colour of the planets, and quotes passages which refer to Saturn as black (μέλας, δνοφερός, σκοτεινός).

accenderet ignes: cf. Verg. *Aen.* 5. 4 *quae tantum accenderit ignem.*

653. **Deucalioneos**: probably not merely an *epitheton ornans*, but = 'such as was the flood of Deucalion in the olden time'. Housman observes in his Astronomical Appendix that Aquarius sometimes was identified with Deucalion (Germ. *Phaen.* 562), so that *Deucalioneos* possibly = *suos*. Other accounts identify him with Ganymede (see Frazer on Ouid. *Fast.* 1. 652 and 2. 145).

fudisset = *defudisset*, see Manil. 1. 272 *post hunc (Capricornum) inflexa defundit Aquarius urna.*

654. **diffuso...aequore**: cf. Ouid. *Met.* 1. 36 *(deus) freta diffudit.*

655. **saeuum**: Bentley, who observes that the double epithet (see Introduction, p. lviii) is worthy of Accius or Pacuuius but not of Lucan, conjectures *tergum...Nemeaei...Leonis* on account of passages like Ouid. *A.A.* 1. 68 *cum sol Herculei terga Leonis adit, Fast.* 2. 77 *medii...terga Leonis*, and Sen. *Oed.* 40 *Titan Leonis terga Nemeaei premens.* This is a possible solution, but see Appendix B for two adjectives followed by one noun in Lucan; and in fact the ecliptic passes not over the Lion's back, but under his stomach. Adjectives such as *saeuus* are stock epithets for lions, cf. 208 and Verg. *Aen.* 9. 792; and indeed *saeuum* may well be regarded as proleptic, cf. Hor. *Epist.* 1. 10. 16–17 *Leonis, | cum semel accepit solem furibundus acutum.* Furthermore, *Nemeaeum Leonem* may be considered to be an entity, for the adjective coheres closely with the noun.

Nemeaeum: Leo had originally been the Nemean lion which Hercules slew. His sign, as Housman observes, is the house of the Sun, who, of course, is in it during July–August.

656. **premeres**: 'were passing over' (Duff).

fluerent: Van Jever's conjecture *furerent* is needless, cf. Sil. 17. 101–2 *fluit undique uictor | Mulciber* and Claud. *Rapt. Pros.* 2. 316 *totoque fluunt incendia uultu.*

656–7. These lines contain the usual commonplace sentiment regarding the final conflagration of the universe; see Appendix B and compare the concluding lines of the *Astronomica* of Manilius: *ipse suas aether flammas sufferre nequiret, | totus et accenso mundus flagraret Olympo.*

657. Lejay compares 2. 413 *succendit Phaethon flagrantibus aethera loris.*

658. **hi cessant ignes**: 'these heavenly bodies are not active now' (Duff), *i.e.* Saturn was not *summo caelo*, and, as Housman observes, 'Lucan was astronomer enough to know that the Sun is not in Leo in the winter'.

658–9. **flagrante minacem...cauda**: the chief star of the conspicuous constellation Scorpio is Antares ('the rival of Mars'), which is bright red in colour and marks the Scorpion's heart; his tail, however, includes a brilliant group of stars (γ, ς, η, θ, ι). Compare Manil. 1. 268 *ardenti fulgentem Scorpion astro.* Scorpio was the feminine house of Mars, and when he was in it war was portended (Manil. 4. 217–29); but, as Housman remarks, he was actually near the boundary between Aquarius and Pisces.

659. **chelas**: the claws of Scorpio encompassed a vacant place which was not at first a separate sign of the Zodiac, so that the complete constellation occupied the space of two signs, cf. Verg. *Georg.* 1. 32–5 and Ouid. *Met.* 2. 195–7 *est locus, in geminos ubi bracchia concauat arcus | Scorpios et cauda flexisque utrimque lacertis | porrigit in spatium signorum membra duorum.* The western part of Scorpio was then the sign Chelae (see Martianus Capella 8. 839), and was not known at Rome as Libra before the first century B.C., so that Libra afterwards was not infrequently called Chelae by the poets, *e.g.* by Manilius in 4. 203. This is not the case here, as Housman observes, for Mars could not be in two signs at once, and *chelas*, like *cauda*, adds merely to the ornamental description of the Scorpion. For the story of Scorpio see Frazer on Ouid. *Fast.* 5. 537.

peruris: see 652n.

660. **Grādiue**: 'the marching god', see Frazer on Ouid. *Fast.* 2. 861.

paras: cf. Verg. *Aen.* 5. 14 *quidue, pater Neptune, paras?*

mitis: see 652n. for this epithet, as well as for *salubre*, and compare Mart. Cap. 8. 885 *stella Iouis salutaris.*

660–1. **in alto...occasu**: 'low down in the western region', *i.e.* in the sixth temple of the dodecatropos. See 651n.

661. **salubre**: see 652n. For this term as opposed to *nocens* (652) compare Sen. *Oed.* 35–6 *sperare poteras sceleribus tantis dari | regnum salubre? fecimus caelum nocens.*

662. **hebet**: Venus was dim because she appeared to be near the Sun at her full phase (superior conjunction), and her rays were

impeded by his, cf. Vitruu. 9. 1. 9. Compare 2. 722 *et iam Plias hebet* (at sunrise), Ouid. *Met.* 5. 444 *alma dies hebetarat sidera*, and Val. Flacc. 5. 370–1 *hebet Arcas et ingens | Iuppiter*.

Cyllenius: Mercury, so called because the god had been born and reared on Mt Cyllene in Arcadia. Compare Verg. *Aen.* 4. 252, etc.

haeret: Mercury is the swiftest of the planets because he is nearest to the Sun, and, as Housman remarks, 'a planet whose regular epithets were *celer* and ὠκύς could not fail to be stationary on such an occasion'. The inferior planets Mercury and Venus move with greater velocity than the earth. When they are between the sun and the earth (*i.e.* at their new phase), their position is called inferior conjunction. Starting from this point (and considered with relation to the sun), the planet appears for a time to move in a clockwise and retrograde direction, but, before it reaches its maximum elongation (*i.e.* the point where the imaginary lines joining the planet to the earth and to the sun are at right angles), it appears to change to a counterclockwise and direct movement. After passing first superior conjunction and then the opposite point of maximum elongation, but before going back to inferior conjunction, it seems to return to a clockwise and retrograde motion. Accordingly, the name 'stationary points' is given to the two positions, each between inferior conjunction and one of the two points of maximum elongation, where the retrograde movement changes to direct or vice-versa, and at which the planet does not seem to move. The apparent progress of an inferior planet is described in Mart. Cap. 8. 880 as *nunc praeteriens nunc consistens aut certe regrediens*. Lucan means that Mercury was now on one of the two stationary points.

663. **caelum Mars solus habet**: Housman observes that Lucan is in error, for 'all the planets were visible, and all in full or normal lustre except Saturn, which was rather near the sun'.

signa: not merely 'constellations' (cf. Housman on Manil. 1. 465), but 'other constellations', *i.e.* apart from Orion. See 31 n.

meatus: a Lucretian word when applied to the heavenly bodies, *e.g.* 1. 128 *solis lunaeque meatus*.

664. **mundo** = *caelo*, see 152 n. and Munro on Lucr. 1. 73 for this frequent meaning, and cf. Manil. 5. 729 *stipatum stellis mundum*. For the local ablative cf. 91 *caelo*.

obscura: Housman remarks that the dim appearance of the rest of the constellations and the comparative brightness of Orion were due to atmospheric conditions which properly had no astrological significance; but that constellation seems to have been a threatening portent when seen too clearly, cf. Sen. *H.F.* 12 *ferro minax hinc terret Orion deos.*

665. Note the asyndeton between this and the preceding line. Similarly between 141 and 142 a conjunction with the sense of 'while' has to be supplied.

ensiferi: Haskins compares Eur. *Ion* 1153 ὅ τε ξιφήρης Ὠρίων. Ovid employs both *ensifer* (*Fast.* 4. 388 *dub.*) and *ensiger* (*A.A.* 2. 56) as epithets of Orion, for whose story see Frazer on *Fast.* 5. 494. Compare also *Met.* 13. 294 *nitidumque Orionis ensem.* The Sword of Orion comprises several stars including θ Orionis and the superb nebula, whence Vergil's *armatumque auro... Oriona* (*Aen.* 3. 517).

fulget: Orion is, of course, a constellation conspicuous for its brilliance, cf. Manil. 5. 723 *mersit et ardentes Orion aureus ignes.*

latus: 'side', *i.e.* 'belt' (Ouid. *Fast.* 6. 787 *zona*), namely the three bright stars δ, ε, and ζ Orionis.

666. **armorum rabies**: cf. Verg. *Aen.* 8. 327 *belli rabies.*

ferrique potestas: cf. 5. 387 *ferri ius.*

667. **confundet ius**: cf. Ouid. *Met.* 6. 585–6 *fasque nefasque | confusura ruit.* Cortius compares Eur. *Suppl.* 311 νόμιμά τε πάσης συγχέοντας Ἑλλάδος.

manu: 'violently', see the Critical Apparatus.

sceleri: see 2 n. Lejay compares Sen. *H.F.* 251–3 *rursus prosperum ac felix scelus | uirtus uocatur, sontibus parent boni, | ius est in armis.*

668. **multosque exibit in annos**: 'will go on for many years', cf. Ouid. *Fast.* 5. 189 *Circus in hunc (mensem) exit* and Sen. *Phoen.* 198–9 *haud ultra mala | exire possunt.* Compare the use of *extrahe* in 672.

669. **furor**: cf. 8.

670. **domino**: Caesar, who is called by Cato in 9. 279 *inuiso... tyranno.* Haskins compares 7. 645–6 *post proelia natis | si dominum, Fortuna, dabas, et bella dedisses.*

ista: see 342 n. Here again *iste* repeats the *hic* of the previous line, so that *pax ista* is the peace which follows *hic furor, i.e.* 'peace in this case'. The commentators quote Cic. *Att.* 7. 5. 4 *pace opus est: ex uictoria cum multa mala tum certe tyrannus exsistet.* Van Jever unnecessarily conjectures *iusta* for *ista*, comparing 4. 365 *iustae...foedera pacis*, but this word is out of place in an anti-Caesarian mouth.

duc = *produc*, 'prolong'. This is probably a reference to the troubles after Caesar's death, cf. 692-4.

671. **continuam**: proleptic.

seriem: cf. Verg. *Aen.* 1. 641-2 *series longissima rerum | per tot ducta uiros*, Ouid. *Met.* 4. 564 *luctu serieque malorum*, and *Pont.* 1. 4. 19 *series inmensa malorum*.

in tempora multa: 'for a long time', cf. 315.

672. **ciuili tantum iam libera bello**: 'free only as long as civil war lasts', *i.e.* until Actium and the final triumph of Octavian.

674. **premunt**: 'are upon them', cf. Verg. *Aen.* 10. 375 *numina nulla premunt* (Haskins).

uertice Pindi: Pindus in Thrace is mentioned by Seneca among the places visited by Bacchus in the company of Silenus and the Bassarids, see *Oed.* 434-5 *Threicio | uertice Pindi*. Pindus and Haemus (680) are coupled by Horace in *Carm.* 1. 12. 6.

675. **Edonis**: 'a Thracian maenad', cf. Ouid. *Met.* 11. 69 *matres Edonidas*. The Edoni, a people of Thrace (see 575 n.) were enthusiastic worshippers of Bacchus, who was himself called *Edonus* by Ovid (*Rem.* 593). The quantity *Edŏnis* instead of Ἠδωνίς is, as Lejay observes, an innovation in Latin poetry which is followed by Silius (4. 776).

Ogygio: 'Theban' from Ogyges, the mythical founder of Thebes. Bacchus was called 'Theban' on account of his connexion with that city, see 574 n. Haskins cites Ouid. *Her.* 10. 48 *qualis ab Ogygio concita Baccha deo*. Compare also Sen. *Oed.* 436-7 *inter matres inpia maenas | comes Ogygio uenit Iaccho*.

Lyaeo: 'wine', cf. 609 *Bacchum*.

676. **attonitam**: either this epithet may be an instance of hypallage (= *attonita*); or *attonita* may be supplied from it with *matrona*, cf. Verg. *Aen.* 7. 580 *attonitae Baccho...matres* and Sen. *Oed.* 1005-6 *attonita et furens* (cf. 695 *infr.*) | *Cadmea mater*; or else it may apply merely to the populace, cf. 3. 97-8 *urbem | attonitam* and Ouid. *Fast.* 4. 304 *attoniti monstro stantque pauentque uiri*.

677. **prodens**: 'revealing', cf. Sen. *Phaedr.* 363 *proditur uultu furor*.

urguentem pectora: cf. Ouid. *Fast.* 2. 803 *positis urguentur pectora palmis*.

678. **Paean**: 'Healer', an epithet of Apollo.

679. **Pangaea**: this mountain overlooked Philippi to the North and the Gulf of Strymon to the South.

679–80. Note the juxtaposition of *niuosis* and *cana*, and see 615 crit. n.

680. Philippos: see the Introduction, p. xxxviii.

681*. quis furor: cf. 8.

682. -que: 'when', see 231 n. and cf. Verg. *Aen.* 2. 692–3 *uix ea fatus erat senior, subitoque fragore | intonuit laeuum.*

hoste: 'a foreign foe', cf. 12 n. The commentators quote Cic. *De Off.* 1. 37 *hostis enim apud maiores nostros is dicebatur quem nunc peregrinum dicimus.*

683. diuersa: 'in a different direction'. The commentators compare Verg. *Aen.* 11. 855 *cur, inquit, diuersus abis?*

primos...ortus: in Verg. *Aen.* 4. 118 this expression means 'the first appearance of the Sun at his rising'. Here it is equivalent to 'the East', and the epithet *primos* appears to be otiose, unless perhaps it is used for the adverb *primum.*

684. Lagei: Lagus was the father of Ptolemy I and consequently the founder of this line of Egyptian monarchs. Here reference is made to the murder of Pompey at the command of Ptolemy XIII (who is described in 8. 692 as *ultima Lageae stirpis perituraque proles*) on Sept. 28, 48 B.C., near Pelusium.

mutatur: 'is exchanged for', so that the line means 'where the waters (see 399 n.) of the Nile flow into the sea'. See the explanation in *C.Q.* xxx, 1936, pp. 62–3. For the ablative after *mutare* cf. 7. 832 *uos (aues), quae Nilo mutare soletis | Threicias hiemes.*

685. hunc: Pompey.

fluminea: not exact, for Pompey was slain and his ashes were buried on the seashore near a place called Mons Casius, see Postgate's edition of Book 8, p. lxiv, and cf. 8. 470, etc.

harena: it is likely that Vergil had the fate of Pompey in mind when he makes Dido curse Aeneas (*Aen.* 4. 620) in the following words: *sed cadat ante diem mediaque inhumatus harena.*

686. dubiam: see 409 n. and cf. 9. 304 (*Syrtes natura*) *in dubio pelagi terraeque reliquit* as well as Sen. *Marc.* 25. 3 *incertarum uada Syrtium.*

687. arentem...Libyen: cf. Ouid. *Met.* 2. 237–8 *tum facta est Libye raptis umoribus aestu | arida.* The matron now visits the scene of the battle of Thapsus, for which see 39 n.

Enyo: see 565 n. and cf. Petron. *Bell. Ciu.* 61–2 *tres tulerat Fortuna duces, quos obruit omnes | armorum strue diuersa feralis Enyo.*

688. Emathias acies: 'the armies that fought in Thessaly', see 1 n. and 106 n.

desuper: 'over and down from', 'down over', a preposition. See *C.Q.* xxx, 1936, p. 63.

688–90. The reference is first to the siege of Massilia and then to the war in Spain which culminated in the battle of Munda, for which see 40n.

689. Compare 3. 299 (*Caesar*) *agmine nubiferam rapto super euolat Alpem* and Ouid. *Met.* 2. 226 *aeriaeque Alpes et nubifer Appenninus*.

691. Cortius rightly explains this line as referring to the end of the civil war upon the death of Caesar in the Senate House. Pothinus, in planning Caesar's murder, recognized that this would happen, if he were successful, in the words (10. 391) *nox haec peraget ciuilia bella.*

692. See 670n.

693. **ponti**: this certainly must be printed, and not Haskins's *Ponti*, which would make Lucan a geographer even worse than he is. The glance is probably at the coasts of Sicily and the campaign against Sextus Pompeius (38–6 B.C.), as well as at Actium (31 B.C.); while the *tellurem nouam* of the next line may be Cisalpine Gaul, the scene of the fighting of 43 B.C. Compare 41–3.

694. **Philippos**: cf. 680. She has seen Pharsalia already and does not want to behold its repetition at Philippi.

695. **lasso**: 'spent' (Duff), cf. Sen. *H.O.* 732 *lassus tumor* (*undarum*).

iacuit: compare the note on which Verg. *Aen.* 3 ends—*i.e.* with the verb *quieuit.*

deserta: cf. 4. 279 *deserat hic feruor mentes.*

CRITICAL APPARATUS

It has been explained already in the Preface that the only passages discussed under this heading are those for which new illustrative matter can be submitted, and that this is in no way a complete Critical Apparatus to the First Book. The MSS in the Bibliothèque Nationale have been examined only for certain passages, and elsewhere I have depended on the réports of Lejay, Hosius, and others.

Abbreviations:

A   Ashburnhamensis, Paris. Bibl. Nat. nouv. acq. lat. 1626, *saec.* ix *ineun.*, a Libri MS. Collated by Lejay.

B   Bern. Stadtbibl. 45, *saec.* x, formerly belonging to P. Daniel and Bongars. Collated by Pfander for Usener.

C   Bern. Stadtbibl. 370, *saec.* x *ineun.*, formerly belonging to Bongars and containing, not the text of the *De Bello Ciuili*, but a commentary, the matter of which is designated below by c. In the Critical Apparatus the symbol C will be reserved for the evidence of the lemmata. The commentary was edited by Usener in 1869.

D   Paris. Bibl. Nat. 8265, *saec.* x *exeun.*, a Colbert MS of uncertain provenance. It contains scholia. Examined by me.

E   Paris. Bibl. Nat. 9346, *saec.* xi *ineun.*, from Echternach. Collated by Simonnet for Lejay.

G   Gemblacensis, Bruxell. Bibl. de Bourgogne 5330, *saec.* x *exeun.* Collated by Usener for Hosius.

M   Montepessulanus, Montpellier. Bibl. de la Faculté de Médecine H. 113, *saec.* ix–x, from Autun (see 436–40 crit. n.). Collated by Steinhart for Hosius.

N   Nostradamensis, Paris. Bibl. Nat. 17901, *saec.* xi *ineun.*, from the chapter of Notre-Dame. Collated by Simonnet for Lejay.

P   Paris. Bibl. Nat. 7502, *saec.* ix, a Colbert MS from Tours (according to E. K. Rand, *A Survey of the Manuscripts of Tours*, Camb. Mass. 1929, i, pp. 176–7). Collated by Simonnet for Lejay.

Q   Paris. Bibl. Nat. 7900 A, *saec.* x, a Puteaneus. Collated by Simonnet for Lejay.

R   Paris. Bibl. Nat. 8040, *saec.* xi *ineun.*, a Colbert MS believed by E. Châtelain (*Paléogr. des Classiques Latins 2me partie*, Paris, 1894–1900, p. 19) to have been at Fleury. Collated by Simonnet for Lejay.

S   Sangermanensis, Paris. Bibl. Nat. 13045, *saec.* xi *med.*, from Saint-Germain-des-Prés. Collated by Simonnet for Lejay.

T   Paris. Bibl. Nat. 8039, *saec.* x, a Colbert MS and formerly a Thuaneus. Collated by Simonnet for Lejay.

U   Leidensis Vossianus xix f. 63, *saéc.* x. Collated by Steinhart for Hosius.

V   Leidensis Vossianus xix f. 51, *saec.* x. Collated by Steinhart for Hosius.

Y   Paris. Bibl. Nat. 10315, *saec.* xii *med. uel exeun.*, from Echternach (see Preface, p. x). Examined by me.

Z   Paris. Bibl. Nat. 10314, *saec.* ix, from Echternach according to H. Omont. Collated by the Conférence de Philologie Latine de l'Institut Catholique for Lejay.

a   Adnotationes super Lucanum in GU multisque aliis codicibus seruatae, according to the edition of Endt (Leipzig, 1909).

c   Commenta found in C.

r   Lond. Brit. Mus. Royal 15 A xxiii, *saec.* xii. Examined by Professor A. Souter for me.

s   Lond. Brit. Mus. Add. 14799, *saec.* xiv–xv. Examined by Professor A. Souter for me.

π   Consensus of later Paris MSS as examined by me.

σ   Other later MSS as designated by Housman on p. xxxvi of his edition.

Ω   Consensus of MSS excluding any specified deviations.

   Statements that Steinhart and Usener collated certain MSS *for* Hosius mean that their collations were utilized by him in his editions. In the notes which follow, symbols such as A′ mean the original reading of the MS in question, where it has been altered subsequently by correction. For reasons of space such corrections will be ignored except in special cases. It has been thought worth while to include the evidence of ABNRT in spite of the belief of Beck (*Untersuch. zu d. Handschr. Lucans*, Munich, 1900), Hosius, and M. Bourgery that they are descendants of Z. This is by no means certain in every case.

   16. **horis** Ω, **auris** Oudendorp. On the ground that latitude, not time of day, is in question, Bentley accepts *auris*, and Lejay and Housman are not unfavourable to it. *Auris* could have become

horis through the intermediate form *oris*. Instances of confusion between these words are not rare, *e.g.* in Val. Flacc. 2. 60 *tacitis ratis ocior horis* editors before Carrio (1565) print *auris* from T, a descendant of V. *Horis*, however, should be retained here and translated as 'hours', 'periods' or 'seasons', cf. Hor. *Carm.* 3. 13. 9 *flagrantis atrox hora Caniculae* and Auson. *Mos.* 180–1 *cum praebuit horas | secretas hominum coetu flagrantior aestus*. Haskins compares Hor. *A.P.* 302 *sub uerni temporis horam* and states that *flagrantibus horis* is 'equivalent to *aestate*'. Cf. 6. 333 *brumalibus horis*, Ouid. *Met.* 4. 199 *brumales...horas*, and Mart. 12. 1. 4 *hora...aestiua*. For the ending of the verse cf 414.

18. **Scythicum glaciali** A′RVrsπ, -co -lem Ω. Lejay defends the latter and more usual reading by observing that *glacialis pontus* = 'the northern sea', while *Scythicus Pontus* = 'the Euxine'. But see the explanatory note throughout. For the defence of *-co -lem* there should be added to Hosius's testimonia *Gloss. Ansil. G.L.* i, p. 268 (J. F. Mountford, *Quotations from Classical Authors in Medieval Latin Glossaries*, Ithaca, 1925, p. 60). Though *-co -lem* is supported by Ouid. *Met.* 2. 224 *nec prosunt Scythiae sua frigora*, Iuu. 2. 1–2 *glacialem Oceanum*, Claud. *Cons. Stil.* 1. 176–7, and Amm. Marc. 31. 2. 1, *-cum -li* ought to be preferred on account of the probable imitation, on the part of Lucan, of Ovid's *glaciali frigore* (*Met.* 9. 582) and *Scythicus Pontus* (*Trist.* 3. 4. 46, 4. 1. 45). For *glaciali frigore* compare also Claud. *Laus Herculis* 125 and Paulinus of Périgueux *Vit. Mart.* 1. 63, 4. 23. This reading has the advantage of crediting Lucan with his favourite device of ending the first half of the line with an adjective and the second with the corresponding noun (cf. 1, 3, 14, etc. and see Cortius on 395), though there are also many lines in support of the *-co -lem* arrangement, *e.g.* 371, where there is in any case a hypallage. For Lucan's fondness for the order exemplified by *-cum -li* see Lejay's *Introduction*, p. lxv.

20. **iacet** Ω, **latet** van Jever, who compares 10. 213–14 *subdita Nili | ora latent*. For the similarity between these two words see 623–4 crit. n. *Iacet* is, however, the true reading, cf. 409, 481, 2. 416–17 *si non per plana iacentis | Aegypti Libycas Nilus stagnaret harenas*, and 4. 106 *sic mundi pars ima iacet*.

31. **erit** Ω, **erat** T′V, Par. 8268 (*saec.* xiii), 8467 (*saec.* xiii).
descendere P′Z′, **discendere** M, **discindere** Ω.

50. **iuuet** Ω, **iuuat** EPR′VYc, Prisc. *G.L.K.* ii, 345, 14. Nettleship in *C.R.* i, 1887, p. 295 approves of *iuuat* (which may indeed be

due to Priscian), but the condition expressed by *iuuet* is appropriately followed by the unconditional prophecy of the future indicatives *cedetur* and *relinquet*. Such unconditional future indicatives are emphatically complimentary to Nero. Compare the construction of Hor. *Carm.* 3. 3. 7–8 *si fractus inlabatur orbis,* | *inpauidum ferient ruinae.*

54. **aduersi** TUVY, **auersi** Ω, Prisc. *G.L.K.* ii, 394, 20. A majority of π is in favour of *aduersi*. *Auersi* is adopted by several editors, including Housman, but the only passage in Lucan alleged in its defence is 8. 337 *auersosque polos alienaque sidera quaeris*, where, however, *auersos polos* is correctly explained by Housman as the eastern hemisphere, and incorrectly by Postgate as the South Pole, or at any rate the southern hemisphere. On the other hand, *aduersi* is the exact word to be used of opposite positions in the celestial sphere, cf. Cic. *Arat.* 186 *procul Arcturo est aduersa parte locata* (*Ara*), and so it appropriately denotes the South in relation to the North. Compare 9. 876 *imus in aduersos axes* (where see Housman), Ouid. *Pont.* 4. 10. 43 *Notus aduerso* (*i.e.* to Boreas) *tepidum qui spirat ab axe*, Manil. 1. 592–3 *quantum a nostro sublimis cardine gyrus* | *distat ab aduerso tantumdem proximus illi*, and Aratus *Phaen.* 25–6 ἀλλ' ὁ μὲν (πόλος) οὐκ ἐπίοπτος, ὁ δ' ἀντίος ἐκ βορέαο | ὑψόθεν ὠκεανοῖο. *Aduersus* and *auersus* are frequently confused, cf. 6. 339.

64. **accipio** DM'PSV, Par. 7936 (*saec.* xiv), 8266 (*saec.* xiii), 8267 (*saec.* xiii), Seru. *Aen.* 1. 8, Prisc. *G.L.K.* iii, 244, 13, **accipiam** Ω. As the apodosis *uelim* is a polite wish, it does not affect the mood of the protasis, which should be indicative to obtain greater emphasis, cf. 50 *supra* and 6. 612–13 *omnia fata laborant* | *si quicquam mutare uelis.*

89. **medium** UV, **medio** Ω. The former reading is to be preferred on account of the better sense (see the explanatory note), for *in medio* would mean merely 'between them'. Those who wish to understand *in medio* as equivalent to 'as a prize' must supply *positum* with *orbem*, cf. Cic. *De Oratore* 1. 3. 12 *in medio posita*, Hor. *Serm.* 1. 2. 108, *Epist.* 1. 12. 7 and Plut. *Brut.* 29 ἄθλον ἐν μέσῳ καὶ λείαν προθέμενοι τὴν πατρίδα. For *in medium* compare Verg. *Georg.* 1. 127, 4. 157, *Aen.* 11. 335, Ouid. *Met.* 4. 41, Liu. 26. 12. 7, Sen. *Ag.* 666, and Cortius's parallel: Aristoph. *Eccl.* 602 τοῦτ' ἐς τὸ μέσον καταθήσει.

101. **geminum** Ωc, **medium** P, schol. Stat. *Theb.* 1. 120. See the note which follows on *male*. *Medium* is due probably to the *medius* of the preceding line.

male UV, **mare** Ω, schol. Stat. *Theb.* 1. 120. *Male*, which is the *lectio difficilior*, is preferred by Cortius (who is therefore criticized by Burman), Lejay, and Postgate, *mare* by most editors, including Housman, who has a helpful note on the use of two synonyms such as *mare* and *fretum*, where one is, for example, nominative and the other accusative in the same clause. [This note is of utility in the illustration of *nec patitur (undas*, not *mare) conferre fretum*.] If *mare* is read, there are in 100–3 four synonyms in rapid succession, namely *undas, mare, fretum*, and *mare*; and Housman in sanctioning the first *mare* forgets that its repetition in 103 (as well as in 110) is as objectionable as that of *rura* in Hor. *Carm.* 4. 5. 17–18, with which he finds fault (*Edition*, p. xxxiii). Gronovius's correction of *male* to *mare* in· Ouid. *Met.* 7. 395, which Heitland (see his *apparatus criticus*) cites in defence of *mare*, not only provides a noun necessary to the construction, but also avoids a repetition of *male* which otherwise would occur two lines later. In fact, the text which the scholiast of Statius's *Thebais* had before him unworthily fathers upon Lucan two unpleasing repetitions in one line, namely *medium* from the preceding and *mare* from the second succeeding verse.

But in the above passage *mare* is not necessary to the construction, for *undas* is the common object of *secat, separat*, and *patitur* by an ἀπὸ κοινοῦ arrangement, while *fretum* is the object of *conferre* and is qualified by *geminum*. For the separation of the adjective *geminum* from its noun compare 5. 680–1 *circumfusa...turba* and 7. 685–6 *infida...Fortuna* (see Heitland, *Introd.* p. cvii). If Ouid. *Her.* 12. 104 *quique maris gemini distinet Isthmos aquas*, Sen. *Ag.* 562–3 *arx...quae spectat mare utrimque geminum*, Thy. 628–9 *maris gemini...fauces Corinthos, Epigr.* 50. 5 *mari gemino semper pulsata Corinthos*, and Stat. *Theb.* 7. 420 *gemini maris incola* all support *geminum...mare*, then *geminum...fretum* is equally well vouched for by Ouid. *Her.* 8. 69 *qua duo porrectus longe freta distinet Isthmos* and Sen. *H.F.* 336 *bina findens Isthmos exilis freta*. For the appropriateness of *male*, especially in juxtaposition with *gracilis*, see the explanatory note.

103. **frangat** Ω, **franget** GM′P′SU. The latter reading is supported by the majority of π. The subjunctive is to be preferred in the apodosis of this conditional sentence.

121. **acta** Ω, **facta** G′S. For *acta* cf. 8. 25 *acta...Sullana (i.e.* Pompey's *acta* in the time of Sulla), *ibid.* 320 *felicibus actis* (also of Pompey),

126. **induit** ΩC, **induat** σ. The indicative is more vigorous than

the subjunctive, just as in English 'Tell me, where are you?' is more emphatic than 'Tell me where you are'. (Roby's example, see his *Grammar*, Part ii, sect. 1761.) Heinsius places a mark of interrogation after *arma*, thus making *quis induit* virtually independent of *scire nefas*, but Housman, who compares 9. 563 *quaere quid est uirtus*, prefers to regard these words as forming a quasi-dependent question.

138. **haerens** Ω, **haeret** AENTZ. Although *haeret* is printed by M. Bourgery, *haerens* should be preferred as balancing 140 *effundens* and linking *pondere fixa suo est* to the five preceding words as closely as the participial phrase with *effundens* is linked to *non frondibus efficit umbram*.

206. **Libyes**: Housman prints the Greek form here in deference to the MSS as in 255, where he remarks that only *Libye* is used in the nominative, whereas both the Greek and the Latin forms are employed in the oblique cases.

209. **iubam et uasto graue** Ω, **iubas et uasto** MRUV, **iubas et uasto grau(a)e** A'P' (*corr.* **iubam** P²). The reading adopted by several editors since Cortius *iubas uasto et graue* is objectionable on account of the *et* postponed to the beginning of the fourth foot, and furthermore *graue* is required as an epithet for *murmur*. See Housman *ad loc.*

229. **it** EPR'SV'Y, Par. 8044 (*saec.* xiv), 8267, 8466 (*saec.* xiii), 8467, **et** Ω. Housman, though preferring *et*, admits that a passage like Sil. 10. 10–1 *uelocius inde | Haemonio Borea pennaque citatior ibat* may justify *it*. For *it* and *ibat* denoting rapid motion after *rapit* cf. Val. Flacc. 4. 45–6 and Stat. *Theb.* 5. 655–60, and for similar asyndeton between *is* and the preceding verb cf. 10. 287–9. The objection to the adoption of *et* is that it must be parallel to the *et* of the following line on the analogy of 5. 405–6 *ocior et caeli flammis et tigride feta | transcurrit*, Verg. *Aen.* 5. 318–19 *Nisus | emicat et uentis et fulminis ocior alis*, and 10. 247–8 *fugit illa per undas | ocior et iaculo et uentos aequante sagitta*; therefore the positive *inpiger* and the comparative *ocior* are left in asyndeton, which is not Lucan's practice, as is manifest at least from 479–80. Such asyndeton as he displays is generally between verbs, participles, or whole sentences, as in 141–2 and 399–401.

246. **gelidos** MS, **gelidus** Ω. A majority of π is in favour of *gelidos*, which Housman prefers on account of 4. 153–4 and 9. 56. Indeed *gelidos artus* has the further qualification of being an Ovidian phrase (*Met.* 4. 247).

247. **tacito** (-ti A'Z) **mutos** Ω, **tacitos muto** GPSV, Par.
8041 A (*saec.* xiii), 8268, 11322 (*saec.* xv), 15146 (*saec.* xiii). The
former reading is supported by the fact that *tacito pectore* occurs
three times in Ovid (*Her.* 13. 89, 21. 201 and *A.A.* 1. 110), cf. also
Verg. *Aen.* 1. 502.

254. **ruentem** G, Par. 8041 (*saec.* xiii), 11322, **furentem** Ω. The
latter reading is due to 250 *furentum* and 255 *furoris.*

260. **tacet** Ω, **iacet** PQ'R'rs, Par. 8041, 8042 (*saec.* xiv), 8266,
–7, –8, 10316 (*saec.* xv). Though Lejay defends *iacet* from 3. 524
iacuit mare and 5. 434 *aequora lenta iacent, tacet* is supported by
Verg. *Aen.* 4. 525 *cum tacet omnis ager,* for Lucan here seems to be
thinking of the general context of this Vergilian passage. Housman's
parallels are not sufficiently close to do much for his defence of
tacet. See the explanatory note for citations from Seneca and
Statius which help to establish *tacet* as the appropriate word.

(In 5. 443 *stagna tacentis aquae,* where the MSS are again divided,
Housman seems to be in error in rejecting *tacentis* for *iacentis,*
which is due probably to *ibid.* 434 (*cit. supr.*). There is no contradiction between *ibid.* 440 *sonantem,* which is within the simile and
is applied to the Maeotis only, not the Euxine, and *tacentis,* which
is outside the simile and is applied to the Ionian sea. (Housman
denies the truth of this last remark, but, even if the simile is
continued to 446, the *tacentis aquae* is that of the Euxine itself,
not the Maeotis.) Compare Prop. 4. 4. 49–50 *tacentes...aquas.* In
Val. Flacc. 3. 732 *flamina conticuere, tacet sine flatibus aequor* (see
642 crit. n.) Burman's *tacet* should replace V's *iacet,* and in Stat.
Silu. 2. 2. 28–9 *nulloque tumultu* | *stagna modesta iacent* the verb
similarly should be changed to *tacent.*)

290. **genero est** Ω, **est genero** PSV. The authority of π is
divided. The verdict of the majority should be upheld, especially
as Lucan (cf. 139) permits the elision of a long syllable before *est.*

304. **transcenderet** Ω, **transcenderit** A'B'DMUZ, Par. 8269
(*saec.* xiii), 8466, [Probus] *G.L.K.* iv, 224, 1. Older editors favour
the former reading, which has been discarded in favour of the latter
in modern editions where, however, no attempt is made to justify
the syntax of *transcenderit.* Even with a present indicative like
concutitur in the apodosis, the imperfect subjunctive in the protasis
is the proper tense to denote a purely imaginary supposition.
Compare Val. Flacc. 5. 408–10 *non aliter, quam si radiantis adirent* |
ora dei..., | *tale iubar per tecta micat.*

305. **ualidae** AB'M'N'PTVZ, Par. 8041 A, **ualido** Ω. The former

reading seems on the whole to be supported by 5. 362–3 *et tu, quo solo stabunt iam robore castra,* | *tiro rudis.*

349–50. The MSS are divided in 349 between **nec** and **neque** and in 350 between **nam neque** and **nam nec**. The second **neque** in the latter line is, apparently, the reading of all the MSS. Housman's rule (unless he has MSS authority entirely against him, as in the case of this second *neque* of 350) is to print *nec* in the second half of the second, third, and fourth feet. Accordingly, to balance the second *neque*, *nam neque* is preferred to *nam nec* in the first foot.

368. **lybies** U, **libiae**, *etc.* Ω. The reading consistent with previous passages is *Libyes*, and the *s* of *sitientis* may have been responsible originally for *Libye(-ae)* by haplography. See 206 crit. n. and 255. Surprise may be felt that Housman did not choose *Libyes* here and also in 5. 39, where it has good MSS authority, for in his comment on the latter passage he even defends such sibilants as would abound there if it were adopted.

381. **castra** Ω, **signa** A′BNR′T′Z, Par. 8042,–3 (*saec.* xiv), 11322. *Castra* is undoubtedly the right reading on account of *metator* in the following line. See 382 n.

389. **piniferae** Ω, **nubiferae** DG′PSV. The authority of π is divided. The former reading is confirmed by Stat. *Theb.* 8. 79 *frondenti...Ossae*, while the latter is not supported by Val. Flacc. 2. 15–16 *in mubem...Ossa redit.*

397. **uogesi** (*uel* **uegesi**) Ω, **uosegi** G²U². There is no reason to ignore the unanimous verdict of the tradition, as is recognized by Heinsius on Sil. 4. 213.

398. **lingonas** YE²a, **lingones** Ωc. P *exhibet* **linguonâs** (*corr.* P′). *Lingones*, as Housman observes, if nominative is in conflict with the meaning, and if accusative does not scan. For the accusative form in *-as* of Gaulish names cf. Tac. *Ann.* 12. 27 *Vangionas ac Nemetas.*

405. **nomine** GMPS, **numine** Ω. Housman observes that the harbour is *named* after Hercules, even though it was sacred to his *numen.* Compare 5. 344 *nostro sub nomine miles,* Lucr. 3. 421 and Munro *ad loc.*

416. **ducat** DMPV, Par. 8041 A, 8266, –7, **tollat** Ω. In addition to the information contained in Housman's note, it may be observed that *ducat* (simple for compound *subducat,* and on that account the more likely reading) is defended by 9. 313–14 *sed rapidus Titan ponto sua lumina pascens* | *aequora subduxit zonae*

uicina perustae, and *tollat* by 10. 260–1 *sol rapit* (*Oceanum*), *atque undae plus quam quod digerat aer* | *tollitur*. *Tollat*, as has been suggested, may be due to a reminiscence on the part of a copyist of Verg. *Aen*. 1. 103 *fluctusque ad sidera tollit*.

420. **aturi**: Lejay's critical note should be consulted for the variants *aturi, atyri, saturi, satyri*, etc. and their MSS authority. While Vibius Sequester vouches for *Atur* or *Atyr* (Riese p. 146), Ausonius (*Mos*. 468, *Par*. 4. 11–12) does so for *Aturrus* and the Greek authorities for Ἀτούριος. The form *Aturi* should be preferred here. The spelling *Atyri* which Housman favours is due merely to dittography on the part of scribes of the final letter of *ripas* and the consequent confusion with the word *satyri*. Note Lucan's quantity *Atūri*.

429. **foedere** E′(G)MSUYc, Par. 14141 (*saec*. xiii), **sanguine** Ω, **funere** Par. 7979 (*saec*. xii). *Funere* in the form *foenere* has been proposed by Havet in *Rev. Phil*. xxxvi, 1912, pp. 193–5. *Pollutus sanguine* may be paralleled by 6. 307 *infando pollutus sanguine Nilus*, and *pollutus foedere* by Ouid. *Met*. 10. 353 *naturae pollue foedus*; but, as M. Bourgery remarks, the dishonour of the Gauls consisted not in slaying their enemies, but in having broken faith (Caes. *B.G*. 5. 27. 10 *illud se polliceri et iure iurando confirmare, tutum iter per fines suos daturum*), cf. Verg. *Aen*. 7. 467 *polluta pace*.

430–5. Schrader objects to these lines on account of the quantity *Batāui*, which is not found elsewhere earlier than Venantius Fortunatus in the sixth century; but see 420 crit. n. for similar shortening of a vowel in a proper name to suit the metre. Another objection is the mention of the Cinga, but see Introduction, p. xli for the justification of the mention here of this river. The scholiasts a and c, however, as well as schol. Iuu. 8. 51 attest the lines.

435. **cana** Ω, **canas** M′Z. In the MSS where it occurs *canas* seems to demand the reading *pendenti*, which is furnished by later hands. But the order *cana pendentes rupe Cebennas* is defended by 371 and Claud. *VI Cons. Hon*. 45 *Tarpeia pendentes rupe Gigantas*. Lejay is the only modern editor to print *canas pendenti*.

436–40. *Pictones inmunes subigunt sua rura, nec ultra*
    instabiles Turones circumsita castra coercent.
    in nebulis, Meduana, tuis marcere perosus
    Andus, iam placida Ligeris recreatur ab unda.
    inclita Caesareis Genabos dissoluitur alis.

The verses 436–9 are found in three only of the older MSS, namely MRT, where they were added marginally at a time apparently not later than 1115; while 440 is not in any known MS, but was first published in 1521 by Accursius in his note on Aus. *Mos.* 468. For a full discussion of all five lines see Lejay, *Introd.* pp. c–cii. Guyet (1575–1655), who is quoted by Oudendorp, stated conjecturally that 436–40 were composed by Marbod, who lived for a long period at Angers, was later bishop of Rennes, and died in 1123 (see F. J. E. Raby, *Secular Latin Poetry*, Oxford 1934, i, pp. 329–37); but all that can be tolerably certain is that the unknown interpolator's intention was to do honour to the valley of the Loire.

The Pictones (Caes. *B.G.* 3. 11) lived near the modern town of Poitou in the departments of ˙Vendée, Deux-Sèvres, and Vienne; the Turones near Tours in Indre et Loire; and the Andes near Angers in Anjou (department of Maine et Loire). The Meduana is the Mayenne, and Genabos (Cenabum according to Rice Holmes, *Caesar's Conquest of Gaul*, 2nd ed. p. 841) was probably the modern Orléans (Rice Holmes, *ibid.* pp. 405–15).

It is unfortunate that Guyet does not specify clearly what prompted him to suggest the authorship of Marbod. The date of the interpolation in the three MSS is nearly as uncertain as its origin, though the script (at any rate in R) would seem to support Lejay's contention that the early years of the twelfth century are most likely. Chatelain in his *Paléogr. des Classiques Latins*, 2me *partie*, pl. clvi reproduces the page in R which contains the added lines, and on p. 19 remarks, apparently without good reason, that they may have been written by Girardus, who gave the MS to Fleury. Dr R. W. Hunt is inclined to believe that the interpolator is probably to be looked for in a school rather than in a monastery, that he flourished, of course, in the valley of the Loire, and that his name might be revealed some day by a study of commentators on Lucan like Anselm (of Laon?) or Arnulf of Orléans who lived during the twelfth century.

453. **datum est** Ω, **datum** E′GPY, **datur** MU. *Datum est* is supported by a majority and *datum* by a minority of π. If the editors print *datum est* in 6. 407, consistency should induce them to follow the majority of the MSS here also.

455. **profundi** Ω, **profundo** P (*corr.* P′). Though Housman prints *profundi*, his inclination to *profundo*, which was merely a muddle on the part of the scribe of P, is hardly justified by 3. 509–10 *profundo...maris*. On the other hand compare Verg. *Georg.* 1. 243 *sub pedibus Styx atra uidet Manesque profundi* and Stat. *Theb.* 1. 297–8 *profundi...Erebi.*

481. **tunc** Ω, Prisc. *G.L.K.* ii, 328, 16, **nunc** MN′P, Par. 8266,–7, 14381 (*saec.* xiv), **hunc** GU. See *C.Q.* xxx, 1936, p. 60 for the reasons why the best attested reading should be restored after two centuries of exile.

The MSS are divided between **alpem** and **alpes**, but the former should be preferred, as it obviates the cacophony with *iacentes*. Lejay on 688 observes that the singular is found before Lucan only in Ouid. *A.A.* 3. 150 *nec quot in Alpe ferae*. Lucan himself uses both the singular and the plural, the former in 688 and 3. 299, the latter in 183, 219, etc.

490. **tum** QSa, **tunc** ΩC. Housman both in his note *ad loc.* and in his 2nd edition of Juvenal (p. xxi n.) discusses the rarity in the best authorities of *tunc* before a guttural.

491. **urg(u)ent** rsσ, **urguet** Ω. Haskins (who reprints the text of Weise), Francken and Housman are the only recent editors to follow Grotius in rejecting *urguet*, for which the influence of *impetus* is responsible in the tradition. *Vrguet* would also leave *incerti* hanging.

531. **denso** Ω, **tenso** AD′EMN′PRUYZC, Par. 8042, –3, Prisc. *G.L.K.* ii, 520, 13 ; iii, 473, 34. The former reading is vindicated by Housman in his edition, and also in *C.R.* xv, 1901, pp. 130–1 and in his edition of Manilius I, p. xxxix, against *tenso*, which is supported by Hosius in *Neue Jahrb.* 1893, p. 340, and Reid in *C.R.* xv, 1901, p. 80.

534. **de** EMRSZ, **e** Ω. *De* is more appropriate, not only because the thunderbolt fell *down* from heaven to earth, but also because it was thought that the sky rises towards the north (see 54 n.).

538. **ore** V′, **orbe** Ω, Isid. *N.R.* 21, 2. *Totoque expalluit ore* is, of course, an Ovidian expression (*Met.* 4. 106, 6. 602). Compare also Manil. 2. 96 *tu* (*Delia*) *quoque fraternis sic reddis curribus ora*.

566. **mouet** Ω, **monet** G′P. Compare Tibull. 1. 6. 45 *haec ubi* (*sacerdos*) *Bellonae motu est agitata*.

567. **sanguineum** MQVZ′, **sanguinei** Ω. The testimony of π is divided. Oudendorp compares Stat. *Theb.* 10. 173 *sanguineosque rotat crines* (*Phryx cruentus*).

569. **magnae** Ω, **uariae** PU. Compare Verg. *Georg.* 1. 476–7 *uox quoque per lucos uolgo exaudita silentes | ingens*.

578. **insonuere** Ω, **intonuere** PUY. Lejay compares Petron. *Bell. Ciu.* 271 *intremuere tubae* and Sil. 12. 181 *insonuere tubae*.

579. **auris** Ω, **umbris** PS′UV, **aruis** D′, Par. 8041, **horis** Heinsius. *Vmbris* is supported by the majority of π and may be

defended by Verg. *Aen*. 6. 264 *umbraeque silentes*, as may *horis* by Val. Flacc. 2. 60 *tacitis...horis* and *aruis* by 260 supr. *rura silent*. But *auris* suggests that the noise of fighting was heightened by the silence of the breezes, cf. Sen. *Med*. 627 *siluere uenti*, Stat. *Theb*. 2. 89 *tacita...aura*, *Ach*. 1. 54 *uenti silent*.

583. **fracto Marium** Ω, **Marium fracto** AMNRTVZ. The former reading is supported by the majority of π. Housman observes that the tomb (in this case the waters of the Anio) was broken by Marius and not by the farmers. Besides, a cogent argument in favour of *fracto Marium* is the correspondence of the adjective (or participle) at the end of the first half of the line with the noun at the end of the second (see 18 crit. n.).

587-8. **motus...monitus** Ω, **monitus...motus** BGM'UV. Though he prints the former reading, Housman following Graeuius suggests that *motus* does not accord so well with *fulminis* as with *pinnae*, but this opinion may be discarded on account of Stat. *Theb*. 5. 586-7 *moti tamen aura cucurrit | fulminis*. The testimony in favour of the latter reading, which is adopted by Heitland, is given on the authority of Lejay.

588. **errantis** ΩC, **uolitantis** A'BMNRZrs. The testimony of π is divided. The former, as Housman observes, is the exquisite word which should be preferred, therefore, to the commonplace *uolitantis*. Similarly the poet Persius (4. 26) employs the expression *quantum non miluus errat*, but Petronius (37. 8) adopts the prosaic equivalent *qua milui uolant*. *Errare* is used of the flight of birds also in Stat. *Silu*. 2. 4. 6, Mart. 1. 53. 7 and Nemes. *Cyn*. 315.

600. **cybeben** AMQZ, **cybelen** Ω. For the spelling see Butler and Barber on Prop. 3. 17. 35-6 (they observe that Bentley on this passage of Lucan was the first to show that '*Cybebe* was the correct form wherever the metre demanded a long penultimate').

602. **festus** Ω, Augustin. *regul. G.L.K*. v, 524, 33, **festis** σ. Housman follows Cortius in adopting *festus*, and shows that *curandis* would have to be understood with *festis* if the latter reading were adopted, or else that *epulis festis* would have to be taken as an instance of a dative for a genitive. The assonance before the penthemimeral and the hephthemimeral caesurae is also objectionable.

608. **numen** ADMNPRTZ, Par. 8266, -8, 15146, **nomen** Ω schol. Iuu. 6. 587. See 405 crit. n. for similar variants. Weber compares Claud. *Rapt. Pros*. 3. 353 *inde timor numenque loco*, to which add Ouid. *A.A*. 1. 203 *date numen eunti* and Sen. *H.O*. 1982

nouum templis additum numen. If *nomen* is adopted, it must allude
to the name *puteal* or *bidental* (see 606–8 n.), but these were regular
terms and would have been taken for granted.

614. **laxo** E′GPQUVc, **largo** Ω. Francken compares 9. 769
iamque sinu laxo nudum sine corpore uolnus, to which add Stat.
Theb. 6. 841–2 *effusaque sanguine laxo | membra natant.*

615. **nigrum** Ω, **dirum** AMN′RTVZr. The former reading is
supported by a majority of π. Housman's objection that *nigrum*
occurs 'fortasse ob *rutilo*' in the tradition is precisely the strongest
argument in its favour, cf. 679–80 *niuosis cana* and Ouid. *Hal.* 129
nigrum niueo portans in corpore uirus. Similarly van Jever wished
to destroy the juxtaposition of *plurimus asperso* in 620 by reading
luridus for *plurimus.* Compare also 6. 547–8 *nigramque per artus |
stillantis tabi saniem* (cf. 624 *infr.*) *uirusque coactum* and see 620n.
For Lucan's forced antitheses consult Heitland, *Introd.* pp.
lxxix–lxxx.

623–4. **iacet…latet** van Jever, **latet…iacet** Ω. This transposition has been adopted in the text on account of Sen. *Oed.* 356
cor marcet aegrum penitus ac mersum latet and 368 *pulmo sanguineus
iacet,* as well as Luc. 3. 644 *qua pulmo iacet.* Lest anyone should
object to the change on account of Claud. *Ruf.* 2. 414–15 *pandit
anhelas | pulmonis latebras,* it may be observed that the latter
passage refers merely to a wound revealing the lungs which are
hidden inside the body, and that *latet* applied to *pulmonis…fibra*
accordingly would involve no omen. Here the omen consisted in
the stillness of the lung, see 623n. (*fibra*).

631. **monetis** V, Par. 8044, 8269, **mouetis** Ω. Van Jever
compares 524 *minaces,* Pseud. Tibull. 3. 4. 5–6 *diui uera monent,
uenturae nuntia sortis | uera monent Tuscis exta probata uiris,* Val.
Flacc. 5. 259–60 *interea auguriis monstrisque minacibus urbem |
territat ante monens semper deus,* and Stat. *Theb.* 3. 627–8 *nam te,
uesane, moneri | ante nefas, unique tacet tibi noster Apollo.*

633. **pectora** Ω, **pectore** A′BMNR′Z, **uiscera** Gac. The
testimony of π is divided between these three variants. To Housman's parallels in defence of *pectora* add Verg. *Aen.* 4. 63–4
pecudumque reclusis | pectoribus inhians spirantia consulit exta.

641. **sequentibus** Bentley, **mouentibus** Ω. Housman in
defending this convincing emendation remarks that the calculations
of astrologers do not move the stars, but follow or observe them
and furnish a description of their motions. Bentley himself compares Stat. *Theb.* 4. 411 *tripode inplicito numerisque sequentibus astra,*

and Housman adds Cic. *Diu.* 1. 36 and 2. 17 for the expression *stellarum cursus* (or *siderum motus*) *numeris persequi.*

642. **cum** MR'VYZ', Par. 7936, 8268, 8466, 11322, **sine** Ω, Prisc. *G.L.K.* iii, 337, 13. *Nulla cum = sine ulla*, just as in 341 *non cum duce = sine duce* and in Sen. *Thy.* 399 *nullo cum strepitu = sine ullo strepitu* (Lejay's parallels). Housman quotes Val. Flacc. 3. 732, which should read *tacet sine flatibus aequor* (see 260 crit. n.); but in printing *iacet* and criticizing *sine* as an interpolation in C, the lost MS of Carrio, he forgets his citation in his note on 260 of *Cons. Liu.* 185 *mutaeque tacent sine uindice leges.* For a defence of *sine* see Löfstedt, *Synt.* ii, p. 211 n.

644. **urbi** Ω, **orbi** PU, Par. 8267. Destruction is being made ready for Rome and for the rest of the world. If *orbi* is read, a tautology ensues; while *urbi* is defended by such contexts as 7. 354–5 *non iratorum populis urbique deorum est | Pompeium seruare ducem.*

667. **manu** Ω, **manus** D'NRSTC, Par. 7936, 8041 A, −2, −3, 8466. *Manu* is a metonymy for *ui,* cf. Sall. *Iug.* 31. 18 *non manu neque ui.*

681. **quot** editor, **quod** A²G¹Q, **quo** G'PS, **quae** A'BEMR, **que** NP² T²Z, **qua** T', **quid** σ. UV are reported by Hosius and Heitland as reading *quid,* but by Francken as attesting *quae. Quo,* which Housman prints, is described by him as a relative, not an interrogative pronoun or an adverb; but either *quo* or *quod* is unsatisfactory for the reason which Francken mentions: 'abruptae insanientis orationi non conuenit, ut haec uno tenore continuentur.' Furthermore *quo* comes awkwardly between the adverbs of 678 and 683. For *quae,* which Housman rejects as otiose, Heitland compares 7. 587 *quod ferrum, Brute, tenebas!* But, if an exclamation is demanded by the tenor of the passage and Housman is justified in remarking '*quae* nihil significat quod non significetur illis *Romanae* et *miscent*', the emendation *quot* (from the variant *quod*) may be nearer the truth than *quid?* which, following Cortius, Hosius, and Lejay print. Compare 5. 327 *tot reddet Fortuna uiros quot tela uacabunt.*

APPENDIX A

SIDVS, SIDERA

15 and 416. The word *sidus* in its general sense of 'heavenly body', whether sun, moon, planet, fixed star, or comet, as well as in its particular sense of any one of these bodies, has not yet received sufficiently detailed treatment from the lexica or from commentators, among whom there are, however, exceptions like Mayor on Plin. *Ep.* 3. 1. 2. The sun is himself a *sidus* (Cic. *N.D.* 2. 92 *ex aethere igitur innumerabiles flammae siderum exsistunt, quorum est princeps sol...deinde reliqua sidera*, Sen. *Marc.* 18. 2 *uidebis uno sidere omnia inplere solem*, as well as Tibull. 2. 1. 47, Ouid. *Met.* 1. 424, *Fast.* 5. 17–18. Considered both at his rising and at his setting, he is *sidus utrumque* (Petron. *Bell. Ciu.* 2). The moon is the *sidus* that is *secundum* to the sun (413), and may too be called *sidus* without any epithet, cf. 6. 479 *inpulsam sidere Tethyn* and Tac. *Ann.* 1. 28. Similarly at 661–2 the planet Venus is called *Veneris sidus*.

There need be no cause for surprise when the poetic plural *sidera* occurs for any of these bodies. It is used of a fixed star (in Verg. *Georg.* 1. 204 *Arcturi sidera*), of a planet (Jupiter in Auson. *Ecl.* 8. 9 *Iouis aurea sidera*, Saturn in Val. Flacc. 2. 364 *Saturnia sidera*, and Mars in Ouid. *Ibis* 215–16 *Martis sidera*), and of the moon (in Ciris 37–8, Merobaudes *Carm.* 1. 13–14 and Boeth. *Cons.* 1. 2. 9), as noted by me in *C.Q.* xxx, 1936, p. 55. For its use with *sol* editors of Lucan at 15 quote Ouid. *Met.* 14. 172–3 *caelumque et sidera solis | respicio* (cf. *Ibis* 32 *lumina solis*). But there is no difficulty in producing examples of *sidera* employed either absolutely, or near a genitive which can be understood with it, as I have done in the above paper, from Manil. 3. 18–19, Val. Flacc. 3. 730–1, 6. 441–2, Stat. *Theb.* 7. 45–6, *Silu.* 5. 3. 96–7 (which is translated correctly by Professor D. A. Slater and Mr J. H. Mozley), and Claud. *Cons. Stil.* 1. 63. Professor W. H. Semple in *C.Q.* xxxi, 1937, pp. 16–17 makes no reference to the last passage, and fails to present a good case for what he calls 'the ordinary meaning of the word' in the others. In the passages from Valerius Flaccus and the *Thebais* of Statius, the practice of theme and variation (see Introduction, p. lix) would appear to settle the matter, while Mr Semple's criticism of my view of the Manilian passage takes no account of the mythological picture of the Sun-God rising every morning in the East and driving his chariot across the sky during the day, until he sets in the West in the evening (cf. Ouid. *Met.* 2. 1–400 *passim*).

Mr Semple's misconception of Manil. 3. 18–19 can be paralleled only by Housman's similar misunderstanding of Luc. 7. 1–3 *segnior, Oceano quam lex aeterna uocabat, | luctificus Titan numquam magis aethera contra | egit equos cursumque polo rapiente retorsit.* The latter's view is cited by Mr Semple, and is to be found in an article entitled *Astrology in Dracontius* (*C.Q.* iv, 1910, pp. 191–5), which unconsciously proves the truth of Quintilian's *nec, si rationem siderum ignoret, poetas intellegat.* The error of Housman's opinion was refuted excellently by H. C. Nutting (*C.W.* xxvi, 1932, pp. 54–5), to whose arguments I would add merely, as conclusive evidence for Lucan's meaning, Ouid. *A.A.* 1. 327–30:

> *non medium rupisset iter curruque retorto*
> *Auroram uersis Phoebus adisset equis.*

For 15 see also *Classical Philology*, xlvi, 1951, pp. 25–31.

APPENDIX B

74
> *omnia mixtis*
> *sidera sideribus concurrent ignea, pontum*
> *astra petent, tellus extendere litora nolet*
> *excutietque fretum,...*

The usual punctuation adopted by editors consists in placing a comma after *concurrent* instead of after *ignea*, as in the text printed above, and Bentley, Housman, Professor Eduard Fraenkel (*Gnomon* ii, 1926, p. 507), and Professor W. H. Semple (*C.Q.* xxxi, 1937, pp. 18–19) also concur in deleting *omnia...concurrent.* Their reasons are (i) the alleged awkwardness both of *omnia mixtis* taken with *sidera sideribus concurrent* and of *sidera* followed by *ignea astra*, and (ii) the fact that Lucan has a break in the sense after the fourth foot only when that foot is a dactyl. In *C.Q.* xxx, 1936, pp. 56–7 *omnia...concurrent* is defended on the grounds (i) that the resemblance of the words *sidera sideribus concurrent* to Sen. *Marc.* 26. 6 and *Ben.* 6. 22 is strongly in favour of their authenticity, and (ii) that *mixtis sideribus* may be a verbal echo of Manil. 4. 386 and

414–15, and *omnia sidera* of Sen. *N.Q.* 3. 29. 1. The repunctuation introduced in the text as shown above is, however, necessary to meet the metrical objection, although it demands that *ignea* as well as *omnia* shall qualify *sidera*. While it is comparatively rare in good poetry to find two adjectives attached to the same noun (see Introduction, p. lviii), double epithet occurs, for instance, at 218 and 655, and for *omnis* with another adjective 2. 431–2, 6. 485–6, and 7. 391–2 may be compared (as well as 79–80 *totaque discors machina*). For *ignea* qualifying *sidera* cf. Cic. *N.D.* 2. 15. 39–40 and Stat. *Theb.* 1. 499.

Housman's objection to *mixtis* with *concurrent* is refuted by 2. 291 *terra labet mixto coeuntis pondere mundi*. The retention of *omnia...concurrent* provides a simile which is the longest in the poem, and is endowed with another sevenfold variation like that of 1–7 (see Introduction, p. lix) in (i) *omnia...ignea*, (ii) *pontum... petent*, (iii) *tellus...nolet*, (iv) *excutietque fretum*, (v) *fratri...ibit*, (vi) *et obliquum...poscet sibi*, and (vii) *totaque discors...mundi*. The theme, of course, is expressed in the clause *cum conpage soluta... iterum chaos*, and denotes the ἐκπύρωσις or final conflagration which Lucan believed to be awaiting the universe. This belief seems to have originated with Heraclitus, and it was a feature of Stoicism (see Arnold, *Roman Stoicism*, Cambridge, 1911, pp. 95–6 and 190–3).

Pontum astra petent means that the celestial bodies will fall into the sea and thereby leave the world in darkness. The Stoics thought that the final conflagration would be accompanied by the complete extinction of all light, cf. 5. 634–6, Sen. *H.F.* 610, *Med.* 9, *H.O.* 1110–15, Claud. *Rapt. Pros.* 1. 115–16, and especially Plin. *Ep.* 6. 20. 15 *plures...aeternam illam et nouissimam noctem mundo interpretabantur.*

Tellus...fretum has been variously misunderstood. Haskins and Lejay, whose explanations essentially repeat that of Farnaby, assume that the negative verb *nolet* negatives *-que*, which accordingly is equivalent to *neque*; *i.e.* the meaning then is 'the land will refuse to stretch out its shores and will not shake off the sea', with which accordingly it will be covered. Common as is this use of the positive for the negative conjunction after *non*, *neque*, etc., no parallel, however, is quoted for its occurrence with a verb like *nolle*. Housman fantastically explains *extendere nolet* as 'will cease to spread out flat' (Duff), *i.e.* 'will begin to raise up', thus ignoring the description of the ultimate deluge in Sen. *N.Q.* 3. 27–8 and attaining an explanation diametrically opposed to the truth.

The editors fail to see that *fretum* is nominative and not accusative (for the latter explanation Ouid. *Fast.* 5. 244 is not a parallel), and that *litora* is the object of *excutiet* as well as of *extendere* by an ἀπὸ κοινοῦ construction. Furthermore, *-que* is strongly positive and indeed adversative to the preceding negation *nolet, i.e.* it is almost equivalent to 'but' (cf. 34, 92, etc.). The result is the secondary theme *tellus...nolet* followed by its variation *excutietque* (*litora*) *fretum*, and the translation should be 'the land will refuse to stretch out its coast-line (*i.e.* will no longer have a demarcated coast-line), the restraint of which the sea will throw off'. The sea will gradually push the shore landwards, cf. Sen. *loc. cit.* 27. 10 *iam enim promouet litus nec continetur suis finibus* and *id.* 28. 3 *ubi litus bis terque prolatum est* (*i.e.* by the sea landwards). Compare the description of Deucalion's flood in 5. 623-4 *litora Tethys* | *noluit ulla pati*, and for *excutiet* cf. 6. 272-3 *sic pleno Padus ore tumens super aggere tutas* | *excurrit ripas et totos* concutit *agros*. The sea, not the land, was supposed to rise heavenwards on occasion, cf. 5. 625 *tum quoque tanta maris moles creuisset in astra*. To the Stoics the *inundatio* (κατακλυσμός) was as important as the *conflagratio* in the final destruction of the universe (cf. Sen. *loc. cit.*).

APPENDIX C

313. *Marcellusque loquax et nomina uana Catones.*

In *C.Q.* xxx, 1936, p. 58 the view is held that Lucan, like Petronius probably in *Bell. Ciu.* 288, is thinking here of all three Marcelli, who at different times were hostile to Caesar, and who were (i) C. Claudius Marcellus, consul in 50 B.C., (ii) C. Claudius Marcellus, consul in 49 B.C. and cousin of (i), (iii) M. Claudius Marcellus, consul in 51 B.C., cousin of (i) and brother of (ii). Just as *Catones* is a good instance of the plural for the singular, so *Marcellus* illustrates the use of the singular for the plural. Compare the employment of the singular of *Decius* for the plural in Prop. 3. 11. 62 and 4. 1. 45 (the former passage is correctly translated by Professor H. E. Butler in the Loeb volume, and its meaning is recognized by Mr E. A. Barber and him in their joint edition). The objection of Professor W. H. Semple in *C.Q.* xxxi, 1937, p. 19, that Hor. *Serm.* 1. 6. 20 *Decio...nouo* refers only to the first Decius, does not hold for the other passages which have just been cited from Propertius, where there is no defining adjective like *nouo* to suggest which one is meant.

The use of the singular of *Marcellus* may have been determined by metrical considerations, which would have made the plural of *loquax* the last word in the line. For the plural *nomina* with *Catones* instead of the singular *nomen* with *Cato* compare Sil. 7. 20–1 (which refers to Fabius Cunctator) *post quam noua nomina lecto | dictatore uigent*, where Ruperti and Mr J. D. Duff are in error. With *nomina uana* compare ´Sen. *Clem.* 1. 9. 10 *nobilium non inania nomina praeferentium*.

Caesar is thinking of occasions when the Marcelli had much to say against him in the Senate, notably on Sept. 29, 51 B.C., when the consul, who was probably better at talking than at acting (Cic. *Fam.* 8. 10. 3 *nosti Marcellum, quam tardus et parum efficax sit*) and so deserved the epithet *loquax*, proposed resolutions about his recall; or the early days of December in the following year, when the consul moved that he should be declared an enemy; or the discussions in the Senate presided over by the new consul of 49 B.C. and his colleague L. Lentulus Crus on Jan. 1, 2, and 7 of that year. Although on this last occasion both the consuls were intent on blocking pro-Caesarian business and instead wasted time in bringing forward endless motions on general policy (Caes. *B.C.* 1. 1 *referunt...de re publica infinite*), Lentulus seems to have been the more abusive (*id.* 1. 2 *omnes conuicio L. Lentuli consulis correpti exagitabantur*, and even *M. Marcellus perterritus conuiciis a sua sententia discessit*).

APPENDIX D

444   *et quibus inmitis placatur sanguine diro*
          Teutates horrensque feris altaribus Esus
          et Taranis: Scythicae non mitior ara Dianae.

Teutates...Esus...Taranis. Caesar (*B.G.* 6. 17, cf. Tac. *Germ.* 9) states that Mercury was the greatest of the Gallic gods, among whom were also Apollo, Mars, Jupiter, and Minerva; but it is extremely rash to imitate and indulge in such identifications as that on the part of scholiasts and commentators on Lucan of Teutates with Mercury, Esus with Mars, and Taranis with Jupiter, or the rival view that Teutates was Mars and Esus Mercury. If Lucan does identify the Gallic with the Roman deities, 'he does what is very rare' (A. D. Nock, *Journ. Egypt. Archaeol.* 15, 1929,

p. 227). It was natural for the Romans on first coming into contact
with barbarian countries to stress resemblances with their own
worship rather than discrepancies, and to identify *e.g.* Taranis, the
deity of thunder and lightning, with Jupiter; but Gallic and
Roman religion, it must be remembered, manifest an entirely
different development.

Works which may be consulted with profit on the subject of
these three gods who compose the Celtic triad are: J. De Witte,
'Le Dieu Tricéphale Gaulois', *Rev. Arch. nouv. sér.* xxx, 1875,
pp. 383–7; J. Rhys, *Lectures on the Origin and Growth of Religion
as illustrated by Celtic Heathendom, Hibbert Lectures* 1886, London,
1888, pp. 44–73; H. d'Arbois de Jubainville, *The Irish Mythological Cycle and Celtic Mythology*, as translated by R. I. Best,
Dublin, 1903, pp. 213–17, and *Les Celtes*, Paris, 1904, pp. 56 and
65–6; J. A. MacCulloch, *The Religion of the Ancient Celts*, Edinburgh, 1911, pp. 20–48; E. Windisch, 'Das Keltische Brittannien',
Abhl. d. phil. hist. Kl. d. k. sächs. Ges. d. Wiss. Bd. xxix (6), Leipzig,
1912, pp. 74–5; and the articles in Paulys *Real-Encyclopädie*.

Teutates seems to have been the national god of the Gauls, and
his name signifies 'god of the *tribe*' (Welsh *tud*, Irish *tuath*, Goth.
thiuda). Esus, according to d'Arbois (*Les Celtes* pp. 65–6), appears
in the Irish name Eogan (from Esu-genos). Taranis, like the Irish
Crom Cruach and Balor, was the god of *thunder* (Welsh *taran*,
Irish *toirneach*). Indeed it has been held by some, including Rhys,
that Taranis was a female deity, because frequently on Gallic altars
representing the triad, one of the three is a goddess. In this case,
the comparison drawn by Lucan between her and Diana is the
more apt.

Lucan's celebrated enumeration of the Celtic triad corresponds
closely to the grouping which is a feature of so many monuments,
the best known of which are the altars in the Musée de Cluny.
According to d'Arbois (*The Irish Mythological Cycle*, p. 216), the
triad represented the sons or perhaps even the doubles of Cernunnos,
the horned god of Night and Death, who was usually represented
in a squatting posture. In the same way it was customary, as on
a bronze monument found at Autun, to portray the deities as
united in a three-headed, squatting, and horned guise, and as
wearing a girdle formed of serpents with rams' heads.

According to Camille Jullian (*Rev. Et. Anc.* iv, 1902, p. 218), the
Carnutes, who dwelt on both sides of the Loire and gave their
name to the modern town of Chartres, are the Gallic tribe of which

Lucan is thinking at the moment; while Pichon (*Les Sources de Lucain*, Paris, 1912, p. 27 n. 3) admits that these verses agree with what is known of their bloody customs. The principle of offering up a life for a life was the basis of the human sacrifices made by the Gauls (Caes. *B.G.* 6. 16. 2), and the practice extended also to the Gauls or Galatae of Asia (Liu. 38. 47. 12). It may be noted that Caesar does not cite an example of human sacrifice, and it is likely that the custom was disappearing in his day. Later, it was officially abolished by a law of Claudius (Suet. *Claud.* 25).

Regarding 446, the punctuation suggested and defended by Ussani (*Glotta* vi, 1914, pp. 71–3) on account of the scholia *a* has been adopted in order to dispose of the supposition of most editors that here is an ellipse of the ablative of comparison, and that the full construction is *et ara Taranis non mitior (arā) Dianae Scythicae* —an explanation which gives a sense which is excellent and similar to that of *Octauia* 979–80 *urbe est nostra mitior Aulis | et Taurorum barbara tellus*, but presents a threefold instead of a fourfold construction and an equally. violent ellipse of the ablative of comparison, for which no satisfactory parallel has been brought forward. Housman and M. Bourgery ignore Ussani's improvement, which gives *non mitior* the meaning of 'just as cruel' (see Introduction, p. lv). The position of *ara* in the line would suggest that it should be taken with *Dianae* rather than *Taranis*, cf. Dracont. *Rom.* 5. 139 *Taurica crudelis mitis tamen ara Dianae* and 10. 177–8 *iam saeuior ara Dianae | coeperat ostendi*. Another objection to the omission of the stop after *Taranis* is the sequence *Teutates...Esus* (both nom.)...*ara Taranis* (gen.). On the other hand, a minor objection to Ussani's punctuation is the comparison which results of Diana with Taranis rather than of Taranis with Diana. Had Lucan written *quo* or *qua* (according to the sex of Taranis) where *non* appears in the line, a straightforward meaning would have been the result. Such a relative could be parsed as an ablative of compendious comparison, for which compare the compendious dative *cui* in 8. 457 *nullas cui (i.e. Cypro) praetulit (Venus) aras*, where *cui = cuius aris*. If *quo* or *qua* had dropped out of the text at an early date, *non* would have been a convenient but thoughtless stop-gap. Similarly in 3. 95–6 *habenti | tam pauidum tibi, Roma, ducem Fortuna pepercit*, *tam* (or *iam*, the reading of some MSS) had been omitted in a MS from which G is descended, and was replaced unintelligently by *non* in that MS.

The reference in *Scythicae...ara Dianae* is in the first instance to the altar of Artemis in the Tauric Chersonese where human victims were sacrificed, see Eur. *Iphigenia in Tauris* passim. Her cult was introduced later into Italy at Nemi, the *Scythicae stagnum nemorale Dianae* of Ouid. *Met.* 14. 331, cf. 3. 86 and Strab. 5. 3. 12, and see Frazer on Ouid. *Fast.* 3. 271. Lucan may be thinking here of its cruelty which made each priest kill his predecessor.

The passage finds a curious echo later in Lact. *Diuin. Inst.* 1. 21. 2–3 *erat lex apud Tauros inhumanam et feram gentem ut Dianae hospites inmolarentur, et id sacrificium multis temporibus celebratum est. Galli Esum atque Teutaten humano cruore placabant. ne Latini quidem huius inmanitatis expertes fuerunt, si quidem Latiaris Iuppiter etiam nunc sanguine colitur humano.* Apparently this calumny was directed by the Fathers of the Christian Church against the cult of Iuppiter Latiaris (see 198 n.); cf. also Porph. *De Abstin.* 2. 56 ἀλλ' ἔτι γε νῦν τίς ἀγνοεῖ κατὰ τὴν μεγάλην πόλιν τῇ τοῦ Λατιαρίου Διὸς ἑορτῇ σφαζόμενον ἄνθρωπον;

INDEX TO THE NOTES

suus replaced by a proper adjective 653

'under its own sway' 155, 407

syllepsis 144, 310, 422, 504

synecdoche 1, 17, 42, 47, 57, 103, 142, 165, 239, 294, 369, 398, 423, 463, 468, 588, 627, 640

synonyms in same context 227, 453–4, 459–60

Syrtis, Syrtidos 367

tacere and *iacere* confused 260*

Tages 637

tamen and *quamuis* both suppressed 292, 577, 579

suppressed after *quamuis* 292, 354

Taranis Appendix D

Tarbelli 421

Tarpeius = Capitolinus 196

temerare similar in meaning to *lacessere* 147

templa (caeli) 155

tentoria 396

Teutates Appendix D

Teutones 254

Thapsus 39, 687

theme and variation 155, 184, 325, 356, 379, 527–8, 529

Thracius 'northern' 389

threefold understood from fourfold construction 504, 551

thunder and lightning, cause of 151, 533

in a clear sky 530

thunderbolts, gathering and burial of 606–8

in a clear sky 533

Thybris, Tiberinus 381

Thyestes 544

tides 409, 413, 417

Titan 15

Titii sodales 602

toga 'civil' or 'private life' 130, 365

= *togatus* or *togati* 365

transference of epithet, *see* hypallage

of idea 212, 413

Treuiri 441

tributaries which lose their name in a greater river 401

triumphs 12

Triumvirate (First) 4, 85

tu, te of two different subjects in the same context 123

tum = tum demum 21

tum, tunc 490*

tumultus 233

tunc = mox, deinde 481

turba of the Roman people 86

Turones 436–40*

uada of the slow motion of a river 399

uagus 336

uallum 517

uelut 'thinking that' 496

uerber (fundae) 229

uictima distinguished from *hostia* 611

uires facere 348

uita = sanguis 363

ullus 'any other' 82, 93–4

umquam 'at any other time' 85

uolgus 'soldiers' 352–3

uolitare and *errare* of birds 588*

utrum omitted 412

Valerius Flaccus 3. 732 260*, 642*

Vangiones 431

Var 404

Vates, Gallic 449

Veneti 409

Venus (planet) 652, 662

verb separated from infinitive which depends upon it 12, 186

Vergil *Georgics* 1. 217–18 15

Aeneid 3. 517 665

Vesta 199

Vestal Virgins 597

Vogesus 397*

Zephyrus 406

zeugma 72–3, 158–9

Zodiac 58, 91, 540, 659

For EU product safety concerns, contact us at Calle de José Abascal, 56–1°,
28003 Madrid, Spain or eugpsr@cambridge.org.

www.ingramcontent.com/pod-product-compliance
Ingram Content Group UK Ltd.
Pitfield, Milton Keynes, MK11 3LW, UK
UKHW020317140625
459647UK00018B/1915